THE

# Way of Life

# METHOD

**How to Heal Your Relationship with Your Dog
and Raise a Sound, Strong, and Spirited Companion
(At Any Age)**

## WAY OF LIFE™
PUBLICATIONS

info@wayoflifetraining.com
7030 Woodbine Ave, Ste 500
Markham, ON, L3R6G2, Canada
(416) 546-5486

ISBN: 978-1-7389009-0-9 (paperback)
ISBN: 978-1-7389009-1-6 (ebook)
ISBN: 978-1-7389009-3-0 (hardcover)
ISBN: 978-1-7389009-2-3 (audiobook)

Ordering Information:
Special discounts are available on quantity purchases by corporations, associations, and others. For details, contact info@wayoflifetraining.com, (416) 546-5486

# THE
# *Way of Life*
# METHOD

How to Heal Your Relationship with Your Dog
and Raise a Sound, Strong, and Spirited Companion
(At Any Age)

SOUHA EZZEDEEN, PHD

*For the dogs and the people who love them*
*enough to reimagine their ways of life.*

# Contents

Introduction ........................................................................................................... 1

## Before We Begin

Chapter 1: Why We Struggle With Behavior Issues ................................................. 9
Chapter 2: The Way Of Life Logic ....................................................................... 25
Chapter 3: Designing Our Way Of Life In Stages ................................................. 51

### STAGE 1: FOUNDATIONS
## Establishing Our Bond

Chapter 4 : Relationship, Mission, and Mindset at Stage 1 .................................. 73
Chapter 5: Managing Space and Boundaries at Stage 1 ........................................ 87
Chapter 6 : Socialization at Stage 1 .................................................................... 113
Chapter 7: Drive Development at Stage 1 ........................................................... 135

### STAGE 2: EXPOSURE
## Growing And Challenging Our Bond

Chapter 8: Relationship, Mission, and Mindset at Stage 2 .................................. 161
Chapter 9: Managing Space and Boundaries at Stage 2 ....................................... 173
Chapter 10: Socialization at Stage 2 ................................................................... 191
Chapter 11: Drive Development at Stage 2 ......................................................... 211

### STAGE 3: INTEGRATION
## Solidifying And Enjoying Our Bond

Chapter 12: Relationship, Mission, and Mindset at Stage 3 ................................ 231
Chapter 13: Managing Space and Boundaries at Stage 3 ..................................... 241
Chapter 14: Socialization at Stage 3 ................................................................... 255
Chapter 15: Drive Development at Stage 3 ......................................................... 267

Epilogue .............................................................................................................. 281
References ............................................................................................................ 289
Glossary ............................................................................................................... 305
Acknowledgments ................................................................................................ 311
About the Author ................................................................................................ 313
Index ................................................................................................................... 315

# Introduction

A lot of times rather than helping people with horse problems,
I am helping horses with people problems.

—**BUCK BRANNAMAN,** Horseman and Clinician

S ummer is here, and we couldn't have asked for better weather. It's still early
and my German shepherd girls, Kizzy and Bruna, and I have the trail near
the cabins almost to ourselves. We stop for a moment, taking in the sights and
sounds, and I draw a deep breath of delight. Kizzy looks up at me smiling. "It's so
beautiful, Mommy."

Bruna circles around me and leans against my leg. "Shall we?" she asks.

For once, we're in a place where it's legal for dogs to be off leash, and the girls are
busy providing lovely examples of dogs deserving of the privilege—Kizzy by running
around us, stomping her feet in joy, while Bruna, equally happy but more reserved,
moves closer to me, circling me or staying right behind.

"Beautiful dogs!" says one woman walking by.

"So well behaved!" says her friend, looking partly impressed and partly mystified.

I marvel at my girls, the liveliness in their sleek bodies and happiness in their
expressions. A rush of pride travels through me, reaching my eyes, and I feel that
familiar sting of bittersweet tears, remembering that things weren't always like this.
Things weren't always this beautiful, this peaceful.

My mind carries me back to the other dogs I'd failed, particularly Maya, my
black German shepherd. I remember the first time I saw her jetting out of the shelter

building like a bullet, pulling my friend Laurie behind her. Laurie was a shelter volunteer and was helping me choose a new companion. Maya was the last one she showed me and the one I took home. She was striking, powerful, beautiful—a big and leggy girl with a gorgeous velvety black coat. They told me I would be her fourth home, that she wasn't even a year old, and that she would be difficult. Deep down, I knew she was more than I could handle, yet I didn't hesitate. Something in her got the better of me. Little did I know this dog would change my life.

Maya proved extremely challenging. She was chronically anxious and paced restlessly. At the dog park, she herded other dogs around, which often escalated to aggression and dog fights with frenzied owners trying to intervene. More than once, the police were called, and I was threatened with being charged and having my dog seized. I eventually kicked the dog park to the curb, but Maya's aggression toward dogs had extended to other avenues by then. She walked horribly on leash and was even more reactive leashed up. I began using a head halter, which aggravated and disgusted her while giving me the illusion of being in control.

I consulted with trainers who recommended we improve upon our obedience and keep socializing her. I was told she needed to be continually exposed to things, given her past as a rescue. I was urged to help Maya "feel safe," so she went with me everywhere and slept in my room from the beginning.

It was suggested that she lacked confidence and that we boost that confidence with sport, so we pursued every sport on the planet. Maya applied herself beautifully and excelled in all disciplines, particularly in obedience, passing her Canine Good Citizen on the first attempt a few months after I adopted her. Outside the structured training arena, however, her anxiety continued—pacing, panting, and submissively urinating whenever I came near her. Unless we were training, she had no interest in me or much else. I could tell that she was deeply unhappy. I was too.

Around that time, I discovered a famous TV personality who emphasized "dog psychology" and "pack leadership," which, in their approach, almost always involved punishment of some kind. In my despair, I remember experiencing an epiphany of sorts. Clearly, I'd failed to be firm enough with Maya! Soon after, I ended up with problems far greater. While Maya's aggression had lessened in frequency, it had heightened in intensity. Under the suppressive effect of corrections, she'd become unpredictable and vindictive. I remember how I felt I'd run out of options.

*I sense Bruna brush against my leg. "Come back," she says.*

*It's not the first time that she's returned me to the here and now, where she and the others dwell. I stroke her cheek, telling her how good she is and thanking her for the apt reminder. I smile with relief, grateful that what is past is past. The three of us walk on as one, happy to be here and in this moment.*

This could be you, and I'd love nothing more than to show you how. But first, if any of my experiences with Maya ring true for you, know that you are not alone. Too many of us lead lives of silent desperation and anguish, sharing our existence with dogs that present behavioral issues. People I talk to every day cannot have company over for fear of what their dogs might do. Many are held hostage by dogs they can't leave behind. Couples I work with report tensions and conflicts over how to best deal with their dogs. Clients tell me how ashamed they feel walking their reactive dogs in public despite their many attempts at getting them to listen.

All feel stressed, frustrated, and overwhelmed, wondering whether they're being good or bad owners. Many doubt that their dog is enjoying a minimum quality of life. And it is indeed true that many of these dogs are not—suffering for being in conflict with their humans, often kept in silent neglect at home, relegated to kennels and garages, tied up outside, if not abandoned, surrendered to a shelter, or euthanized.

Indeed, we have been witnessing unprecedented levels of canine behavioral issues, affecting dogs of all ages, breeds, backgrounds, and ways of life. Dysfunctions such as anxiety, leash reactivity, fear, separation anxiety, and resource guarding, among others, have sadly become part of the mainstream conversation around dogs.

In seeking answers to these problems, people spend hours scouring the internet, reading books and blogs, watching videos, and listening to podcasts, trying to figure out why their dogs are having issues and how to resolve those issues. Billions are spent on tools, trainers, and increasingly, medication. Yet trying to put a Band-Aid on the dog's behavior doesn't work because it isn't the behavior that's really the problem.

Rather, it's our very bond with our dogs that's been wounded and waiting to be healed.

We know the influence of relationships on well-being for us humans. We know that healthy bonds heal and support us physically and psychologically. Yet, when we talk about canine behavioral issues, why aren't we talking about the quality of our relationships with our dogs as a factor?

Dogs are not born neurotic and dysfunctional. They are not inherently anxious or aggressive but rather are collectively rebelling against the expectations we have placed on them and the unnatural ways of life we are asking them to live. Our relationships with them are not what they could be because we've forgotten that they're dogs. All they've been doing is trying to remind us.

If behavioral issues reflect issues of bond, it follows that they can't be fixed through training alone, and that's regardless of the training approach. Bonds are the result of trust, and in each moment and with each way-of-life decision, we are coming across as either worthy or unworthy of that trust. All our way-of-life decisions constitute our raising of the dog. Therefore, instead of problem-solving via training, we heal issues and cultivate bond via rearing.

This book introduces the Way of Life method as the ultimate guide to canine rearing and recovery from behavioral issues. The Way of Life method examines not only our daily raising and training practices with our dogs but also our mindset and relationship over time. It offers a different way of living with dogs, one that isn't difficult as much as it is different.

The Way of Life method helps improve existing relationships and get started right with a new dog, puppies included. If you happen to be dealing with behavioral issues, following this process will help you get a handle on the chaos—end your dog's troubles, restore your relationship, and assist you in raising a sound, strong, and spirited dog (at any age).

# The Way of Life Method

Think back to when you first brought home your dog or puppy. Most of us integrate the new family member right away, playing with them, beginning training, taking them places, and having friends over to meet them. For a dog of any age and from any background, this new environment is intimidating at best.

Don't be fooled by appearances—dogs don't show people they don't know how they really feel. They're in a new environment, one where the folks in charge are still strangers and the rules of conduct still unknown. It is natural for dogs to be suspicious and stressed. Unless managed carefully in times of transition, the overwhelm and uncertainty they feel will lead to anxiety, and then problems start to emerge.

In contrast, the Way of Life method describes a planned and deliberate approach to introducing new dogs to our life and home and addressing behavior issues with existing dogs. This method features a three-stage template that follows the rearing stages observed in mother dogs, wolf packs, and sophisticated and social mammalian species across the spectrum, humans included. They reflect the maturation of our dogs, the expansion of their worlds, and the deepening of our relationships with them across childhood, adolescence, and adulthood.

→  Stage 1 is Foundations. It starts off at childhood "in the den," where foundations for our bond are established. Here we take charge of the dog's life, almost micromanaging to ensure nothing but successful experiences, which will begin restoring our troubled dog's self-esteem. We put an end to conflict and turmoil and bring back structure, safety, and success.

→  Stage 2 is Exposure and introduces "the rendezvous," where our firmly established bond is challenged and strengthened. When we expose our adolescent dog in measured ways, this challenges and strengthens our relationship, and the more the dog succeeds in these endeavors, the better they feel, and the more they earn integration into our homes.

→  Stage 3 is Integration and speaks to the idea of life "in the pack." Following successful education, exposure, and maturation of the dog into adulthood, we solidify our bond and finally get to enjoy the product of our rearing. We continue to expand our dog's world, and we free the dog. We have the trust and bond to go as far as our dog will take us. At this point, we have dogs that are honest about their preferences and personality, and aren't afraid to love us fully.

Instead of trying to fix problems, the three-stage Way of Life method helps us raise sound dogs that don't have problems. They're immune to dysfunction just as a healthy body fights off disease. The result of all this is more than well-trained or well-behaved dogs. It's dogs that are sound, strong, and spirited—knowing they are seen, understood, and raised as dogs.

# How to Use This Book

This book is organized into four parts. In the opening chapters, I set the framework for the Way of Life method and the three-stage process I've just introduced. Chapter 1 describes how we explain behavior issues and how we go about dealing with them. Chapter 2 will walk you through the logic behind this book, connecting the dots between behavioral issues, relationships, and way of life. In chapter 3, I describe how wolves raise their cubs, offering the basis for the three-stage rearing process presented here.

Then we'll go through each of the three rearing stages: Stage 1—Foundations, Stage 2—Exposure, and Stage 3—Integration. Each stage includes four chapters, one devoted to each of the four pillars that constitute our Way of Life: 1) mission, relationship, and mindset; 2) managing space and boundaries; 3) socialization; and 4) developing drives through exercise, training, and sport.

Throughout the chapters, you'll find reflection questions, exercises, and activities for you and your dog. You'll also find stories of dogs I've worked with presenting a range of issues and the path we took for a healed way of life. At the back, you'll find an extensive list of references and a glossary to help with any terms you may need clarified.

I recommend you read the entire book first to get the logic of why we're doing what we're doing. When you feel ready to challenge this process, go back to the top and read with application to your situation in mind. I strongly suggest you keep a companion notebook to track your activities and progress, and write down your observations and answers to the reflection questions.

## A Little About Me

My earliest interactions with animals took place in the garden of my grandmother's Mount Lebanon villa, overlooking Beirut and the Mediterranean Sea. With her dogs standing guard a few feet away, Teta, or "granny" in Lebanese dialect, loved showing me how to scoop up frogs sleeping in the leaves of her bean plants, hold them in my hands so they wouldn't slither out, and put them back gingerly.

Teta was always surrounded by animals—her chickens, stray dogs, and cats. I never saw her coddle these animals, and yet they adored her. I never saw her train or direct them, and yet they behaved. I never saw her make a big deal of the dogs nor socialize them the way we do these days. When people visited, they paid no mind to the dogs, and the dogs didn't mind visitors either.

Though it was years before I could have animals in my own life, I never forgot Teta's almost innate understanding of them and how easily she shared her life with them. Years of graduate education toward becoming an academic hijacked much of my 20s. Today, I'm a behavioral scientist holding a PhD in management and organizational behavior, fields that have informed my work with dogs from a different angle.

Organizational behavior is essentially the study of people in organizations and what drives their performance. In organizational behavior, we study leaders and followers, teamwork and group dynamics, motivation and learning, and attachment and relationships, to name a few. We explore how individuals and organizations interact. Dogs are embedded in organizations—families, cultures, and societies that create a context or situation for dogs. And just as with people, situations can bring out the best or the worst in our dogs. Therefore, instead of working with behavior as most of my dog training colleagues do, I work with the context and relationships behind behavior. I work with organizational behavior.

For years, I studied under different trainers, worked with my own dogs, fostered rescue dogs, boarded touchy dogs, and coached acquaintances and friends for free, welcoming every bit of experience I could get my hands on.

I was mentored by incredible individuals—sport instructors and decorated competitors such as Kathy Warner, Christopher Rollox, and Karin Apfel, trailblazing veterinarians such as the late Sharon Kopinak, and especially master dog trainer and breeder Sam Malatesta. He changed my entire outlook on dogs just as I hope to change yours. Last but not least, my dog Maya who blessed me with the motivation to change, as painful as it sometimes was.

For having been so fortunate to develop such knowledge, I knew it had to be shared and founded Way of Life Dog Training in 2019, putting to use my now 20-plus years of experience to coach people and their dogs officially. Based in Toronto, Canada, I coach clients in-person and remotely, working with dog owners across Canada, the U.S., and beyond. This book is an extension of that mission and of my desire to share its message with a broader audience.

# BEFORE WE BEGIN

# CHAPTER 1

# *Why We Struggle With Behavior Issues*

No animal is an island. Thought and feeling intertwine with ecology and life history.
Society is where the mind's life takes place.

—**NATIONAL GEOGRAPHIC,** *Inside Animal Minds: What They Think, Feel, and Know*

*M*aya's heavy breathing wakes me up yet again. I look over, and though it's dark, I see her up, panting and looking at me intently. I thought our long hike on the Appalachian trail the day before might have tuckered her out so she could sleep, but her anxiety is ever present, as it had been since I brought her home a few weeks earlier.

*I fall back on my pillow and utter a few curse words. I'd done everything I could for this dog. We'd started an obedience class soon after I adopted her. I exercised her consistently and took every opportunity to socialize her. We were patients at the best vet clinic in town and regulars at the dog park. About twice a week, Maya and my other dog, Rama, visited a day care with large meadows, a pool, and other dogs to play with when I worked long days at the university.*

*I didn't know what to make of Maya's anxiousness and extreme aggression toward other dogs. My girl was intelligent and affectionate but also terribly hard to handle—willful, strong, and oblivious to anything I did or said. It was five years of a conflicted existence with Maya before I met Sam Malatesta, who would go on to be my mentor and most influential teacher for the next decade. No one new to Sam forgets their first experience at one of his seminars, witnessing him and his dogs loose around him. He did not have to say much, yet they each took position around him, aware of but unfazed by the surrounding traffic. When he moved, they moved along, and when he settled, they would as well. Sam was known to say that to have dogs like that requires we be "worth looking at." When we fix ourselves and become worthy in the eyes of our dogs, we fix our dogs.*

*Recognizing that I wasn't "worth looking at" in Maya's eyes was a hard pill to swallow, but it also made complete sense to me. I came to see that Maya didn't just need me to act differently, she needed me to think and feel differently. The guilt was crushing at first, but I eventually felt a sense of relief, even elation, knowing that if I'd screwed things up so badly, I could also do something about them.*

*Maya gave me yet another chance. This time, she knew I finally may be getting it. I went back to square one, treating her as if she'd just been adopted and we were new to each other. We worked on basics, just she and I, for several weeks. Eventually we were ready to get back out there, and gradually, we expanded our world and our experiences. By then, Maya's trust was on the mend, and she felt safe enough to show me just how much she had under the hood. Once in class at Sam's, she was bit by a touchy client and did not react, beelining to me instead.*

*The once-aggressive dog had become the dog I could rely on to help settle in some of my fosters. Thanks to such stability, we were able to resume sports and went on to try sheep herding, an activity I'd long dreamed of pursuing. She became my sidekick, coming to the office and running errands with me. We so enjoyed these golden years, her leisurely off-leash walks, therapeutic swims, and late nights on the couch, reveling in the intimacy we'd both longed for.*

One of the reasons it was difficult helping Maya all those years ago and why so many people still struggle with behavior issues, despite the plethora of trainers, training tools, and techniques available, is because we remain fundamentally misguided about why dogs "misbehave." In this chapter, I explain that we continue to struggle with behavior issues because we do not acknowledge way of life as the root cause. Because of this superficial understanding, our interventions (also detailed here) remain just as superficial.

# How We Explain Behavior Issues

Generally, we tend to attribute behavior issues to the dog's background, breed, predatory identity, personality, or some underlying physical or psychological condition. Let's look at each one of these explanations and explore how they fit into the puzzle of behavior, and more importantly, how they don't.

## Background

Regarding background, we tend to emphasize a dog's early experiences—for example, experiences from whelping to weaning, quality of maternal care, and interactions with littermates and breeders. Vets and behaviorists emphasize the critical socialization period—roughly between three and 16 weeks—and many seem to think that dogs are ruined if they suffered adverse experiences or were not socialized enough during that time.

Having been mentored by a breeder for nearly a decade, I know that these early periods when the pup is vulnerable and impressionable no doubt constitute a critical life period. However, that does not mean our relationship with our dogs cannot make up for whatever was experienced during that time. One of my clients picked up an orphaned puppy off the streets; he was small enough to fit in the palm of her hands, and she bathed him in a cooking pot. He'd not had the benefit of being raised and weaned by his mother, but my client, diligent in her attitude and way of life, more than made up for that compromised beginning. It's never too late to heal a dog.

It's also common to justify poor behavior on grounds that the dog is a rescue. I'm no stranger to the pain witnessed in rescue and shelter dogs, including puppy mill dogs (and moms) and dogs enduring abuse, neglect, starvation, and exposure to the elements. And let's not forget the many dogs that were adopted as pets, spoiled, messed with, and then discarded. No doubt, the impact of a traumatic situation can be heartbreaking and long lasting. Dogs that have been hurt in any way are changed and unfortunately will probably not become what they could have been without the harm.

But as trainer and author Suzanne Clothier put it, "Sometimes the dog's history becomes baggage that the human carts along for the dog's entire life."[1] Many people think the dog is ruined, and that's just that. Others think that trying to improve these dogs' behavior would be stressful and that they've endured enough. One client told me she was raised in a home that took on many rescues but allowed these dogs to act out their dysfunctions, whether they guarded their food or hated kids. Her parents believed that their behavior was just who they were and that loving them meant accepting them. In my experience, after working with dogs from all kinds of backgrounds, this is simply not the case. Dogs can and want to change. In fact, they're relieved when we challenge them and give them the chance to lay down the burdens they've been carrying.

## Breed

We also blame the breed for dysfunctional behavior. One vivid example that comes to mind are clients who thought their corgi's nipping at their ankles was breed related and normal. I quickly explained that it was normal for corgis to nip sheep and cows but that something's off when they're nipping at people! Over the years, I've heard the range of statements attributing behavior to breed:

*"We have a husky, so we don't let him off leash."*

*"We have a pair of Portuguese water dogs. They love people and pull us to go say hi."*

*"We've never let our greyhound loose because we're afraid she won't come back."*

---

1    Suzanne Clothier, "If Only That Hadn't Happened, This Dog Would Be Fine," Suzanne Clothier Relationship Centered Training, accessed April 17, 2023, https://suzanneclothier. com/article/hadnt-happened-dog-fine/.

*"We have boxers, and boxers really need to be trained so we started early."*

*"We have a German shepherd, so we're not surprised that she's a little high strung."*

*"We were told that cockapoos can get 'cockapoo rage.' Do you have experience with that?"*

In her 2018 book *Meet Your Dog*, Kim Brophey describes several breed groups, their background, characteristics, and the problem behaviors that owners might need help with. (See insert for popular varieties using Brophey's classification.) With guardians, for example, one could be dealing with aggression and territoriality. Herding types such as border collies and corgis can chase after moving objects, bark excessively, and nip at the feet of people and other animals. With toy dogs, owners might complain of excessive barking and separation anxiety.

Of course, breed is a powerful shaper of behavior—so much so, in fact, that I often recommend that my clients with mutts get genetic testing done on their dogs so we have a better idea of what we could be dealing with. Over hundreds, if not thousands, of years, dogs have both evolved and been selected for specific functions in response to specific local needs. This has produced astonishing genetic mutations resulting in breeds for protection, hunting, retrieving, livestock herding and guarding, and more. With these sharpened capacities come breed-specific needs and tendencies, which can be wonderful when channeled correctly or a nightmare in the wrong hands.

## *Breed Group Characteristics And Examples*[2]

**Bulldogs:** Tracing their ancestry to ancient Rome, these stocky and muscular breeds were originally used as gladiators and bull-baiters for cruel human entertainment.

*Examples:* American bulldog, boxer, bull terrier, French bulldog

2   Kim Brophey, *Meet Your Dog: The Game Changing Guide to Understanding Your Dog's Behavior* (New York: Chronicle Books), 2018.

**Guardians:** Guardians represent large and courageous breeds of dogs developed as early as 1100 BC. They were bred to protect herds and properties and were used in war as well.
*Examples:* Bernese mountain dog, cane corso, Great Pyrenees, Newfoundland

**Gun dogs:** Gun dogs are a particular type of hunting dog designed to hunt fowl, assisting hunters in locating and exposing prey, without killing or damaging the kill.
*Examples:* cocker spaniel, English pointer, golden retriever, Portuguese water dog

**Herding dogs:** Herding dogs have been around for as long as humans have raised livestock, helping round up, sort, and move stock working closely with the human shepherd.
*Examples:* Belgian Malinois, border collie, Cardigan Welsh corgi,
German shepherd

**Natural dogs:** Considered the first dogs of the world, these sledding and guarding breeds represent early evolutions away from ancestral wolves, maintaining strong instinctual behaviors.
*Examples:* Akita, Alaskan malamute, chow chow, Siberian husky

**Scent hounds:** Scent hounds date back to the Middle Ages. They were developed for their extraordinary scenting abilities, originally used in hunting and increasingly in search and rescue.
*Examples:* basset hound, beagle, bloodhound, coonhound, English foxhound

**Sight hounds:** Sight hounds are among the first groups of dogs developed for a specific purpose, in this case the ability to spot prey at a distance and the speed to apprehend it.
*Examples:* Afghan hound, basenji, greyhound, saluki

**Terriers:** Terriers are bold and tenacious breeds designed as pest control. Their size and agility helped them keep human settlements rodent-free and disease-free, contributing to our health and survival.
*Examples:* Airedale, cairn, Jack Russell, West Highland

**Toy dogs:** The smallest breeds of the dog world served as companions to aristocrats, monks, and emperors, providing heat and comfort, a magnet for fleas, and an alarm system in one tiny package.

*Examples:* bichon frise, Cavalier King Charles spaniel, chihuahua, Maltese

---

Given that today, most people with dogs own them as pets as opposed to workers, it is no wonder so many dogs have problems. Our way of life is a far cry from how dogs lived throughout most of their history, causing them a collective state of culture shock. They've gone from animals with a purpose to pampered pets with no objective. The range of behavioral issues we see is in great part a marker of this change and our failure to adequately prepare our dogs for their new job as "pet"—a job that they are not genetically prepared for.

At the same time, tremendous variations exist within any given breed. Each individual dog is a greater or lesser representation of that breed's general tendencies. Let's also not forget how much trouble breed-related thinking has gotten us into—from choosing a breed based on its good qualities without appreciating what it takes to draw those out, all the way to idiotic bans on breeds considered dangerous. Breed alone is not cause for behavioral issues; rather, it is a three-way interaction between the dog's breed, the dog as a unique representation of its breed, and the dog's context or way of life.

## Predatory Identity

Another excuse seeks to justify behavior on grounds that because dogs are predators at the core, they will always act as such. We routinely hear people allege that it is normal for dogs to act savagely simply because they're dogs. We apply this thinking to behaviors such as resource guarding, territoriality, or aggression toward wildlife, for example.

I believe that dogs are predators at heart and that their essential predatory identity should be kept front and center. But this means appreciating their wild legacy and following in their rearing ways; it has nothing to do with allowing viciousness on the grounds that "it's a dog!" A few days before I sat down to write this section, an incident occurred in my home that only confirmed my conviction that dogs being predators at the core doesn't mean they need to act viciously.

I had let three dogs—Bob, Kizzy, and Nejra—out for the morning pee break as I worked around my kitchen overlooking the yard. I heard Bob barking feverishly and went to the glass door to look. I couldn't quite see him, but Kizzy and Nejra both had their hackles up. When I moved a little closer, I saw that the three dogs had formed a triangle around a raccoon. The most predatory of the three, Bob, barked the loudest but stood his ground. None of the dogs appeared to want to attack the animal, but they weren't about to leave it to its devices either. Once my mind registered the situation, I quietly called the dogs inside as if I'd not seen a thing. One after the other, they made their way back in. There was no bloodshed. No gang attacks. No dogs piling on an innocent animal. They simply cornered the raccoon until I could step in.

The truth is that in the wild, predators don't hunt for sport. They don't kill for fun. Wolves go hungry before they hunt—it's a dangerous proposition, and they know they could die trying. They also know when to call off a hunt, as most hunts don't end successfully. They know they need to preserve whatever energy they have. They are not eager to put themselves in danger because they have responsibilities and family members who rely on them. They are self-preserving, knowing the safety and well-being of others is at stake.

Our dogs *are* predators, and that is something I revere about them. But they are not primitive. When dogs act ruthlessly, without reason or instruction, they have been raised to be incapable of thought and their instincts are veering wildly off the natural track. By endangering themselves in needless killing, they are in essence acting immaturely, neither thinking nor self-preserving. Real predators don't need to prove they're predators. They simply are.

## Personality

Another way we explain a dog's behavior is through the dog's supposed "personality." When clients describe their dogs as "a little timid" or "a bit of an a-hole," I see those issues masking a deeper malaise. Clients will label their dog as a "bully" or "meany," when I know that dog is just trying to deal with a situation. I've also heard and read more than one expert who asserted statements along the lines of "some dogs are just plain bullies." Some dogs "can never be off leash." Some dogs are "just mean."

Of course, dogs have their individual personalities and tendencies—just like people. But any time I hear a person call their dog something less than flattering, I know there's more going on beneath. I suspect a fair bit of projection as well; these labels are a coping mechanism that helps us unload our own limitations onto our dog. This gives us a convenient way out of taking responsibility and confronting our issues head on.

## Physical or Psychological Condition

No doubt, pain and discomfort can cause dogs to feel a sense of weakness, vulnerability, and stress, driving a range of behavioral issues. Regardless of what issues we're dealing with, the absolute first thing is to rule out potential medical conditions. Changes in behavior are usually the earliest signs of illness, especially if these changes are acute and sudden. If that is what you are experiencing, it is crucial you schedule an appointment with your vet. But please keep in mind that both our culture and the medical community can be quick to insist that there must be something psychologically or physically wrong with a dog that's acting out, without ever thinking about way of life.

Not long ago, I was on a call with a new client who was at a loss trying to figure out the cause of her giant-breed dog's behavior. She recounted dealing with a steady progression of behavioral issues, beginning with leash aggression that was followed by "bullying" other dogs in off-leash areas, possessiveness over toys, poor recall, and uncontrollable "manic" behavior upon meeting new people and dogs. Initially, my client strongly believed her dog was psychologically unwell and was running scores of medical tests, trying to identify a medical condition that could explain the dysfunctional behavior. She was not considering how their way of life together could be a cause for her dog's anxiety and misbehavior. Surely, there could be something wrong medically; however, my conversations with this client quickly revealed issues in the way of life that no doubt contributed to the escalation.

We also apply psychological labels to our dogs, such as fear aggressive, insecure, anxious, territorial aggressive, and so on. While these descriptions have their place in our discussions around behavioral issues, again they do not take us to the root cause. I remember a client once exclaiming with great enthusiasm, "I knew it was anxiety!" after I'd introduced this idea about where behavioral issues stem from.

Just slapping a label on a dog isn't enough, though. Let's keep in mind that anxiety is not something inherent in the dog; rather, it is the dog's response to a troubling situation. In addition, labeling dogs can even be dangerous, as once we think we've figured out what's wrong with *them*, they may not only be doomed to that label forever, but we're now even less likely to consider contextual factors. Yet such is the extent of our collective myopia when it comes to dogs and their ways of life. We believe that dogs are anxious, aggressive, or possessive because *they* must be sick in some way. To truly help our dogs, we must consider *our* part in this, which includes looking at the expectations we place on dogs and the problematic ways of life we subject them to.

# How We Deal with Behavior Issues

Behavioral issues exist—no matter what you believe to be the underlying cause. In the traditional world of dog training, there are five general approaches to dealing with issues, including behavior modification through various forms of conditioning, participating in dog sports, increasing the dog's exposure to things, using tools of control, and medicating the dog. Let's take a look.

## Modifying Behavior

The world of dog training is painfully behaviorist. In other words, it is dominated by a perspective that focuses on outwardly expressed behavior and devises ways of "modifying" that behavior.

Behaviorism essentially sees people and animals as products of their learning experiences, "learning" being the result of associations between events and their outcomes. The behaviorist movement began with the famous works of Ivan Pavlov, which established learned associations between events or what's become known as "classical conditioning."

Later, Thorndike's law of effect and the lab experiments of B.F. Skinner developed stimulus-response theory, also known as "operant conditioning" and referred to as "learning theory" in the dog training industry. This perspective holds that dogs learn by associating behaviors with consequences, and these consequences act as reinforcers of behaviors.

For example, you might have heard of positive reinforcement, which involves associating a desired behavior with a pleasant outcome. It is one of four modes of reinforcement, the others being negative reinforcement, positive punishment, and negative punishment. (See glossary.) Of course, there are differences in the effects of these reinforcements and how they are experienced by the dog.

As a result, it's interesting to note the animosities between those who emphasize positive reinforcement, advocating for a "force-free" approach to training dogs, versus those who identify as "balanced" trainers, meaning they use both rewards and punishments. From my perspective, however, all these trainers remain behaviorists. All are focused on surface behavior, which they attempt to modify either with carrots, sticks, or both. None are looking beyond the surface to understand the root cause.

We're obsessed with behavior and take it at face value. Meanwhile, when looking at organizational behavior, we know that similar attitudes can manifest as different behaviors. Equally, similar behaviors can be expressions of different underlying attitudes. By believing that behavior defines dogs, we end up judging them unfairly: A dog appearing aggressive toward dogs must hate dogs. A dog barking in the crate must not like the crate. A dog appearing afraid must be a fearful dog. A dog refusing food must be low in food drive etc.

Because we think the problem is the visible behavior, we work on modifying that behavior by applying various forms of reinforcement and using different techniques such as desensitization, shaping, and counterconditioning. Just about every problem in dog training seems to have a behavior modification protocol available for it.

Take for example the case of leash aggression or reactivity, where a dog reacts violently or aggressively toward other dogs or people while being walked on leash. The idea of behavior modification involves teaching a behavior that would be considered incompatible with the unwanted behavior—for example, looking at the person instead. So we proceed to teach dogs the watch me command or to condition an autowatch. Take this quote by McConnell and London: "… if you teach your dog to react to the sight of another dog by looking at you, instead of lunging toward the dog, your problem is basically solved."[3]

As I see it, my problem is not "basically solved." It is simply being conditioned into something different via repeated associations. Trainers who follow those strategies don't realize that conditioning dogs also causes problems—such as dogs becoming needy, jumpy, and anxious because they're now addicted to our reinforcement. Dogs that are conditioned often become reactive because we have undermined their innate capacity to think. In addition, because the root cause is overlooked, it is only a matter of time before the angst that's been suppressed via conditioning shows up elsewhere.

This narrow perspective in the mainstream world of dog training has resulted in many thinking that there should be simple solutions for their problems. This limited view also portrays a limited vision of what's possible with dogs. One of my clients with a once fearful and reactive Aussie was told by the behaviorists she consulted that the issues could not be fixed, only managed. I told her I wasn't surprised they would think so given that the only tool available to them is behavior modification. With an approach focused on the context that enables behavior, rather than just the visible behavior, change is possible for any dog.

---

3    Patricia B. McConnell & Karen B. London, *Feisty Fido: Help for the Leash-Reactive Dog (2nd ed.)* (Black Earth: McConnell Publishing Ltd., 2009), 4.

## Participating in Dog Sports

People who are active in dog sports often feel great passion for their discipline. They also tend to be folks who take their dogs seriously and have a lot of investment in how their dogs behave. It's common for these folks to think that participation in canine sports and such activities will solve behavioral issues and that sport will help boost the confidence of an insecure dog or channel the high drives of another. Yet, the fact remains that behavioral issues are as prevalent in these spaces as any. Simply put, participation in dog sports will sweeten an already healthy bond, but alone it won't solve our problems.

Instead, the pressure of sport on both handler and dog will stress a bond that's already fragile. We have dogs being put in challenging situations without the relationship prerequisite. With the right foundations, however, sport is a wonderful way of strengthening dogs and boosting our bonds with them.

## Ramping Up Socialization

A common misconception is that dogs misbehave because they've not been socialized enough. If they're acting out around other people or dogs, it must be because they haven't been given enough opportunities to be around people and dogs, right? Wrong. Often, the problem is that they've been socialized excessively and incorrectly, and this is a major problem that I see with many—if not all—dogs that I work with.

We think we're helping our dogs by constantly exposing them to new things, people, and dogs. I've heard countless owners tell me they thought taking their dogs to day cares, dog parks, puppy or breed-specific playgroups and meet-ups, pack walks, and so on would be great ways to socialize their dogs and help their behavioral issues. They are baffled to see these issues only get worse.

As I explain later, we need to have a strong relationship base with our dog before we go out into the world. We need to mean something to our dogs for them to be open to socializing, and that takes time.

# Prescribing Medications

Aided by growth in veterinary behavior specialties, it's becoming increasingly common and normalized to have dogs on long-term psychotropic medication, prescribed for a range of behavioral issues. I am not saying that our veterinarians don't have our dogs' best interest at heart. Veterinary medicine is a difficult career, and vet professionals are doing this work because they love animals and want to help them. But as with human medicine, especially in the West, there is an emphasis on solving problems that pop up instead of looking to cure the root cause. And while vets are incredibly knowledgeable in many aspects of animal health, that does not make them experts on behavior and relationships with those animals. Yet, medication has become an acceptable way of dealing with behavioral issues. Medicating a dog is potentially less work than going back to Foundations, but there are also many adverse effects.

It is argued that medication decreases stress and aids the dog's ability to recover from stressful episodes. It is said that meds help dogs cope and allow learning to take place. In my view, numbing dogs' feelings of anxiety and fear misses two important points. One, learning is ultimately an emotional experience that dogs must go through, otherwise they will never transcend the normal apprehension associated with learning something new. Two, learning is a relational experience—when dogs are in the company of a trusted teacher, they learn better and feel more secure, knowing they have someone to rely on.

There is no learning without experiencing some discomfort—that's a normal part of growth, a positive stress. When we choose to medicate dogs over the long term, not only are we compromising their learning, we're also overlooking the way of life behind their behavior. We're ultimately saying that they're the ones that are the problem. My preference is to clean up the situation first and then assess if there was really a need for meds. With that said, if you have a dog on medication, I urge you to not take them off these meds without consulting your vet first.

## Shopping for the "Perfect Tool"

We live in a consumer-driven world; capitalism sadly runs much of our lives and this affects our dogs too. There is a beast of a marketing machine targeting dog owners who are desperate to find solutions. Walk into any pet store, and you will find not only a dizzying array of toys, foods, treats, and clothing items but also various tools meant to manage behavior.

Dogs with fears of loud noises? A ThunderShirt or a pair of ThunderCaps should do the trick. There are calming collars for dogs with anxiety and puzzle bowls for fast-feeding dogs. But by far, we see a variety of tools designed to exert control over dogs and prevent them from pulling. These include tools such as prong collars, choke chains, electronic collars, head halters, and no-pull harnesses, among others.

If these tools work, it's because they hurt. Without exception, these tools cause dogs discomfort or pain, while giving many owners the false impression that they've solved their problem. Suppressing dogs with such tools does not make them safer; it only frustrates them and invites further problems while yet again helping us overlook and not take responsibility for way of life.

In sum, the excuses we're making for our dogs' issues and the limited ways we've tried to deal with them have run their course. These misguided beliefs and assumptions mean we are unable to address our situation effectively. And worst of all, there are consequences to all this misunderstanding: endless frustration, unnecessary spending, and preventable relinquishment and euthanasia—these are heartbreaks I want to spare you.

While our dogs and their behaviors are a product of conditioning, remember that we, too, are a product of conditioning. Society and the prevailing culture around dogs have also conditioned us into believing certain things about dogs—

things that simply aren't true and that ask dogs to behave in ways inconsistent with what they are.

I'm giving you permission to bust out of the mold and look at our culture around dogs with a little more distance, while acknowledging that this can be difficult. We need to look beyond behavior and accept that simply modifying behavior through conditioning, sport, tools, or medication will not solve our issues. Dogs are much more than their breed or background. What we might see as unchangeable personality traits or deep-seated psychological conditions are their best attempts to cope and not really who they are at the core.

So if these long-held beliefs about dogs, their behavior, and how to change it are flawed, then where do we turn? This is where the Way of Life method comes in. In the next chapter, we'll discuss the five ideas of the logic underlying the Way of Life method.

# For Reflection

1. What drew you to a life with dogs?

2. How would you characterize your relationships with your past dogs (if any) and your present dog?

3. What is the breed of your current dog, and to what extent is your dog representative of their breed(s)?

4. How would you describe your dog's behavior at this time? Which aspects do you love, and which do you struggle with?

5. Which solutions have you attempted for behavioral issues, and in which ways were they successful or unsuccessful?

# CHAPTER 2

# The Way Of Life Logic

The questions we don't ask become the puzzles we don't solve.

**—A. J. DARKHOLME,** author and poet

T*obey, a Siberian-Labrador mix a little under two years old, was brought to me with separation anxiety concerns. Along with millions of others in Canada and around the world, Tobey's owner had shifted to working from home during the pandemic lockdowns. Being a fit and active person, she hiked daily and thought that a dog could share her active lifestyle and enjoyment of being out in nature. Soon enough, she brought young pup Tobey home. She, her partner, and Tobey spent much of these isolating times exclusively together.*

*During this period, many dog owners, new as well as experienced, developed strong feelings of attachment toward their dogs, and this client was no exception. But, at about a year old, Tobey began to act up when left alone. Complaints from building management about his barking soon streamed in. My client and her partner tried working on Tobey's increasing issues but could not sustain their efforts as they separated a few months later. The change was difficult for both my client and Tobey and left her having to deal with his issues on her own.*

*She tried what she could, including a bark collar, a camera, and having family members or pet sitters come stay with Tobey whenever she had to be away. None of it helped. As we started working together, she came to learn that separation issues reflect a lack of maturity in the dog and in the human-dog bond. She needed to go deeper into the nature of their relationship and the way of life that produced it.*

*We went to work, first on the practical aspects of their way of life including regulating Tobey's movements and access to things, returning him to a consistent schedule focused on down time in the crate and solo time on her apartment's balcony. When out and about, my client protected Tobey's space from intrusion, returning them both to a place of intimacy. She showed him that she had a handle on the environment, and he could just relax. During this time, she used the garage and stairwell of her building astutely to exercise Tobey, protecting him from outside influence. He also boarded with me several times, which allowed him to vocalize all he wanted, ride out the stress of separation, and recover from it. The experience also gave him a break from his busy urban environment and sent his confidence soaring.*

*Already, we're seeing a marked decrease of anxiety in Tobey. A large and powerful dog, he's now more manageable when he and his owner are out in the world. At home, he's calmer and increasingly capable of being on his own. When a dog's way of life is sound, the dog will be too. It is only a matter of time before my client and her dog can enjoy the relationship they were meant to have.*

Way of life is a powerful determinant of dogs' attitude and behavior. Therefore, we can't possibly ask our dogs to change while keeping their way of life as is. In this chapter, I will walk you through the Way of Life logic with the following five key lessons:

1.  Problem behaviors are not inherent in dogs; rather, they are about dogs' way of life.

2.  Our relationships with our dogs are a fundamental aspect *and* product of our way of life.

3.  Rearing dogs is not the same thing as training dogs.

4.  Way of life is an ongoing commitment and it is based on four pillars.

5.  Our way of life follows rearing and relationship stages observed in dogs, wolves, other animals, and humans.

# 1.  Problem behaviors are not inherent in dogs; rather, they are about dogs' way of life.

One of the most important steps to take toward addressing behavioral issues is to look beyond behavior and to recognize that it's almost never just about the behavior. We could be dealing with a mild case of food aggression, a little possession around toys, a severe fear of strangers, extreme leash reactivity, or inordinately high sound sensitivity. And while it's easy to see the symptom of the problem as the problem itself, believe me: working on the behavior isn't what's going to fix things.

As discussed in chapter 1, we have a tendency to attribute behavior to the dog's background, breed, or personality. Of course, these are critical contributors to behavior, but we overlook the power of a dog's way of life. We, as the owners and guardians of our dogs, seem unaware of how much discretion we have over that way of life and, therefore, how much influence we have over our dog's behavior.

A focus of much organizational behavior research is the influence of the person versus the situation on individual behavior. Gary Johns, a leading organizational behavior scholar and expert on context forces, argues that it makes no sense to judge the behavior of individuals without attention to situation. His research suggests that context and setting are far more powerful determinants of behavior than personality or other individual factors.[4] I know the same is true of dogs.

---

4   Gary Johns, "The Essential Impact of Context on Organizational Behavior," *Academy of Management Review* 31, no. 2 (2006): 386–408, https://doi.org/10.5465/amr.2006.20208687.

We say things like "the dog is aggressive," "the dog has separation anxiety," "the dog is anxious," or "the dog is reactive." You now know that these labels don't address the context driving the outward behavior. Until we investigate a dog's way of life and begin the process of reengineering that life, let's not pass judgment on any dog.

I hope this key lesson frees you from the thinking that we don't have control over the situation, because we do. We know from our relationships with humans that it is wiser for us to change our own attitude rather than attempt to change others. This entire time, we've been trying to change dogs while leaving their way of life—the root cause of their behavior—unexamined and unchanged. Any time we've attempted to change dogs—whether through training, coercive tools, or medication—what are we saying? We're saying the problem lies with the dog. This lesson asks us to reframe that belief.

## 2.  Our relationships with our dogs are a fundamental aspect *and* product of our way of life.

There are many aspects to a dog's way of life, and we'll get to those in the fourth key lesson. Most important, though, is the quality of the bond between the dog and person. This is where it's helpful to talk about another school of thought in psychology, attachment theory. Unlike stimulus-response (operant conditioning) theory, which is concerned with behavior and behavior modification through reinforcement, attachment theory is concerned with attachments and how they drive behavior.

Attachment theory is a product of the joint work of John Bowlby and his student Mary Salter Ainsworth. Bowlby and Ainsworth theorized that attachment performs a natural and healthy function in childhood as well as adulthood and that attachments constitute a fundamental aspect of human functioning.

Attachment theory draws on concepts from many fields, including developmental psychology, psychoanalysis, and ethology, or the study of animals under natural conditions. Notably, Bowlby was inspired by the ethologist Konrad

Lorenz and his concept of imprinting. He later advanced the controversial notion that family experiences are a fundamental cause of emotional turmoil, revolutionizing thinking about bond and its impact on development.

Later, Ainsworth advanced the concept of the attachment figure, or "mother," as a "secure base," from which the infant can explore the world. She tested these ideas empirically by developing the strange situation test, a laboratory procedure frequently used in both human and animal studies where the impact of separation from the attachment figure is assessed. She discovered different reactions to separation, reflecting varied attachment styles resulting from early interactions with the attachment figure.

Namely, insecure attachments result in distress and separation anxiety while secure relationships empower an individual's autonomy and agency. For people—and dogs too—this secure base is one that they can always return to, knowing support and guidance are available there. Thus, secure attachment predicts creativity, autonomy, and exploration.

In times of stress, an individual's attachment style, the product of that individual's early experiences with intimate relationships, gets activated. Those who have a secure attachment style will deal with things better than those who do not. What does this mean? It's the quality of our attachments that dictates how we behave when faced with stressful situations. If we have secure attachments, we are more likely to take things in stride and carry on.

In the same vein, a strong human-dog bond enables dogs to handle the challenges and stresses of human society without fear, anxiety, or reactivity. Dogs with secure attachments, meaning dogs that have been raised to feel safe, are less likely to experience stress. They are likely to deal better with known culprits of anxiety and misbehavior, such as thunderstorms or fireworks, and social situations, like meeting new people or going places.

## 3. Rearing dogs is not the same thing as training dogs.

The next key lesson is that the relationships we have with our dogs are not just the result of training but a product of rearing (which I'll sometimes call "raising" or "upbringing"). While training teaches skills through conditioning, rearing instills character traits through the way of life. Each moment of every day, we are managing and interacting with our dogs in various ways, and whether we know it or not, we are sending messages and instilling attitudes through these actions that may or may not better our relationship. All these are acts of rearing our dogs.

And yet, hardly anyone talks about rearing dogs anymore. I recall attending a conference surrounding the theme of aggression in dogs and hardly hearing the words "rearing" or "raising." Every possible reason for aggression was discussed except the possibility that we may have failed in rearing the dog. When one attendee asked a related question, a well-known behaviorist quickly responded that "we don't want to blame the adopters." It's unfortunate that encouraging people to take responsibility is seen as blame instead of enlightening and empowering.

When I think about training, I think about mechanical cue-behavior-consequence sequences. I ask the dog for something. The dog does it. The dog gets rewarded. This is how we teach behaviors such as sit, down, come, and so on. Here, we are conditioning the dog—creating enough repeated associations as to form a stimulus-behavior relationship. There is no thought. There is no heart—only mechanics, a simple programming of the dog's mind. There are many in the dog training community who believe that programming dogs to do things is all that's needed for well-behaved dogs. If that were the case, all one would need when working with reactivity, for example, are cues such as watch me or leave it. If you've ever seen a dog being told a command over and over again to no avail, you know this isn't true.

In my view, training is essential to teach skills that may not be entirely natural or easy to the dog—for example, in work or sport. But nurturing a true bond requires that we rear our dogs, and rearing involves much more than training. When we focus on rearing, the dog is de-emphasized in favor of us, the people doing the rearing. When we focus on rearing, the attention shifts from the dog learning something to *becoming* something—a certain kind of animal endowed with specific traits, a dog with a certain attitude. There are three traits that I work to instill in dogs: *soundness*, *strength*, and *spiritedness*.

Notice I didn't say friendliness. I didn't say sociability. I didn't even say politeness, biddability, or obedience. Without a foundation of soundness, strength, and spiritedness, none of these other qualities can be developed. Let's look at what these mean.

## Soundness

Sound dogs are thoughtful, calm, and balanced. Because they can think, they can discriminate between situations and understand that some behaviors are acceptable in some places but not others. Sound dogs are nonconfrontational and nonreactive. Instead of succumbing to the fight-or-flight response, they think and seek out their person should any doubt or stress arise in their minds. "Sound" means they take in situations before responding; there is a space for thought between stimulus and action.

## Strength

A life with humans in the twenty-first century is not exactly easy on dogs. Cultivating their strength helps build resilience against all sorts of stressors, including fireworks, thunderstorms, traffic and construction noises, our long working hours in and outside the home, and a public that feels entitled to invade their personal space. When we have strength, we don't have separation anxiety. When we have strength, we can encounter stressful periods, and our dogs ride things out with us. When we have strength, the holiday noises are annoying, but they're not cause for panic. The dog feels less stressed overall and can sustain a certain amount of stress. As decreasing stress is a factor for longevity, you're also doing yourself and your dog a favor by cultivating strength.

## Spiritedness

Having bestowed upon our dogs the gifts of being able to think (soundness) and deal with life (strength), we have now instilled confidence and spirit in them. Spirited dogs aren't afraid to be who they are. They can "be dogs" in all the wonderful ways this may manifest. They're not afraid to make mistakes. They're not afraid to push boundaries. They're not afraid to be playful. They can let their guard down, be who they are, and love us with all they have.

When dogs are sound, strong, and spirited, they are able, consequently, to manifest the following capabilities, allowing them to be the great companions we want them to be:

→ **Functionally obedient.** The first clue that something's off in our way of life is when we're killing ourselves training dogs to obey and behave. When we are mindful of our way of life and create a real relationship with our dogs, they become what I call "functionally obedient." In other words, they behave without us having to ask. They act out of sound judgment, not because behaviors have been trained into them. They stay close without cues or leashes and without having to be constantly told.

→ **Tolerant of social situations.** Dogs are predators at the core and central to this identity is selectivity and suspicion in social interactions. Dogs don't have to be social butterflies or particularly extroverted, but they might have to accept a degree of socializing. When dogs are raised to be sound, they can be trusted to seek us out if uncomfortable rather than take matters in their own hands (or paws, as it were).

→ **Nonconfrontational.** Sound, strong, and spirited dogs do not have an axe to grind. They don't go looking for trouble, get into arguments, or fight with others. They are too good to fight, too sound for the drama. Should they come across people or animals looking for trouble, they withdraw rather than engage. Yet too many dog owners still consider this kind of dog submissive. Meanwhile, the bully that's looking for trouble is seen as dominant as opposed to neurotic and insecure.

→ **Healthily bonded.** When we raise our dogs with these traits, we unlock the doors to their hearts. Dogs are able to form deep and meaningful attachments with humans who enhance their capacity to think, boost their self-esteem, and let them be dogs. At the same time, this bond is not a codependent one. Our dogs are okay if we're gone during the day or if we travel. They're even okay if we're not okay.

→ **Open to new experiences.** When dogs are bonded to us, they are open to new experiences that are safely introduced by those they trust. Sound, strong, and spirited dogs will also be more receptive to those things: "I like you, so I'm probably going to like this!" Yet too often, we misinterpret a dog's reactions as fear or aggression, when it might simply be the case that the dog was introduced too soon, without the requisite relationship.

The result of a healthy approach to rearing is that we become the ultimate incentive for the dog. Dogs now want to do things in gratitude and appreciation. "You make me want to be a better dog," says the dog that's raised with soundness, strength, and spiritedness in mind. Rather than programming dogs through training and conditioning, we create a way of life that helps unlock their natural intelligence and unearth their real personality.

## 4. Way of life is an ongoing commitment and it is based on four pillars.

Now you know that we are raising our dogs in each moment and with every interaction—not just during training sessions. To me, this is the core of Way of Life. It is not a one-and-done system. It is both the experience and result of the myriad decisions we make on behalf of our dogs. Our way-of-life decisions, whether conscious or subconscious, create a context, and the dog is a product of that context.

There are four pillars that I focus on in the Way of Life method:

→ Relationship, mission, and mindset

→ Managing space and boundaries

→ Socialization

→ Drive development through exercise, training, and sport

These pillars constitute essential aspects in the way of life. Across the three stages—Foundations, Exposure, and Integration—we'll be visiting these individually and building on them. Let's take a look at each.

# Relationship, Mission, and Mindset

At each of the three stages, we are starting with a particular relationship. We also have a specific mission, along with the need to cultivate a mindset that supports that mission. Basically, each stage requires us to have a certain attitude toward the dog and to not only act but also feel, think, and relate in ways that support our mission.

As you learned in the second key lesson, the nature and quality of the relationship between us and our dog is a powerful part of our way of life. Our relationship is in part driven by our mindset about dogs—our attitudes toward them and how we perceive and relate to them—for example, if we feel sorry for the dog, worry about the dog, or desperately want the dog to get better. These relationship dynamics create a powerful social and psychological context for our dogs, one that may or may not support the resolution of behavioral issues and the rearing of sound, strong, and spirited canines. When working with a dog, think of your attitudes, thoughts, and feelings toward that dog as equally if not more important than any other tool in your kit.

I realize the challenge involved in harnessing one's thoughts and feelings. That challenge is compounded when we have a household with multiple members, each one holding different attitudes and behaviors toward the dog. I work frequently with families whose members do not see eye to eye on dealing with the dog, which leads to arguments and ultimately confusion for the dog. When we rethink the dog's way of life, we need everyone on board. This is a collective commitment: families need to choose to make a difference in their own lives as well as that of their dog. I have worked with several clients who felt that their family ties grew deeper as they aligned themselves for the benefit of the dog and their family unit.

## The Family Hierarchy

The family hierarchy is a model that helps us understand relationship dynamics and, ultimately, our goal in raising our dogs.

Organizations of any kind entail some form of hierarchy, meaning a structuring of authority and responsibility distributed differently among members. Companies, governments, nonprofits, and organizations of all kinds consist of hierarchies. Human clans, tribes, and families are organized around hierarchies. Just about every cohabitating animal in the animal kingdom lives within a hierarchy of some kind, be they pods of whales, herds of deer, troops of monkeys, or bands of coyotes. And of course there are wolf packs, which epitomize hierarchy, organization, and collaboration for the good of all.

While I cover wolf packs and their connection to dogs in greater detail in the next chapter, keep in mind for now that the hierarchy and social structure present in any familial organization is meant to ensure bonds, cooperation, and survival. Dogs are wired for the idea of someone being in charge, someone exercising authority, power, and presence so that they can simply be dogs. A sense of law and order is essential for dogs' psychological well-being.

The five hierarchical levels found in wolf packs are shown in the illustration. These levels represent growth from infancy to adulthood as well as roles and responsibilities within the pack.

When wolf cubs begin life, they are at Level 1: Infant Cubs, the lowest level of the hierarchy. They need everything provided to them and cannot make decisions or be in charge of any part of pack life. As they mature, they progress in strength and mental capacity to Level 2: Adolescents and Yearlings. They are still learning but are beginning to be incorporated into the pack. Wolves are generally considered adults at two years old, reaching Level 3: Adult, where they take on responsibility for some part of pack life. Some adults rise to pack leadership, reaching Level 5: Alpha. In large enough packs, there is shared leadership between alphas (Level 5) and the seconds-in-command or leaders-in-training at Level 4: Beta.

For some, the terms "alpha" and "beta" will bring up the much maligned and controversial notion of dominance. Unfortunately, the existence of ranks within wolf packs, meant to ensure safety and survival for all, has led some dog trainers to find justification for abusive and harsh techniques. These harmful approaches reflect the belief we held for the longest time that we needed to be dominant over our dogs. Many sadly still think this way. Yet, this is based on a misunderstanding of dynamics in captive wolf packs—"captive" being the key word.

Indeed, dysfunctional dominance dynamics played out in these random assemblages of disparate wolves. Being captive, the wolves lacked family connections and natural experiences that create real bonds, turning some into domineering bullies and others into beating posts. You'll notice in the description above that nowhere did I mention "omega" as one of the ranks. In a healthy hierarchy, these scapegoats who absorb everyone else's stress simply do not exist.

In wild wolf packs, there is a definite order with a clear mission: to grow and mature the young members into fully functioning adults. No pack could survive if the young stayed immature or if some members were allowed to stay insecure and weak. They all need to grow and fill a role for the cycle of life to continue. This means that the hierarchy is dynamic rather than static. By the same token, you can think of your own family—people and dogs—as taking on roles within this hierarchy. As dog owners, we, too, have a mission to act as the leaders of our hierarchy so that we can grow the young ones in our charge to the highest level possible.

Therefore, we do not need to be dominant over our dogs, but we do need to be dominant *for* our dogs—"dominant" meaning being parents, leaders, and guides. I mean, aren't we the ones in charge? We are, and the dogs know it. Any time we have a conflict with our dog, it is helpful to ask, who is the one really in charge here—the human or the dog? Where are we on the family hierarchy, and where is the dog?

Our goal as effective leaders is twofold: to be a Level 4 or 5 and to motivate our dogs to move up to a Level 3. To do this, we have to be the ones in charge of the way of life. This requires that we carry ourselves with gentle power and authority and that we not be afraid of that. Our dogs are looking to us to fulfill that leader role—to be a reliable and consistent safe space for them—and yet we continue to look outside ourselves for the answer to behavioral issues.

Unfortunately, the damage inflicted by trainers who resort to outdated dominance thinking has led some in the dog training community to claim that dominance does not exist and that we don't need to be leaders for our dogs. But in rejecting the idea of dominance, we ended up throwing out the baby with the bathwater. When we said, "We don't need to be dominant," this also came to mean "it doesn't matter what we represent to our dogs" and "who and what we are to our dogs is irrelevant."

This is a core reason why so many of us are struggling. We are oblivious to just how much we matter to our dogs and how crucial it is that we exemplify the kinds of leaders and stewards they can trust. For me, those who are truly dominant, as opposed to domineering, are simply in charge of the care of others and have the strength that allows others to thrive knowing they are safe and guided. At the core of our leadership is our aim to mature our dogs to that healthy level of adulthood.

## LEVELS OF THE FAMILY HIERARCHY

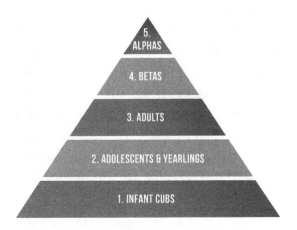

While it's evident that we need to mature a puppy into a healthy adult, in reality, the same goes for any dog with issues. While mainstream training sees behavioral issues as behaviors to be changed or conditioned into something else, I view them as reflecting a lack of maturity in the relationship and, by extension, in the dog. They reflect a dog who's been kept infantile as opposed to raised to be sound, strong, and spirited. When dogs are coddled and allowed to remain neurotic and dysfunctional, on some level we are failing in our job at maturing them. When we mature dogs and ask them to behave as grown-ups, behavioral issues simply cannot exist.

Think about it this way: dogs *want* to mature. Working up the social hierarchy is pure instinct for dogs. When we keep them stuck in their behavioral issues, i.e. immature, we are creating a deep, almost existential conflict between us. It's the most natural thing for them to grow and follow a worthy leader in doing so. The Way of Life method is not just for your dog; it will also teach *you* to become that worthy leader.

## Managing Space and Boundaries

Let's now move to a more practical aspect of way of life: the degree of freedom and choice that we grant our dogs. Lately, there's been growing emphasis on giving dogs greater agency. I could not agree more with the idea of dogs being able to exercise choice and live as freely as possible, but there's a time and place for this. Dogs deserve freedom and choice when they are mature enough (free of behavioral issues) to handle that choice.

Space and boundaries decisions pertain to how much structure dogs have in any given situation—for example, whether and how much dogs are confined, whether we have a leash on them, whether they can go where they wish, or whether they can exercise a degree of choice. This is important because although we can teach dogs what we want them to learn, they can also learn things we did not want them to when we are lax in our management. This is often referred to as "inadvertent training" or "unintended learning."

Here's the thing: The level of freedom granted to a dog is an endorsement of that dog's general attitude and behavior. When my poorly behaved dog has the freedom to go from one place to another, one person to another, to make this decision and that one, I am validating the dog and expressing my approval.

"Wait a minute," says the dog. "We fight when I try to do what I want outside, but when I come home, I do what I want without any repercussions! What's going on here?"

Managing dogs at the start so that they can be truly free is a cornerstone of this approach. As they progress through the stages, we start to expand their world. Eventually, we can do more and go more places successfully, allowing our dogs to practice greater levels of responsible freedom.

## The Three Circles

A helpful model to manage space and boundaries is the concept of the three circles, developed by my former mentor, Sam Malatesta. Take a look at the illustration, which shows three concentric circles. According to Sam, dogs "slice" specific environments into these three circles, and each one carries specific significance.

The largest circle is the territorial circle. This outer circle is the boundary of the space that you're in, a.k.a. the territorial line. Boundaries include the fence line of your home and yard, the walls of a room including doors and windows, the walls in the inside of our vehicle, and so on. Beyond the territorial line is another "world," and our dogs know that. So we need to instill in dogs the understanding that we do not hang out by these territorial lines nor leave one territory for another without permission.

The next circle is the tranquil circle, the 10- to 15-foot-radius around us. We don't need our dogs to be right at our side all the time, but we don't want them hitting the territorial line either. Rather, we want them within the tranquil circle, in our orbit. When out and about with their moms, puppies orbit around their mothers at about this radius. From the beginning, we work on preserving that same instinct toward us.

The third and smallest of the three circles is the space immediately around our body, the inner circle. Sam often refers to this as the "handler-dog box" and emphasizes that "nothing goes in and nothing goes out, without my permission." Our dog cannot leave this box without asking and us allowing it. No one can come into the box and touch our dog without our explicit permission or invitation.

I want you to imagine for a moment whether a mother wolf or mother dog would allow an intruder near her cubs. Picture the wrath of that mom if something were to come near her babies. And yet, we allow people to violate that circle all the time, touching our dogs, looking at our dogs, or allowing their dogs into our personal space. On a deep level, our dogs are looking to us to provide security from that. Dogs thrive on safety and knowing that both the inner and tranquil circles are places where nothing can hurt or disrupt them.

Throughout the exercises in each stage, we will lean on the three circles to help strengthen our dogs' understanding of what is expected in each space.

THE

# THREE CIRCLES

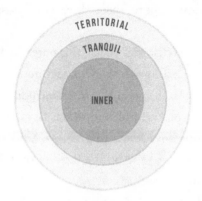

# Socialization

I speak to clients all the time who say they can't wait to have their puppy's shots completed so they can start socializing. Countless adopters of new rescue or shelter dogs have told me the first thing they're going to do is socialize their dogs to help them get over their difficult pasts. What does "socialization" mean anyway? And why do we think socialization will make dogs not be afraid of things?

The lack of rigor in our understanding of what socialization is has translated into a plethora of practices that have hurt both humans and dogs. Sam Malatesta refers to these practices as "forced socialization"[5] while trainer Denise Fenzi describes them as "hyper socialization," which she says produces dogs that become "hyper greeters." She goes on to say that such dogs "cannot function if they are not allowed to interact with every dog and person they see. No greeting?

---

5   Sam Malatesta and Souha Ezzedeen, "One with Dog: Sam Malatesta's Whelping Box Approach to Rearing and Training Dogs," (unpublished manuscript, Canadian Intellectual Property Office: Copyright Registration #1130736, 2016), 27.

They scream, whine, and pull frantically on their leashes toward the object of their desire—and show lots of frustration at being held back."[6]

Mainstream socialization generally involves early, intense, and frequent exposure of pups to all sorts of things. In other words, the more the better. For many, this has meant taking new puppies and dogs everywhere we go, having them meet everyone, and having everyone come play with them. It's meant practices like "pass the puppy." It's meant asking people to treat and touch our dogs. It's meant that as a society we find it normal to go interrupt strangers, asking to pet their dogs.

The idea that we ought to socialize in such fast and furious ways is in great part responsible for the rise of dog parks, doggy day cares, puppy playgroups, and breed gatherings in our culture. People feel awful when their dogs don't take well to these situations, not realizing that it is this kind of socialization that's responsible for the fear, timidity, and reactivity experienced by so many. About two decades ago, I, too, had fallen for this nonsense and did a lot of harm to my dog's stability and our bond.

Many trainers, breeders, academics, and veterinarians have relentlessly advocated for this extreme socialization, bolstered by arguments surrounding critical or "sensitive" socialization periods.[7] This is based on the idea that puppies are very impressionable and best able to learn about the social and physical world during the first three or four months of life. Yet, one must ask, "What exactly is the puppy absorbing during this critical time?"

There is also a belief that once that period is over, that's it. "If this time passes without your puppy having adequate exposure … she may be at increased risk for developing fear, timidity, aggression,"[8] warns a brochure found in veterinary offices. This not only is inaccurate but also paints a rather pessimistic picture of dogs, their resilience, and lifelong capacity for learning.

---

6    Denise Fenzi. "Socialization in the World of COVID," Denise Fenzi Blog, September 21, 2020, https://denisefenzi.com/2020/09/socialization-in-the-world-of-covid/.

7    Zazie Todd, "Why You Need to Socialize Your Puppy," Companion Animal Psychology, February 25, 2015, https://www.companionanimalpsychology.com/2015/02/why-you-need-to-socialize-your-puppy.html.

8    American Animal Hospital Association, "The Social Scene: Introducing Your Puppy to the World," Pet Behavior Brochure Series, 2016.

## The Levels of Socialization

Our goal here is not to merely train dogs as much as it is to raise them to be sound, strong, and spirited by being deliberate in our way of life. Socialization is one critical pillar in our way of life, so it is essential we be subtle about what we mean by it.

Often, the meaning and goals of socialization are confused with the levels of socialization, which refer to degrees of exposure to and levels of engagement with the world. We need to start at the beginning and progress along the rungs of exposure as our dogs mature and our bonds deepen.

## LEVELS OF SOCIALIZATION

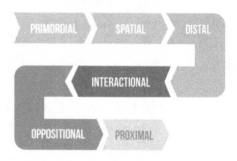

The first level of socialization, primordial, is the socialization between us and our dog—no one else. It is what allows us the bonding foundation that will help us socialize at the next levels. Spatial socialization is about experiencing different spaces and environments. At the distal level, the dog is exposed to people, animals, and things, inside and outside the home, at a safe distance. At the proximal level, we are physically close to people, animals, and things, while still expecting our dog to ignore them. At the interactional level, the dog engages and interacts physically and psychologically with people and animals.

Last, at the oppositional level, we have interactions that the dog could experience as uncomfortable or invasive. One way to appreciate the extent of this oppositional socialization is to think of it as exposures where we're asking the dog to hold back from being a dog. For example, dogs are protective of their space, and we're asking them to tolerate space invasions when we expose them to oppositional socialization. Beginning with primordial socialization, we will bolster and build upon the levels of socialization throughout the three stages.

# Drive Development

The final pillar in our approach is developing and harnessing canine drives through exercise, training, and sport. I think of the canine drives as push buttons on dogs' engines, what gets them going, grabs their attention, and keeps them engaged. Is it treats? Is it a good game of tug? Is it our physical or verbal affection?

Trainers talk a lot about the canine drives and how to grow dogs' motivation to do things. One of the very first books on dog training I ever read was Jack and Wendy Volhard's *Dog Training for Dummies*, which emphasized the management of these drives, what it takes to awaken or settle a dog's drives, and how to "switch" from one drive to another. Given the power of drives in shaping behavior, knowledge of drives and how to harness them is a critical aspect of handling dogs successfully and therefore one of the core elements underlying Way of Life.

## The Canine Drives

Canine drives are inherited from dogs' wolf ancestors (whom we'll learn more about in the next chapter). They generally fall into the following four categories: food, prey, pack, and defense drives. Throughout the three stages, we harness

THE
FOUR CANINE DRIVES

these drives by following a deliberate progression from food drive to prey drive to pack drive and then defense drive.

Food drive is a dog's very first sense of enthusiasm and motivation for a goal. When those cubs are newborn, the mother is not teaching them hunting skills; rather, she is feeding them, building their food drive.

The next drive that emerges as pups and cubs mature is prey drive, which includes various related drives such as the drive to sniff things out, a.k.a. hunt drive, or chase after things, a.k.a. offensive drive. While food drive is a juvenile drive, prey drive is an adolescent and emerging-adult drive.

Pack drive is about being oriented toward the family and is the sign of a maturing dog or wolf. The motivation to please, to connect, to bond, and to belong is one that comes with growth. It is a desire and joy to please without food, toys, or other incentives and is a hallmark of maturity in the dog and depth in our bond.

Last, defense drive is the desire to defend, to alert, and to protect. It is very much related to pack drive. It is only true attachment and loyalty that causes dogs to want to protect. Sometimes people with new dogs interpret their dogs barking at strangers or other dogs as being protective of them. I am quick to correct them that the dog doesn't have a bond to protect just yet. A healthy defense drive follows a healthy relationship, and that's generally not what we have when we're getting started.

These drives are natural and innate to dogs, but they can be dysfunctional, such as a dog that is aggressive about their food bowl or that trees every squirrel they see. Sound, strong, and spirited dogs display all of these drives in healthy ways, in having a healthy appetite, playing, forming deep attachments, and protecting in a self-assured way. In the Way of Life method, we work on fostering drives through exercise, training, and sport.

## Exercise

Dogs, regardless of breed, tend to be intensely physical creatures. While there are wide variations in need for physical stimulation, all dogs are happier and healthier if their bodies are exercised and kept lean, strong, and fit. When dogs are tired and their bodies are awash in endorphins, they can't help but feel better. This means that exercise is a crucial part of a healthy dog with active drives.

When dogs experience physical exertion, this awakens their desire to eat (food drive), which is why it's essential for dogs that are withdrawn and fearful to exercise safely. Eventually, this kind of exertion will open their appetites for food and then their enjoyment of toys and play. At the same time, there's exercise that supports our goals and exercise that doesn't. Say you're out on a jog and you allow every person on the trail to check out your dog. The dog is getting exercise, but the inappropriate socialization is defeating the purpose of the exercise. So, we adapt exercise to each of the three stages.

## Training

While exercise like running or playing fetch is physical, training is a form of mental exercise. Training can include day-to-day commands, tricks for fun, or cues for more complex behaviors in work and sport. In training, dogs realize that they can "work" to have their needs met; they can obey cues for food or perform for play. The sense of having a measure of control strengthens dogs and, in turn, their drives. The more experience dogs have with a given activity, sport, or discipline, the more they gain confidence and sharpen these drives.

Still, I hope you can appreciate by now that the Way of Life method is about all pieces of the puzzle working together. Just as with other aspects, training is layered across the three stages. In Foundations, we don't train in the traditional sense; rather, we work on setting up dogs to succeed, and we watch for good behavior and reward it instead of requesting it. As we get into Exposure, we build on this and introduce cues and rewards to build a language that the dog can understand and respond to.

## Sport

Each dog comes with drives derived from their breed legacy and personality. Hands down, sport is one of the best ways of harnessing dogs' drives and growing these drives to help dogs fully express their genetic potential and unique capacity. No matter the breed, your dog's drives can be stimulated and satisfied in one of the many sports available, and we will discuss how participation in sport will also evolve across the stages.

## 5. Our way of life follows rearing and relationship stages observed in dogs, wolves, other animals, and humans.

The final key lesson I want you to consider is that the way of life needs to be designed along stages that reflect the dog's development and the unfolding of our relationship. This is at the heart of raising a dog.

How do we know how to raise? We look to dogs. We look to wolves. We look to the animal. Our job is to transpose their innate rearing logic into how we rear our dogs. By seeing how animals raise their young naturally, we can distill that wisdom into a set of practices to help us raise our dogs. As these ways are baked into their DNA, our approach instinctively resonates with them. They can tell we get it.

It was my decade-long mentor, Sam Malatesta, who taught me to look to the canine kind for guidance. Sam was an experienced breeder who approached his craft a little differently than others. Instead of interfering with his breeding moms and their rearing, he observed them with some distance. He was endlessly fascinated by the behavior of the mother dog and how she did things with her babies. He'd often be asked, "How many males and females, Sam?"

"Not sure," he'd reply. Unlike other breeders who almost tell the mothers what to do and rescue rejected runts, Sam left his moms alone and respected their decisions. He knew the mothers knew better than anyone which pups were fit for life and which ones weren't.

Sam's brilliance was to observe breeding after breeding, litter after litter, mother after mother, eventually noting patterns and stages of rearing. Sam noticed that all the mother dogs, regardless of age, experience, personality, or inclination for mothering, reared their babies the same way. He was humble before the mother dog, learned from her ways, and therefore gained insight into how *we* can relate to our dogs so they can feel the same trust, joy, and confidence that pups feel in the presence of their moms.

From these decades of observations, Sam distilled a rearing template that formed his whelping box theory (see insert)—an outline of the behavior of mother and pups during the eight-week period from whelping (giving birth) to weaning (a puppy's transition from milk to solid food). The whelping box theory essentially translates the rearing ways of the mother dog for us, as the humans who will be taking over. Its insights are the bedrock to my approach, and importantly, it doesn't just apply to puppies. The three stages can be used to help us heal our relationships with our dogs, help them recover from behavioral issues, and rear sound, strong, and spirited dogs at any age.

---

## The Weekly Progression Of The Whelping Box Theory

**WEEK 1:** Pups are born, forcefully expulsed from the warm belly of their mother into a world where they must fend for themselves. Any breeder knows that not all puppies are going to make it. At birth, puppies cannot hear nor see, but they instinctively crawl toward their mother, their source of heat and nourishment and key to their survival. The mother dog ignores those pups who cannot make it to her. Those that do wiggle their way get fed, licked, and groomed. She does not punish, but she does ask her little ones to work their way in. She's also not always with her pups. She leaves to relieve herself and catch a break here and there, instilling independence and self-reliance early on.

**WEEK 2:** By now, the pups who were too weak to make it to their mother have passed away. The strong ones start opening their eyes and begin to get a little pushy with each other, displaying the first signs of competition within the litter. At this point, the mother dog will allow a friendly stranger to be present but will protect her puppies should the interaction evolve beyond that.

**WEEK 3:** The pups continue to develop—their eyes are fully open, their bodies stronger and more coordinated. Their vocal cords are getting lots of practice with much barking, whining, and whimpering going on. They continue to be driven by hunger and motivated by food, but at this point, predatory instincts start to kick in. This is seen in the roughhousing, pinning down, nipping, and other games of dominance that occur naturally between littermates.

**WEEK 4:** About midway into the rearing period, the mother dog starts spending longer periods of time away from her brood. She is more comfortable with not only the breeder handling her pups but also with friendly strangers. This is also the time when the pups start to get weaned off their mother's food, and the mother nurses standing up instead of lying down, which requires greater effort on the part of the growing pups. The pups' prey drive, honed through play with their mom and each other, continues to develop. While earlier, she would have allowed these games to proceed without interference, at this point she introduces discipline, becoming a little more protective of the soft pups and more assertive with the strong ones. The pups' defense drive starts to emerge; we see the pups now barking and growling at strangers.

**WEEK 5:** The puppies are weaned off their mother and attempts to feed off her are no longer permitted. Her interactions with her babies at this point are about weaning them and challenging them in play as opposed to feeding them. She will also exercise greater discipline and dominance over these bold and growing pups. This is not only to strengthen them but to prepare them to separate from her. Pups can be moved outside to a pen, creating a very different environment for the puppies and again reinforcing that separation from their mom, though she is still around to check on them.

**WEEKS 6–8:** Weaning continues in full force with the mother dog present but not nearly as involved as she once was. Still, when they are together, their mother is ever the epicenter. Where she goes, they follow, and she remains their source of safety and validation. The pups are exposed to visitors and other adult dogs that are suitable to socialize with impressionable young ones. Puppies begin to display their unique personalities as they adapt more and more to a human world. After all, going to their new homes with the humans they will call their own is only days away.

---

In sum, the Way of Life logic can be represented by five key lessons:

1.  Behavioral issues are not necessarily inherent in dogs; rather, they are about dogs' way of life. Our relationships with our dogs are a central aspect and consequence of that way of life.

2.  Rearing simply means we're conscious of our way of life and the kind of dogs it produces.

3.  Our aim is much more than training for skills; it is about rearing for the attitudes of soundness, strength, and spiritedness.

4.  Way of Life is an ongoing commitment based on four pillars: relationship, mission, and mindset; managing space and boundaries; socialization; and drive development through exercise, training, and sport.

5.  Way of Life is organized along rearing and relationship stages observed in dogs, wolves, other animals, and humans.

Having studied the mother dog under Sam's mentorship, I found myself wanting to go deeper and find out about how our dogs' ancestors raised their young. I went on to learn how wolves rear their cubs, finding inspiration and structure for my own three-stage methodology, all of which we'll explore in the next chapter.

# For Reflection

1.  What is your understanding of the word "relationship?" How do you feel human-human relationships differ from human-canine relationships?

2.  What are your goals for your dogs and for your relationship with them? To what extent do these goals feel accessible to you right now? What are you nervous about? What are you excited about?

3.  What is your understanding of training dogs versus the idea of rearing them?

4.  What is one thing in this chapter that really surprised you or offered a contradiction to what you previously understood about dogs?

5.  Make a list of what happens on an average day in your dog's life, then label each action or activity with the pillar that it falls into. How are each of the four pillars currently represented in your dog's life? What areas might need work?

# CHAPTER 3

# Designing Our Way Of Life In Stages

Man, in character, is more like a wolf…than he is any other animal.

—**CARVETH READ,** philosopher and logician

*I*t's a few months into my long-awaited sabbatical from the university, and I am about to cross an item off my bucket list: a visit to the Haliburton Forest Wolf Centre—a museum and wolf sanctuary only a few hours away from my home. My mother, our four dogs, and I take an enchanting drive north to the Centre and arrive at our inn, greeted by beautiful weather and a tolerable amount of visitors. We settle our things and get the dogs squared away, feeding them and letting them rest after the trip.

Haliburton Forest is a 100,000-acre forest that provides all kinds of recreational activities along with housing a research facility, three sawmills, and educational center. The Wolf Centre offers museum exhibits that showcase our checkered past with wolves—upon entering, we see various medieval tools of trapping and torture and pelts hanging on the walls. Walking deeper into the building, we arrive at a huge one-way window overlooking the woods where the wolves tend to hang out.

I approached the glass as near as I could, short of fogging my view with my breath. It is a few moments before I catch a sight of one of the wolves—Onyx, the *alpha male. Not too far from him, Luna, the aging but still beautiful alpha female, is curled up in comfort. Though these wolves are captive, they are wolves all the same. Their fascinating exquisiteness, graceful and assured movements, and hypnotic gazes fill me with awe.*

*I couldn't help but see in them the suffering that their ancestors had experienced for generations. When I read accounts of what was done and continues to happen, I am left breathless at the brutality levied against wolves. I feel the pain and loss they've felt for centuries, relentlessly hunted down by a conqueror at war with nature, at odds with his own soul. Meanwhile, the Indigenous people of this land knew the wolf as "Brother."*

*Symbols of freedom, icons of wilderness, keystone species, apex predators—there are so many words to describe this animal with whom we have much in common, this animal that we have lived alongside and adapted into the dogs we share our lives with today. I stand there, my eyes burning with a sense of deep emotional and spiritual connection to these animals, a bond that I know millions around the world share.*

*Later that night, we attend a talk on wolves and participate in a wolf howl— quietly walking from the lecture hall to the sanctuary, eventually howling in unison in hopes that the wolves would howl back. Our guide says that the wolves don't always, but that night, they did.*

*I know I was on some level changed by this experience. I go back home a few days later that much more intent on writing this book and sharing a method inspired by wolves. If I can only show the world just how much wolves have to teach us about enjoying deep bonds with our dogs, I tell myself, maybe they, too, might have a chance to live in peace.*

Consider the three stages—Foundations, Exposure, and Integration—for a moment and then think about how most of us bring new dogs home and integrate them right away. They have access to every corner of our residence and all the people and pets in it. They go where we go, meet who we meet, constantly exposed to new and different situations without any foundation or education. It's demoralizing and demotivating for dogs when they're not given the chance to work for their privileges. Big and small, workers or lap dogs, all dogs descend from noble animals that got nothing in life easily or freely—wolves. And when they miss out on the chance of earning their place, they are stripped of their natural strength.

Despite millennia of trials and travails, wolves have endured. They have survived around the globe and across the ages, the difficulty of their existence softened by the strength of the pack, their family. Wolves are driven by a love for their own that is unseen in other parts of nature. They display a level of loyalty that puts many humans to shame and have an iron will to not only survive but thrive. For the longest time, when watching wildlife documentaries, I would root for the prey animal running for its life. Now, I root for the hunting predators that are just trying to live and could die trying.

Be it the mother dog or wolf packs, our canid cousins are masters at raising their young. They are deliberate about how they do things, designing their way of life around stages. If we stop to consider for a moment, don't we do the same raising our young? Doesn't our own rearing flow through stages? When babies are born, parents are often quite protective of them and can keep them to themselves for a long time. Then they become toddlers and their world expands considerably, their personalities revealing themselves more acutely. Soon enough, they're off to kindergarten, progress through the school system, and then might continue with university and graduate education before becoming increasingly integrated in society, by working and starting families.

For some reason, though, we don't apply this wise thinking to our companion dogs. I feel blessed to have learned to look to the animal for answers and to see the wisdom of working in stages. I studied wolves and their rearing ways for several years before I sat down to write this book, finding in their wisdom inspiration and structure for the approach I outline here.

I know many of us in the world of dogs admire and cherish wolves and are gutted to see them hunted down and so savagely persecuted. We see them in our dogs. We see our dogs in them. We know they gave us dogs, and we know we owe them life. We owe them voice. We owe them regard for the gifts they've passed on to our dogs. And, as they are masters at raising their young and building powerful and long-lasting family bonds, we have much to learn from their ancient ways.

# Wolf and Human

One of the key reasons that humans and wolves gravitated toward, domesticated, and helped each other survive is due to the many similarities we share.

At the most basic level, we share what is called the "mammalian factor"—general characteristics that mammals display such as engaging in acts of affection like kissing, touching, playing, and tickling. Wolves and humans are in the minority of mammalian species that form pair bonds and mate for life. Mammals show unique personalities and a level of intelligence that allows them to be flexible and adaptable, including the capacity to bond with other species.

Further, mammalian life is endowed with culture, meaning a particular way of life. We share with wolves the practice of social organization, which manifests in leadership and authority structures, families, and boundaries. We establish order and hierarchy in our lives and organize our existence around the raising of our young.

Humans and wolves also value territory and boundaries. We are both very much tribal and territorial. Wolves are particularly big on boundaries. Marking the territorial boundaries is part of the lupine way of life, and just as they risk death during hunts, wolves are also killed by other wolves in battles over territory. We humans have done the same, though I hope that one day we'll transcend this tendency.

Whether in wolf packs or human society, the formation of unique and complex personalities is another aspect that we share, and this includes traits such as independence, intelligence, ambition, seriousness, and playfulness. Wolf observers and writers such as Farley Mowat and Rick McIntyre describe wolves as possessing traits that we see in dogs and ourselves—for example, having presence or being conscientious, thoughtful, affectionate, kind, and passionate.[9] And just like us, wolves' personalities are shaped by nature as well as nurture.

While humans are the ultimate predator, wolves are undisputed apex predators in their environments. They regulate the behavior and movement of the herd animals constituting their prey. In culling the weak, old, and diseased, they keep herds to an ecologically appropriate size and aid in the very survival of these animals and the ecosystems they call home.

Wolves are also extraordinary hunters, developing collaborative hunting skills to take down much larger animals even when outnumbered—something that humans have also been doing since hunter-gatherer times.

Just as we identify with specific groups of people such as our families or nations, wolves identify with their pack. Wolf packs range in size and can include this year's cubs, last year's yearlings, young adults who have yet to leave, and sometimes grandparents, aunts, and uncles. Both wolves and humans don't normally breed with relatives and can adopt orphaned pups. In wolves as in humans, there is evidence of communal nursing and communal denning. Unlike most mammalian species, human males and male wolves—rather than just the females—feed their offspring. Wolves bury their dead pups, grieve losses, and do so for a long time. Just as we recognize the voices of those we love, wolves recognize the howls of their family members.

In wolves, family bonds are crucial and are forged and strengthened through daily trials such as hunts, dealing with the elements, and defending territory. Bonds are also strengthened in celebration through successful hunts and births. That's why domineering behaviors are seen so starkly in captive wolves—they lack the opportunities presented by life in the wild to face common challenges and strengthen their bonds.

Wolves and humans also play as a means of solidifying bonds. There can be bickering and arguing, but we return to the ties that bind us. We are also

---

9    Rick McIntyre, *The Reign of Wolf 21: The Saga of Yellowstone's Legendary Druid Pack* (Vancouver: Greystone Books Ltd.), 2020.
Rick McIntyre, *The Rise of Wolf 8: Witnessing the Triumph of Yellowstone's Underdog* (Vancouver: Greystone Books Ltd.), 2019.
Farley Mowat, *Never Cry Wolf: The Amazing True Story of Life Among Arctic Wolves* (New York: Penguin Modern Canadian Classics), 1963.

both neotenic, retaining juvenile tendencies well into adulthood and sharing an enduring propensity toward having fun and playing games as ways of strengthening our ties.

# Wolf and Dog

Discussing wolves in the context of dogs is common but also controversial. Those who oppose wolf-dog comparisons argue, and rightfully so, that dogs aren't wolves and wolves aren't dogs. Yet this tendency to reject wolf-dog comparisons has been pushed to the extreme, going as far as thinking of dogs and wolves as entirely different species, which is simply not true.

The fact remains that dogs and wolves are both canids that share genetic characteristics. Technically, wolves (*Canis lupus*) are a parent classification for dogs (*Canis lupus familiaris*), meaning dogs are descendants of wolves. Dogs have much in common with their wild ancestors, including suspicion of strangers and deep bonds with family members. Dogs and wolves share instincts and skills that have served humans in various capacities including tracking, scenting, herding, and protection. Dogs and wolves have the capacity to possess, protect, hunt, and kill. They also love deeply and would do anything for their family. Another trait I believe they both share is muting their personalities when they're unsure of a person or situation. I know without a doubt that dogs rarely show their underbelly or display their true colors unless in loved and trusted company.

At the same time, I don't entirely blame people for insisting on the differences. Comparisons with wolves have unfortunately justified all sorts of meanness and cruelty toward dogs. If dogs are like these wild animals, then we can justifiably be hard on them and dominate them, right? This prevalent and misinformed idea is based on the occasional rituals of intimidation and dominance seen in wolf packs, particularly captive ones, as mentioned in chapter 2. Indeed, much of what we have learned about such events was derived from observations of captive wolves that are much less compassionate and cooperative than their wild counterparts whose very survival depends on cooperation. So I for one am not inclined to ignore the wisdom of wolves.

There are also other differences that you might find surprising. Wolves have a much larger brain and are more prosocial than dogs; in other words, wolves are more likely to help and share than dogs are. We all know of stories of competition, if not full-on hostility and aggression, in multidog households. Wolves care about each other and are attentive to each other, while dogs are first and foremost attentive to humans. There is collaboration and interdependence among wolves, while there is competition and independence among dogs.

When we keep our dogs' wild lineage in mind, it helps remind us of their primal nature. When we treat dogs exclusively as pets, we overlook that wild identity. By relentlessly training and programming obedience and performance in our dogs and having expectations of them that do not align with their core canid identity, we strip them of their instinctive nature. We're treating them as something other than dogs. This alone is the cause of myriad issues.

# Shared Leadership in the Wolf Pack

Wolf packs consist of complex family structures of adult members, yearlings, and cubs—the family hierarchy as discussed in chapter 2. At the top are the leaders and seconds-in-command, also known as the alphas and the betas. The alphas include a breeding male and female. Alphas rise to their status by displaying extraordinary social, tactical, and physical skills. They are considered the keepers of the wisdom and the models of a pack's shared identity and culture. Indeed, both human societies and wolf packs manifest unique cultures through shared norms, values, and rules of conduct. These are often enforced and passed on generation after generation by leaders and elders. When either of the alphas die, the process of knowledge transition is damaged, endangering the entire pack.

In contrast to the image of violent and domineering alphas, true leaders extend empathy, embody valor, and show benevolence and mercy. They lead by example, modeling sensitivity and wisdom. Those who rise because they were larger, stronger, and ruthless do not make effective leaders and are eventually taken down.

For the longest time, the fascination was with the alpha males—their size, power, and majesty—resulting in an overestimation of their role in the pack.

Wolf biologists had been predominantly men and were biased toward the males (shocking, I know). But closer observations by a new and more open-minded generation of wolf researchers are proving just how much influence the females wield. In fact, there exists a parallel hierarchy of males and females within the pack and shared leadership between alpha males and females, each assuming different roles. The alpha males take on political and ritualistic roles—they deal with rival packs, protect territorial boundaries, rally the pack around their deep howls, and motivate and inspire the members.

At the same time, there is a code of deference from the male structure to the female structure, resulting in wolf packs being predominantly matriarchal societies. Thus, new light is being shed on the role and importance of the alpha female, who assumes reproductive leadership of the pack. It is the alpha female who chooses who mates with her, and it may not always be the existing breeding male. She chooses the den site, decides when the pack will hunt, and where pups will be raised. She directs the pack's travels, and her personality sets the tone for the culture and character of the pack. The entire life of the pack is structured around the alpha female coming in estrous, giving birth, and spending weeks in the den with her newborns, the entrance to which is protected by the alpha male and other pack members.

---

## The Power of the Alpha Female

*Kingdom of the White Wolf* is a terrific National Geographic documentary miniseries on the arctic wolves of Ellesmere Island in the Canadian high arctic, providing a poignant example of the importance of the alpha female. Through the documentation and lens of explorer and photographer Ronan Donovan, we are able to appreciate truly wild wolves who have lived there for about 10,000 years and have never known human cruelty.

Donovan was able to locate a pack that accepted his presence, allowing him to film for the duration of the three-month summer period when the weather and light are more forgiving for humans. He named the pack the Polygon pack due to the polygon-shaped water formations surrounding their den.

He identified the breeding pair—the alpha female, an older wolf he dubbed White Scarf, and the alpha male, Clean Coat. With their pups grown up enough to leave the den site and travel, White Scarf led her family on a hunting journey, occasionally stopping and regrouping at various rendezvous sites.

Upon leading her pack on one last successful hunt, she was seen retreating quietly, limping away while everyone was sound asleep after their big meal. One of her daughters, One Eye, followed her but returned without her. Presumed dead, White Scarf's absence threw the pack into disarray and depression. They found themselves unable to work together and could not coordinate a successful hunt in her absence. This was all despite Clean Coat, the widower alpha male, still being around. It wasn't until One Eye stepped into the role of her late mother that order was gradually restored. Such is the centrality of the alpha female.

**SOURCE**

Gerber, Tony, director. *Kingdom of the White Wolf,* featuring Ronan Donovan. National Geographic, 2019. https://www.disneyplus.com/series/kingdom-of-the-white-wolf/

# A Wolf's Life in Stages

Like the mother dog discussed in the previous chapter, the wolf pack takes their cubs from the den to dispersal, growing them from a state of utter vulnerability and helplessness at birth to a place of strength and independence when it's time for the cubs to find their place in the pack or leave for a new one.

Instead of raising a pup from whelping to weaning over an eight-week period as is done with dogs, the work of the wolf family extends over a period of one to two years. While the mother dog is preparing a puppy for life with human beings, the wolf pack is preparing cubs for life in the wild. There are greater dangers and higher-order technical and social skills required.

In wolves (and one could also say in humans), young ones are reared through three stages: infant, adolescent, and adult. Connecting the dots between these rearing patterns and the unique relationship we have with our dogs as animals and companions, I devised a rearing program for our dogs that mirrors these growth stages. Let's look at these three stages and how they align with the process we'll be following for rearing our dogs.

## Stage 1: Cubs in the Den/Foundations

In the first stage, the denning stage, the cubs are born in the seclusion of their den. Wolf litters vary in size but usually include an average of four to seven pups. Planning ahead, the mother wolf will have chosen a suitable denning site, a safe space to give birth and leave the cubs when she steps out. Wolves around the world den differently according to geographic landscape. Wolves in warmer climates hide above ground while North American gray wolves can dig dens under log jams, in depressions around trees, and in rock formations. The denning stage lasts approximately two months. The den site constitutes the hub of social activity for the duration of that time. The mother remains with her cubs for the entire denning period, stepping out only occasionally.

While dens vary, they are essentially private chambers that allow for a safe birth and protection of the pups for several weeks while they're vulnerable and fully dependent on their mom. Dens are often chosen near water sources. Food surplus is cashed around the den should the mother need to eat while the others are away hunting. Packs are generally reluctant to hunt too close to the den for fear of attracting other predators to the cubs. Therefore, moms need to be strategic about the den site—preferably one that is both hidden and easy to keep an eye on from afar. As a result, good denning sites tend to be used generation after generation.

During the first three weeks of life, the cubs are only in the den and interact with only their mother, though other females might come in occasionally to check on them. The alpha male will also smell them briefly when he brings food to his mate. All members remain vigilant, guarding the site and leaving the mother food. She in turn is imprinting herself as the source of the cubs' survival and the provider of milk, warmth, and all things good. The cubs are in this dark and snug space, leading a very simple life. Early on, they also learn to be on their own because mom, while always close, does leave the den at times. They sleep huddled on each other for warmth when she's gone and beeline to her when she's around to feed. These first few weeks are almost an extension of the gestation period, a continued pregnancy allowing the cubs to gain their senses and grow rapidly. This is necessary because they are quite small when born due to how many cubs are in a litter.

At around three weeks, a significant change occurs. The cubs' eyes open, and they start making brief appearances at the head of the den, seeing the outside world in snapshots, and then going back in for more feeding and sleeping. This is the first time that the members of the pack can catch brief glimpses of them at a distance. Soon enough, the cubs tumble out of the den for short visits to spaces right around the den and visit more directly with the other members of the family.

During that time, the cubs will also be gradually weaned off their mother's milk and will experience eating food for the first time. Instinctively, they lick the faces of pack members, triggering the regurgitation of partly digested food that is easier than solids on the cubs' developing digestive systems. Large males can carry up to 20 pounds of meat to regurgitate to eager cubs.

At this stage, they're still too wobbly and too young to travel. Thus, the denning stage is a time of incubation and preparation for the intense period of education that is to follow. It is also a time of vulnerability, as the pack is tied to the den, having to protect the site and feed the nursing mother at all costs. The wolves cannot go far to hunt, and at the same time, the smell of fresh kill near the den could draw predators. By the time the cubs are old enough to leave, it is a momentous occasion indeed.

Similarly, at Stage 1 (Foundations) with our dogs—no matter their age—we are in a space akin to the den. Our goal is to start at the basics or go back to basics. Beginning with a solid decompression, we create Foundations based on simplicity and success. We are establishing a relationship and preparing the dog for the schooling and socialization to come. The control is tight, and the places we go are limited. We have an infant on our hands and need to retain control of things. There is no freedom, and there can't be choice.

This does not just apply to new puppies. If you have just rescued a dog with noted issues, this is the place to start—keeping it simple and building from there. If you have raised your dog from puppyhood and are having problems, those shaky foundations need mending, which means scaling back on liberties the dog had and returning to basics.

## Stage 2: Adolescents at the Rendezvous/Exposure

At around eight to 10 weeks old, the cubs have outgrown the den site and are ready to travel with the pack. This is a key transition in the life of the pack, which is now able to move more freely to hunt. But this doesn't mean that the cubs are now integrated into the pack. Rather, they are moved to locations called "rendezvous sites" across their travels.

The pups tend to be a little shy on their very first excursions away from the den. They stay close to their mother, but soon enough, their curiosity, wild nature, and trust in their family help them explore in safe proximity as they journey to these rendezvous sites. Sometimes, just getting to that first location is a challenge for these cubs.

Rendezvous sites are like open-air nurseries providing a secure place to rest, regroup, and leave cubs alone or with caregivers who often include yearlings, the cubs' siblings from last year's litter. During this time, adults can go about grown-up business such as game explorations, hunting, and marking and defending territory. Rendezvous sites can include holes and burrows to hide the cubs from predators. They can be old coyote dens with tunnels that the curious cubs can explore. For about a year, the various rendezvous sites along the journey of the pack form the locus of the cubs' education and socialization.

The cubs spend time playing on their own or with each other: games of ambush, chasing, tackling, wrestling, sparring, pinning, tossing and catching, sliding down snowbanks, and tug-of-war with sticks, bones, and hides. They explore nearby areas under caretakers' watchful eyes. They follow tracks and run after prey animals only to scurry back home to safety. They learn to hunt rodents such as voles, entertaining themselves, feeding themselves, and learning basic hunting, arguably the most important skill of all. They practice mousing, hearing rodents move beneath them and rearing up like foxes. Sometimes they get so much into this game that they ignore the adults returning with food to regurgitate to them. It's a lot more fun working for it!

The cubs learn to interact with pack members, to play, socialize, and bond with their elders. They learn about the family hierarchy and come to understand the prevailing chain of command. They learn simply by watching their siblings, their parents, aunts and uncles, modeling after their behavior. It's worth mentioning the enthusiasm that the adults, particularly the yearlings, display around the cubs. Yearlings love to play with their younger siblings and are tremendously active in the rearing of these cubs. Adults will purposefully lose when playing with the young cubs to help them build confidence. At the same time, they keep an eye out for predators, protect the cubs, and nudge them to safety when appropriate. All this socialization integrates the wolf cubs into the family structure and serves as an apprenticeship for the yearlings to tend to their own offspring one day.

A second round of weaning occurs later when the cubs experience their first meal of fresh kill as opposed to regurgitated food or the small rodents they learned to hunt. The alpha female sees to it that the pups eat first, while the others wait their turn, alpha male included. Feeding behaviors that some consider aggressive—lip curls, snarls, chasing members away from the kill (or pretending to)—are in fact ritualistic and serve to diffuse, as opposed to foment, tension by ensuring that all get their fair share. Transitioning to fresh kill for the cubs takes time, however. When they continue to ask adults to regurgitate food, they are disciplined with more emphasis than ever before—pinned down consistently until a mild warning such as a hard stare or lip curl does it. They're being asked to join the others at the table. They're being told it's time to grow up.

As the cubs mature, they begin to venture out with the roving adults. At four months old, they can travel quite far from the rendezvous site. As the cubs mature and are more involved in hunts, they begin to acquire the elements and skills involved in a successful hunting sequence. They learn about the prey animals to pursue, their prey species model. At first the cubs only watch, but from about six months onward, they become increasingly helpful assistants in hunts. And as they approach the end of their first year, they "test" the herd with their family, running the prey animals for hours sometimes, wearing them down to sort out the targets—the weak, old, and sick elements—until it's time to make room for the mature and skilled adults to deal the final strike.

What does this mean for us? Following a successful period of structure and simplicity, one allowing us to establish healthy foundations, we transition to Stage 2 (Exposure). Our mission is to expand the dog's world, ramp up their education and begin actively training, including addressing behavioral issues more directly. Because we have strong foundations, we are a team learning together at Stage 2. We have a dog that is eager for more and looks to us for cues, having been appropriately decompressed and prepared. Successful exposures mean the dog goes places with us and deals well. The dog learns things easily, listens and pays attention, and responds appropriately to increasingly difficult situations.

## Stage 3: Yearlings in the Pack/Integration

When the adolescent cubs reach seven to eight months old, they are grown and educated enough to leave their rendezvous sites and join their families in the nomadic life of the next several months. In these travels, the cubs learn about territory, boundaries, and the dangers of encroaching on rival packs. By the end of their first year of life, they will have reached 90% of their adult size and are fully integrated into the pack, actively participating in all aspects of pack life while continuing to learn from their elders.

These yearlings are part of a larger hunting strategy, true members of a team. They see how the spry and speedy females run the prey to exhaustion while the big and powerful males deal the fatal blows. They learn about the hunts that are worth pursuing and those too dangerous to risk. They learn that most hunting attempts end in failure and that they need to conserve their energy to try again. They learn that injuries and even death could occur. They learn that when successful, they will need to fight other animals looking to leach off their effort, including bears, coyotes, foxes, and birds of prey.

Sometimes, these young adults will stay with their parents a little longer, assisting them with cubs while continuing to learn from them and be nurtured by them. As with the famous Wolf 21 (see insert), they might stay longer to help their family should there be a need, gaining more experience and fostering deeper bonds. Young adults reach the peak of their physical ability and hunting proficiency at two years.

But there now remains a final lesson to be learned when these young adults will experience the mating season for the first time. Indeed, maturity can mean integration and promotion up the ranks; it can also mean separation and independence. As the mating season approaches, the alphas are deeply engaged with one another in bonding rituals. They are also more aggressive toward members of their own sex, blocking any courting attempts. It's important to understand the ecological wisdom of wolves and that they know what their environments, or prey base, can sustain and reproduce accordingly.

These stresses will cause some yearlings to bide their time, stepping back from leadership and waiting for their parents to pass on. Others take the great risk of striking out to start their own pack, seeking new territory and inviting a mate in, or finding a mate and together seeking new territory.

The idea of the lone wolf has been exaggerated, as the only time a wolf would be alone or choose to be alone is when it reaches the age to seek a mate. These young wolves are called "dispersers." Just like Wolf 21 and his adoptive dad, Wolf 8 (see insert), a disperser can be accepted into an existing pack and elevated to pack leader. At times, this quest for independence fails, and the prodigals come back home to resume their previous positions. In other instances, they return to challenge the existing order.

The growth, learning, maturation, and strengthening of the wolf cubs allow them to gradually take their place as full-fledged participants in the pack. By the same token, the accumulation of successful exposures is what allows us to move into Stage 3 (Integration) and begin integrating our dog into our home. This is also where we allow ourselves to feel and express the love we had inside all along. The dog needs to know we are the teachers (Stage 1) and then go to school (Stage 2), before becoming a full-time member of our home (Stage 3). This is deeply meaningful and powerful for our dogs.

At Stage 3, our mission is to solidify the dog's learning to an off-leash level while intensifying exposure and continuing to develop the dog's drives. Many people I work with are satisfied with the incredible progress that can be made at Stage 1 and 2 alone. But my mission is to ensure the dog's capability to be free under all sorts of circumstances, which means we must continue to manage and lead. We have a dog that's been thoroughly educated now, one worthy of being integrated and deserving of our full approval, one capable of being free.

---

## Yellowstone Legends

After years of planning and preparation, wolves were reintroduced on January 12, 1995, to Yellowstone National Park from where they'd been nearly eradicated for almost a century. Fourteen wild wolves were brought in by truck from Alberta, Canada, and held in acclimation pens for several weeks before being released. To keep track of the wolves and the success of the reintroduction, the new wolves and others captured over the years were collared, numbered, and alphabetized M or F according to sex. Their stories, told in books and documentaries, symbolize hope, survival against the odds, and the power of family bonds. Below are a few of these legendary wolves.

### WOLF 8M

Wolf 8M was only a cub when he made the journey from Canada to Yellowstone. Upon arrival, he and his family spent the first 10 weeks in an acclimation pen before being released. With nothing better to do, Wolf 8's three brothers relentlessly picked on 8, displaying the domineering and bullying behaviors common among wolves in captivity. They were black, big, and strong. He was small, gray, and looked more like a coyote.

8's life became a little more normal once the pen gates were opened, but he'd become a different wolf, showing signs that he'd been made tougher by these experiences. As a young male, he dispersed, looked for a family to call his own, and stumbled upon young 21 and his siblings, who had lost their dad and desperately needed a new alpha male. Being still young himself, 8 quickly won over the hearts of the younglings. It wasn't long after that that their widowed mother welcomed Wolf 8 as her new mate, adoptive father to her cubs, and her pack's new alpha. They in turn increasingly saw 8 as their hero, and this was particularly true of 21, who adored his adoptive dad.

With his devotion to family putting the fire in his belly, Wolf 8 revealed what a good partner and parent were. He began to show the strength, courage, and loyalty that is the stuff of legends: fighting off much stronger rival alphas; battling other Yellowstone predators, including grizzlies, coyotes, and mountain lions; hunting bravely and effectively; and raising generations of Yellowstone wolves.

## WOLF 21M

Wolf 21M was a large and powerful wolf just like his biological father, Wolf 10, from whom he'd also inherited his remarkably playful attitude. After the demise of 10 and later being adopted and raised by Wolf 8, 21 stayed one year longer than most yearlings do, supporting his new dad and growing family, performing solo hunts, acting as his dad's bodyguard, and compassionately tending to sickly cubs. The two males shared a deep and lasting bond, and the cubs adored 21 as they would a favorite uncle. Wolf 21 also learned from Wolf 8 and saw him as a model. One cannot appreciate the force of nature that Wolf 21 was without recognizing the influence that Wolf 8 had on him.

When he struck out on his own, just like his dad, Wolf 21 came across a pack in need of a new male. This pack, however, was a troubled one, led by a ruthless and domineering female, Wolf 40, who kept a short leash on the other members, particularly her sister 42, whom she constantly bullied. Wolf 21 wasn't welcomed easily, but his social skills, playfulness, peacemaking attitude, and assertiveness won over the Druid Peak pack, which would become his own. With both 8 and 21, it was their demeanor with the cubs that won over their widowed moms.

The eventual demise of 40 freed Wolf 21, with his equally clever and courageous mate Wolf 42 at his side, to reign as alpha of the Druid Peak pack for more than six years, a pack that reached 38 wolves at one time. He was an enormous wolf, weighing around 130 pounds as an adult. He never lost a fight and never killed an enemy. He was magnanimous and merciful, and he showered affection on his mate and youngsters. One of the things 21 was known for was his skill at raising his offspring, often pretending to lose in wrestling matches with his cubs and yearlings, building their confidence and strengthening their bonds.

## WOLF 826F (ALSO KNOWN AS WOLF 06)

Wolf 826F was given the nickname "06" after the year of her birth (2006). She epitomized the beauty, strength, and intelligence of the alpha female wolf and was followed and loved by many.

When she was shot and killed by a hunter on the edge of Yellowstone National Park while trying to find her beloved mate who'd also been shot, she was mourned by millions around the world. Her death stirred new controversy and renewed debate around the protection of wolves in Yellowstone and beyond.

For about two years, 06 was the undisputed alpha female of the Lamar Canyon pack, which she had founded after leaving her natal Agate pack. A granddaughter of Wolf 21, she was a fourth-generation wolf after wolves were reintroduced to Yellowstone.

She was also a kind and doting mother who modeled wisdom and mercy. 06 was an unusually large female, a formidable hunter able to hunt elk on her own. She was an astute fighter who once managed to divert an extraordinarily large rival pack away from her den.

While she had many suitors, she took her time deciding on the right partner, eventually choosing brothers 754M and 755M to be her mates. These two boys were quite young at the time. Looking after a litter of newborns with inexperienced mates put the onus on 06 to care for all of them, and she did. Not only that, 06 never lost a cub in its first year of life, a rare feat of parenting and one that sealed her contribution to Yellowstone National Park's ecological development.

## SOURCES

Blakeslee, Nate. *American Wolf: A True Story of Survival and Obsession in the West*. New York: Broadway Books, 2017.
McIntyre, Rick. *The Alpha Female Wolf: The Fierce Legacy of Yellowstone's 06*. Vancouver: Greystone Books, 2022.
McIntyre, Rick. *The Reign of Wolf 21: The Saga of Yellowstone's Legendary Druid Pack*. Vancouver: Greystone Books, 2020.

McIntyre, Rick. *The Rise of Wolf 8: Witnessing the Triumph of Yellowstone's Underdog.* Vancouver: Greystone Books, 2019.

# Three Rearing Stages

Let's take a moment to reflect on how we do things with our dogs and how that compares to how mother dogs and wolf packs rear their young. Mother dogs give birth in a whelping box and keep things simple for a while, imprinting themselves as the source of all things good, all things nourishing and safe. Mother wolves give birth in dens, and because the cubs are born so tiny and helpless, they need that close and intimate contact for several weeks before they're ready to take on the world.

What do we do when we bring new dogs home? We take them everywhere. We introduce them to everyone. We show them everything without having a minimum rapport with them. We call this "socialization." A few months into this pattern, troubles begin, but we fail to see the connection between these troubles and how we started. We need to ask why we're in such a rush while moms and dads across the animal world—including ourselves with our own young—take their time.

## Three Rearing & Relationship Stages

| Stage 1: Foundations | Stage 2: Exposure | Stage 3: Integration |
|---|---|---|
| *Establishing Our Bond* | *Growing and Challenging Our Bond* | *Solidifying and Enjoying Our Bond* |
| "In the Den" | "At the Rendezvous" | "In the Pack" |
| Youth/Childhood | Adolescence/Teenage | Adulthood |
| Preschool | School | Graduation |
| Structure & Simplicity | Education & Expansion | Freedom & Choice |
| Primordial, Spatial, Distal | Proximal, Interactional, Oppositional | All Socialization Levels |
| Food & Prey Drives | Prey & Pack Drives | Drives in Balance |
| Informal/On Leash Training | Formal/On & Off Leash Training | On- & Off-Leash Versatility |

There are few things I enjoy as much as preparing dogs (Stage 1), showing them the world (Stage 2), and with time and maturation, integrating them into my life and home (Stage 3). While these stages are progressive, we're always doing a little of each stage at any one time. For example, our dogs live with us and are therefore already somewhat integrated into our homes (Stage 3). Any time we're handling our dogs, we are exposing them to things (Stage 2). But the question is one of degree and what is being emphasized at each stage, which we unpack in the next three parts of the book.

Without wolves, we would not have our beloved dogs. And as you now know, there is so much we can learn about way of life from both our canine companions and their ancestors. Now let's find out more about Stage 1, where our goal is to establish foundations for a strong and healthy bond with our dog.

# For Reflection

1.  What are your thoughts and feelings about wolves? How about other canid species such as coyotes and foxes?

2.  In which ways are humans and wolves similar? In which ways are dogs and wolves similar and different?

3.  How does your attitude toward your dogs, and dogs in general, shift when you are reminded of their wild origins?

4.  Which aspects of wolf life and behavior resonated with you? Which ones surprised you?

5.  Looking at your dogs as objectively as you can, where do you see the pet? Where do you see the predator?

# ESTABLISHING OUR BOND

# CHAPTER 4

# Relationship, Mission, and Mindset at Stage 1

All suffering comes from attachment.

—**SIDDHĀRTHA GAUTAMA,** Indian mystic also known as the Buddha

*M*y client didn't have much experience with dogs but had dreamed of having one since childhood. Finally, she settled on a breed suited to apartment living, saved up enough for a puppy, and read and researched all she could. But when she brought home Bean, her new Havanese–shih tzu mix puppy, she found herself at a loss about what to do.

She'd had Bean for three days when we spoke. She tearfully described him as agitated and averse to her attention, saying that he'd nipped her several times already. My client was heartbroken, thinking Bean didn't love her.

I paused before saying, "He doesn't know you yet." Silence ensued.

I explained that Bean and all dogs need a little time and that things need to be done a certain way at the start to avoid having behavioral issues down the road. I also explained that we can always go back to these foundations, improve on them, and get back up again. "Dogs are forgiving," I added.

*My words hit her like a brick to her forehead, and she began crying. "I'm appalled!" she exclaimed. "How could I have been so off-base? How could I have not known this?"*

*I reassured her that she certainly was not alone. The practice of bringing new dogs home without giving them the benefit of an adjustment period is common and responsible for many of the problems experienced later. She happened to call three days in, but others call three months or three years in, not seeing the connection between how they got started and what they're now dealing with.*

*Once over her initial turmoil, my client went to work with Bean to set him up on the right foundations. Her stance shifted to raising Bean, who is now a happy, playful, and outgoing companion. Among other things, he has coped well with losing one of his eyes, and when his owner had to go out of town and left him with me for a weekend, he took it in remarkable stride. I told her that he won the prize for the best-behaved dog I ever boarded. Such is the power of healthy foundations.*

Be they domesticated puppies or wild cubs, dogs' first few days of life are simple, safe, and restricted to intimate spaces. Puppies and cubs need to decompress from the change of environment that comes with birth. They have much growing up to do, with mom's care and under her watchful eye. The change of environment experienced by these babies should not be underestimated. It is a shock to be born, a radical change of environment. We hear it in wailing babies and squealing pups.

Similarly, the adoption or acquisition of a new dog is akin to a new birth, an opportunity to do things right from the start and right any wrongs that might have previously occurred. As well, when we change up the way of life to help our dog and our relationship with them, that, too, is akin to a birth of something new. The first day I went back to square one with Maya, after five years of a difficult life together, really felt like the first day we had something healthy going on. We are creating a new way of life, which means we're going to be changing things—in our dogs and in ourselves. A hallmark of healthy foundations is an adjustment to this momentous change.

If the issues we're dealing with are present in a new puppy, a new rescue, or a rehomed dog, their adoption into our life is also a big change for all family members and a unique opportunity to get started right. If we've had our problematic dog for some time, we're shifting what the dog has come to expect. Dogs are sensitive to change and will need to adjust and decompress from their past lives. We are the center of their world, and when they feel that they can't lean on us, that results in a conflicted state that's extremely stressful for a dog. At the same time, during Stage 1 they will protest the loss of their past privileges, and that, too, is normal. A successful adjustment to the changes—for example, by getting the hang of the new routine and showing signs of improvement—is one of the ways we know we're on the right track.

So Foundations is focused on decompression from the change in way of life and then building (or rebuilding) a healthy foundational relationship that is based on safety and success. We're creating a solid base that will support the dog's learning and experiences at Exposure (Stage 2) and then allow the dog to hone the attitudes and behaviors necessary to be fully included in our home at Integration (Stage 3).

If you look at any mammal across the world, you'll see that early stages of development are kept simple. Mothers of many species bond with their babies by restricting them to a private and protected space. Following in the wise ways of mothers domestic and wild, we, too, keep things simple and restricted for our dogs at the start.

# The Juvenile Stage

When working through Stage 1, keep in mind that the dogs are in the "childhood" stage. They're still babies, toddlers, puppies, juveniles—whatever word works for you to remember their innocence, ignorance, and vulnerability.

New rescues or adult dogs presenting behavioral issues may not physically be puppies, but they do not know us, our family, or the ways of our life. In that sense, they are children, ignorant and defenseless. Many of them have challenging backgrounds and difficult pasts that have stunted their growth. They have much mental and psychological growing up to do.

How about the dog we've had for a few years? Well, that dog is in childhood too because conflicts and poor relationships stress dogs, and stress hinders development. The difficulties we've experienced with our dog mean the dog is not nearly as mature as they could be. As discussed in chapter 2 with the family hierarchy, our job as leaders of the family is to mature the dog along.

# Relationship

The notion that the dog in Foundations is akin to a juvenile has implications for the nature of our relationship. In this state, our bond is fragile, and we need to keep things structured, simple, and successful. (See Mission below.)

We all know that the relationships we enjoy with children are qualitatively different from those we enjoy with adolescents or adults. Like new parents holding their newborn for the first time, we are also "meeting" our dogs for the first time at Foundations. In these early days of rearing, I don't know the dog, and the dog doesn't know me. Foundations mean we are strangers to each other, and this can sometimes be difficult to stomach.

When we're all giddy and excited about our new dog—taking them here and there, posing for pictures, letting other people hold them and exclaim over them—this is the opposite of the balance and calmness that the dog is looking for at this stage. Us being in charge is what helps calm dogs and lets them trust, nothing less. Our goal is to act as parents, guardians, leaders—the folks in charge—which is the basis of a healthy relationship dynamic. I can't emphasize enough how safe and good that makes dogs feel.

This can be easy to overlook, just like my client did when she first brought Bean home. Just because we're feeding and housing the dogs and like them well enough doesn't mean that we have a relationship. It takes longer for dogs to bond than people realize. I've come to appreciate the suspicious nature of this animal, and when you combine that with a checkered past with humans, I understand why they would not trust so easily.

Therefore, we're also getting rid of the expectation that there's going to be a whole lot of love and affection in these early stages. It's too early for pack drive, basically. With a new dog, that dog doesn't know us, so it's a little too soon for "love" and affection. I'll often hear people who just got their dog tell me how much they're bonded already, but there is not a chance that this is the full story. Dogs are predators at the core, and they don't bond so easily. In those first few days and weeks, they're thrilled that you're a kind person instead of a mean one, which might appear to you as love. But it isn't yet. This is more of a survival instinct than love.

Similarly, I'll hear people say that the dog is being protective—that, too, is premature defensive drive, which is more anxiety than it is real defensiveness. If a dog is relatively new to you, or in a conflicted relationship with you, would they want to protect you, do you think?

The same is true of an existing dog. You might worry that a change in way of life will undermine the bond you currently share with your dog. Clients often tell me how wonderful, sweet, and affectionate their dog is, how they snuggle on the couch at night, and how well-behaved the dog is inside the house. But then we're briefed on the problems manifesting in the dog.

Dogs can sense our approval and the disconnect between that approval and how they're behaving. So if you snuggle on the couch and have your dog in your bed at night, but it is barking at the neighborhood dogs on every walk, we have a situation that's dissonant for the dog. The privileges inside are clearly not commensurate with the behavior outside.

If you're experiencing behavioral issues, how healthy can your bond be? If we have a dog with issues, the bond is weak and compromised. It's not possible for a genuinely healthy bond and behavioral issues to coexist. Healthy bonds are the antithesis to behavioral issues. Therefore, the Foundations stage means looking at our dogs with fresh eyes and giving them the chance to appreciate us anew.

# Mission

Our mission at Stage 1 is threefold:

1.  To decompress dogs through the change in their way of life

2.  To instill safety through simplicity and structure

3.  To build (or rebuild) strength and self-esteem through successful experiences

Together, these endeavors begin the process of establishing foundations for our bond and our life together.

If we happen to be using restrictive tools, anything from prong collars to head halters, we set those aside. These tools use design mechanics to control the dog in a way that we have not earned. While they might be helpful in controlling the dog, they suppress the dog, adding to the very negative pressure that we want to get rid of, the kind of pressure that makes dogs reactive and potentially dangerous.

With clients who have dogs on psychotropic medications prescribed as a long-term solution for behavioral issues, we work with their veterinarian to gradually wean the dog off the meds as we introduce our new way of life and watch the benefits kick in.

# 1.   Decompressing From the Change

Decompression is an important aspect of Foundations because change has a greater effect on dogs than we realize. If we appreciated just how sensitive dogs are, we would be a lot more careful in what we did with them as they're experiencing changes. Remember that they are creatures of home and turf, that being within versus outside territorial boundaries is genetically a big deal.

"Decompression" simply means to release pressure, and for us that means giving dogs physical and mental space to reset themselves. The main way we decompress dogs in Foundations is by setting predictable schedules, crating them, giving them alone time, and providing good doses of physical exercise without expecting them to be particularly obedient or social.

With any kind of dog, think of all the changes they have gone through before and since they have lived with you. By rejigging our way of life, we're creating a different environment for a dog. That period of transition can be stressful as everyone adjusts. Because change is stressful, clarity and capacity to learn are compromised, and we need to give the dog some time to regain composure and recover from the stress of the change.

## 2.  Instilling Safety and Simplicity Through Structure

At the core of any behavioral issue is a dog who's not feeling safe. Subjecting them to a simple and predictable schedule is, of course, pressuring for the dog, the way a boot camp would be. But don't be fooled by any apparent resistance; you will see with time the sense of safety the dog gains with routine. You know you're making headway when you can tell they're learning the schedule. At this point, when the dog is seen as a juvenile, they thrive on knowing what to expect, will adjust to the new routine, and feel incredibly good for braving the change.

A crucial aspect of structure is containing dogs and keeping them separated from humans and other pets for a fair bit of the time. Just as puppies in the den spend their time separated from the pack, our dogs are also separated from the family except for scheduled outings. This isolation is precisely what helps the dog experience our contact, when the dog receives it, as a form of imprinting. The dog can bond without distractions from any other sources.

The separation is not just physical, however. It is also psychological. We need to feel a certain way at this stage, including being more neutral toward a dog whose behavior we're trying to fix. When I have a dog giving me problems, I'm more detached and less enamored when interacting with that dog. The expression "polite indifference" resonates with many of my students. The dog gets less of me because we're having difficulties. This is a good source of pressure because it instills in the dog the desire to work for my approval.

Too often, clients with new pups will come for advice but don't like hearing about the structure I recommend at the start. But then we talk again eight months down the road about problems that could have been avoided. There can be such a thing as too much human meddling, when we are doing so much with our dogs that we rid them of their natural instincts and then wonder why we're having difficulties. Much of my work is about restoring dogs to a more natural state of "dogness."

## 3.  Building Strength Through Success

When dealing with behavioral issues of any kind, we have dogs who not only feel unsafe, but also lack self-confidence and self-esteem. Whether withdrawn or reactive, they lack strength. Dogs that are quick to react lack the mental and psychological muscle to modulate their responses, and they know it. Going back to the family hierarchy, we're working from the low levels, assuming we have a "child" on our hands. Therefore, we set aside any expectations of understanding or obedience at this stage. We assume the dog doesn't know much of anything, so we don't even ask.

That's why we keep things simple and restricted to safe spaces. We handle our dog in such a way that there are only two words that can come out of our mouth: "Good dog!" And if something goes a bit awry, we keep our mouth shut. We are reengineering the dogs' experiences of being with us, shifting from conflicted to harmonious.

At this stage, we see to it that the dog doesn't get to practice behaviors that create conflict—keeping them away from sources of reactivity or fear and returning to simple and successful. As an example, if your fearful dog only wants to go so far as the grass around your building, that's as far as you will be going for some time. Rebuild your dog's self-esteem with experiences they can handle. At the same time, you must start to push when you notice improvements in confidence.

We also set aside expectations that the dog be social with anyone beyond the household. Do mother dogs or mother wolves socialize their babies with strangers? Of course, we've got to go to the vet sometimes or perhaps the groomers. But everything that isn't necessary should be cut out at the start. Intimacy is not built in a crowd, and that's why it's essential to create a private space to get to know one another or to get reacquainted.

In this privacy, we imprint ourselves as the people that matter, the people who can be trusted. We choose our activities carefully, pushing the pause button on socialization outside the immediate family circle and not taking dogs to places that could overwhelm, trigger, or upset them. We keep things simple at the start with a goal of controlled, successful fun. We work with food and prey drives as our common language. We develop these drives, which will help us when it's time to leave the den and transition to Exposure.

# Mindset

The first piece of mindset at Foundations is realizing that you are on a journey of change, just like your dog. And just like dogs, we find change challenging.

Many people who contact me find the idea of changing how they live with their dogs daunting. We are attached to how things are, even if they're dysfunctional. So at Foundations, cultivate the idea that we, too, need to give ourselves time to adjust. It's a big deal when there's a new dog in the house. We all need to go into decompression mode for some time. If we've lived with our dog a certain way and aren't too happy with the results, we will need to mourn the past. I sure did with Maya, but knowing that the changes would benefit us both, I worked to adjust to the new reality.

At this point, let's try to not think of ourselves as the owners, moms, or dads of the dog just yet. Our concern is establishing foundations for a relationship instead of going for the relationship itself. Whether our dogs love us at this point is not our primary concern. A conscious parent is concerned about doing what's right for their child and is less concerned with whether the child says they like them.

Let's be the ones in charge as conscious handlers. The idea of thinking of ourselves as the dog's foster parent, trainer, or handler are helpful in introducing greater distance between us and the dog. Think of the dog as not ours but destined for someone else—that they're not ours to love. Almost automatically, this helps us become more objective. Use a label that works for you to capture an impartial as opposed to a sentimental or emotional stance.

Crating the dog significantly at the start is not just for the dog. It also benefits us as it allows us the mental and psychological space to be more detached, neutral, and less emotional about the dog—a state that I assure you is essential to your recovery effort. The dog cannot get better if they feel you're in love. This signals to them that they can do no wrong and their behavior is acceptable.

One client with an Italian greyhound thought lapdogs needed to be around their person all the time. She was taken aback when we discussed Romeo's schedule, particularly how much time in the crate I was asking for. She resisted at first but eventually agreed as her frustration with Romeo's peeing, zooming, and shredding reached her limits. A few days into the new program, she couldn't help but notice a calmer dog—a happier dog—which meant the humans in the house were also happier.

Thinking of ourselves as professional handlers and trainers also helps us keep our thoughts and feelings in check when we're dealing with our dogs. If our hands are shaking and we have tears in our eyes while crating the dog or if we're reluctant to have them put away so much, the dog is going to sense that conflict. We need to commit and approach all aspects of this way of life with confidence, seen by our dogs as sure-footed leaders worth trusting.

Not too long ago, I had clients with an anxious and hard-to-handle mastiff. They were a couple who did not see eye to eye on the handling of the dog and argued with the dog around. This is a key piece of the Foundations mindset: the states in which the dog sees us. Our dogs are not in a state where they can see us upset. They're "children", remember? Good parents take the argument away from the child or, better yet, find a way to resolve things without arguing.

One longtime friend of mine recently adopted a dog that truly has a temperament of gold—happy, outgoing, smart, social, the whole bit. Despite a tough start in one of the southern states, the challenge of the transport to Canada, time in a foster home, and then activity restrictions as she recovered from heartworm, Mary was a sweetheart. My friend assumed this meant the dog was stable and began allowing her off leash while the dog was still immature and their relationship still fragile. She allowed herself to like the dog and express lots of affection, which I recognize can be hard to avoid with such a lovely temperament and endearing personality. But trouble was on the horizon, and soon my friend shared with me that Mary was taking off after squirrels and not always coming back when called. "Stop delighting in her so much," I said.

Our attitudes toward dogs are a substantive part of their way of life, and dogs are extremely attuned to our feelings. At this stage, the mindset is all about cultivating that polite indifference. It doesn't mean we don't love our dogs or care for their needs; it only means we are giving them the space to see us as that stable leader they can trust and rely on.

## Moving to the Next Stage

Transitions along the stages should be gradual and almost seamless, but there are signs that we're ready to start exposing our dog a little more. Generally, we will note that the dog has become accustomed to the new way of life. The dog knows the schedule, enjoys their time in the crate, and appears to relax. Our exercises (explored in the next three chapters) are coming along nicely; we're both enjoying them and getting the hang of them. We're starting to get to know the dog. The dog is starting to know us.

Because the dog has been allowed to decompress, we see a more clearheaded and focused dog, one who is now more workable and trainable. The dog's true nature is gradually arising. A dog who started withdrawn and shy has become a little more outgoing and bolder, perhaps even a little bratty. Making things simple and successful has boosted their confidence, and they feel good about themselves for a change. A dog who started anxious and hyper has become calmer, more settled, and thoughtful. Both are now ready for more.

In one of the next chapters, you'll hear about Murphy—a behavioral foster I had for 14 months. The reason he ended up with me was that his hyperactive and anxious behavior coupled with physical strength made it impossible to adopt him out. As we made headway in decompressing Murphy and creating new foundations for him, it was clear that his true personality was almost the opposite of what he had presented under the stress of the shelter. All this dog wanted was permission to relax and smell the roses. When he started to show me how laid-back he was, I knew we were ready to move things along.

We want the dog's food drive to be active, their bodies lean and exercised. We want them interested in food across the levels of socialization that we work with at Stage 1, including when it's just us at home (primordial), when we're in a new place (spatial), and when there are people and/or animals at a distance (distal). We also want them to show keen progress toward prey drive and increasing interest in games of tug and ball.

How long does this take? This is a legitimate question, but it varies based on a host of factors. With Murphy, for example, it was about six weeks of decompression and another five months before his foundations had been renovated and he was ready for adoption. In the case of Molly the cockapoo, whom you'll read about in chapter 10, the concerns were manageable, and she was a mature little dog who just wanted some space. The owners were extremely keen, and it only took a few weeks at Stage 1 before they moved into Stage 2. Nimbus, an extremely anxious German shepherd we'll meet in chapter 13, has taken two years for Foundations work, and now he's ready for more direction at Exposure.

Keep in mind that it's not just the dog who decides how long this takes. It's up to us as well because dogs come around much faster without our pressure and agendas. When we have the right attitude and are confident in this process, when we're not needy of the dog nor are we watching the clock, things will click into place. Without exception, dogs have a way of showing us they're ready for more. It is our job to detach and observe so that we can notice and respond accordingly.

Whether with a new dog or an existing dog with issues, our relationship is in infancy and is still fragile. Regardless of age or background, we relate to our dog as a juvenile to be guided rather than an educated dog that can be disciplined. At Stage 1, we keep things simple to decompress from the change. We establish structures that reinforce safety. We control the environment to ensure nothing but successful experiences to begin rebuilding the dog's self-esteem. In the next chapter, we get down to the practical matter of managing space and boundaries at Foundations.

# For Reflection

1.  How would you describe your role and attitude toward your dog since you met?

2.  Summarize and recognize your accomplishments with your dogs to date. Identify the challenges and growth opportunities that still lie ahead.

3.  At Stage 1, we are asked to think of our dogs as juveniles. How does seeing your dog this way change your perception? How does it change your practical approach to dealing with the dog?

4.  What is your mission for Stage 1? What are the changes you will have to make—in your household and in yourself—to create a successful physical and psychological environment for your dog?

5.  Which aspects of Stage 1 feel accessible to you, and which parts are you excited about? Which aspects feel challenging? What are you apprehensive or nervous about?

# CHAPTER 5

# Managing Space and Boundaries at Stage 1

Good training is almost invisible.

—**SAM MALATESTA,** master dog trainer, breeder, and developer of the whelping box theory

*M*onica was a rescue dog whom I'd volunteered to foster. This dog had spent some time in an open shelter where the animals are constantly with each other and able to roam, so she was never contained nor crated until she took the plane to fly to Canada from overseas.

Before she came to me, she spent some time with a foster affiliated with the rescue that brought in Monica. The foster parent had Monica for a few days for vetting before I could collect her. Like many foster parents, this foster home was not particularly well versed in the mechanics of decompression and Foundations. The foster home gave Monica free range, thinking that's what she needed and deserved, only to struggle with walking her and holding her still for vetting.

When she was finally able to join us, I proceeded to Foundations work—decompressing, reestablishing safety through simplicity and structure, and ensuring successful experiences to boost self-esteem. During the day, Monica took well to the crate, barking only on occasion. Her difficulty was at night, and she barked consistently in the middle of the night those first few weeks, making it impossible *for us to sleep. She barked so much overnight that she almost wore me down. But I carried on because I knew she had demons that needed to be expressed.*

*Despite her troubles at night, I was validated by seeing how much happier and lighter she was in her day-to-day disposition and in our interactions. We experienced that deep improvement about three weeks into her time with me when I had to take her to the vet for follow-ups to clear her for adoption. This was our first time visiting the vet together and leaving the neighborhood.*

*The vet couldn't believe her eyes when she saw Monica calm, relaxed, and pleasant to be handled for examination. This check-up came after a long wait, as rescue dogs seen on a pro bono basis need to wait their turn, sometimes for several hours. "This is not the dog I saw three weeks ago," she said. Monica also knew that she'd just handled something that the best of dogs can struggle with and was clearly proud of herself for this accomplishment. She could also feel everyone else's pride and approval. I know without a doubt that these experiences gave her the strength to adjust to her new home a few weeks later.*

Our mission at Stage 1 is for dogs to see us and respect us as a safe base and to appreciate us as instrumental in developing their strength. In these early days, remember the dog does not know us, and we do not know the dog. How much freedom should we give a dog we do not know? How much freedom should be granted to a dog with behavioral issues?

I remember Finn, a rescue black Lab mix that had endured abuse and was understandably a little tense and shaken. This client brought him home with neither a leash nor a plan, thinking that the best course of action was to let him choose what he wanted. What did the dog do? He ran to the nearest hiding place, finding refuge under a bed. This was followed by the ordeal of trying to get him out. First impressions are powerful, so take charge from the get-go.

Before you begin, there are some basic supplies you will need. All these supplies are ones that you'll use throughout the three stages and your dog's entire life. Have these on hand—before you get the dog if possible. Here's what I recommend:

→   Large house crate (see the insert "Crating Q&A")

→   Snug car crate or some form of containment during transport

→   Barriers and baby gates

→   Exercise pens for indoor/outdoor use

→   Long drag line for indoors, at least six feet so you can step on it if needed

→   10–15-foot line for outdoor activities

→   Secure collar/Martingale collar

→   Regular harness (not the no-pull variety)

→   Small, easy-to-consume, tasty treats

→   Treat pouch

→   Chew bones appropriate to dog strength and size (e.g., antlers, buffalo horns)

→   Puzzle toys (e.g., Kong)

→   Tug toys

→   Mat for inside the crate

→   Mat or bed for outside the crate

At Stage 1, we are serious about space, and that's putting it mildly. We manage the dog closely and leave little to chance. The control is tight, regimented, and almost militaristic, especially at the start when decompressing. What does this look like?

→   The dog is on a predictable, consistent schedule.

→   The dog is crated or contained for significant amounts of time.

→   When the dog is out, it is for supervised sessions leashed or on the drag line.

Let's dive into each of these elements.

# A Predictable Schedule

Having dogs contained and on a consistent schedule helps meet one of their most fundamental needs, the need for predictability and safety. This is especially important in the early stages of our relationship with our dogs. When the dogs eventually understand what's expected, this reduces their apprehension and boosts their confidence. As they mature under our guidance, they will be able to handle changes to their schedule.

When I ask clients if they're on a schedule of sorts, they'll say, "Yes! Yes, sure, we're on a schedule!" And I'll say, "Could you write it down?" And that's when they realize that they're not really on a schedule. Let's begin by setting a realistic schedule.

Once the schedule is set, stick to it as closely as possible in these early weeks and months. Of course, some flexibility is necessary, but if you can commit to a routine, this process will be easier for the dog to understand, and you'll make progress faster.

At Stage 1, the dog's schedule is primarily down time in the crate, alternating with sessions outside the crate. Importantly, there should be a specific plan as to the time, duration, and purpose of these outings. It should not just be aimless time to wander. We have an agenda for each session, which can include time for dogs to do their business, exercise and play sessions outside the house, socialization sessions, and grooming.

Generally, I recommend that the dog have between three and five daily outings, averaging 30 minutes with some sessions longer (for example, the session where we aim to exercise the dog) or shorter (for example, the last outing before bedtime). I also recommend selecting one day a week where you keep things very simple, like a weekly rest day. Simplicity and consistency are key!

**Activity:** *Writing Up A Schedule*

Come together with any other members in your household to draft your Stage 1 schedule. Design the schedule accounting for work, family, and community obligations. If your home houses multiple family members or roommates, take this opportunity to work as a cohesive unit, sharing your schedules, and taking responsibility for the shifts in the schedule that work for your availability and your capacity. Make sure everyone has a copy and discuss in advance any changes to the schedule.

Include these events:

→ **Crate time:** Aim for two- to six-hour stretches in the crate.

→ **Solo time:** Provide alone time in a backyard, on a balcony, x-pen, or behind a baby gate.

→ **Outings:** Provide three to five outings daily. Specify outing length, time, and activities. Aim for outings to be at least 30 minutes, depending on activity. The very first and very last outings can be short. Outings dedicated to vigorous exercise should be longer.

→ **Meals:** Feed according to your dog's age and health at a specific time in the privacy of their crate.

To get you started, here's a sample schedule that you can use when first beginning this process with your dog. This schedule is an example of a more restrictive decompression schedule, but as the dog adjusts, you can start to loosen up and do more, such as going for hikes or car rides. Adjust as needed.

## Sample Stage 1 Schedule

**OUTING 1: 7:30 AM—8:00 AM**
Wake up and take out of crate
Walk in yard/quiet area for pee break
Hang out quietly
Return to crate with breakfast

**OUTING 2: 1:00 PM—2:30 PM**
Take out of crate
Walk in yard/quiet area for pee break
Vigorous exercise in yard/quiet area

Solo time in yard/quiet area

Return to crate with chew toys

**OUTING 3: 6:00 PM—7:00 PM**

Take out of crate

Walk in yard/quiet area for pee break

Solo time in yard/quiet area

Return to crate with dinner

**OUTING 4: 10:00 PM—10:30 PM**

Take out of crate

Walk in yard/quiet area for pee break

Return to crate for the night

# Crating

Crating is essential to raising sound, strong, and spirited dogs, but it also helps dogs throughout life in myriad ways. (See insert.) This tends to be a sticking point for many clients I first meet with, but I cannot stress enough the importance of crating heavily as a key part of the Foundations stage.

A properly sized crate offers dogs a continuation of gestation period or that time in the womb. It is safe, quiet, dark, and a space all their own. It is a necessary part of rearing for stability and bond, and this ultimately helps grow the dogs' autonomy and capacity to choose wisely. If people refuse to crate their dogs in the early stage, foundations cannot be built. It's that simple.

---

## *15 Benefits of Crating*

1. Facilitates puppy house-training

2. Holds young dogs undergoing training

3. Prevents and corrects bad habits

4.  Provides a zone of safety and rest

5.  Offers downtime to aid in the learning process

6.  Assists in safe introductions and gradual socialization

7.  Facilitates the management of multiple-dog households

8.  Supports dogs in riding out stressors of any kind

9.  Aids in the development of self-esteem and independence

10. Keeps dogs safe at training venues and events

11. Enhances boarding success

12. Prepares for overnight hospital stays

13. Promotes recovery from surgery or illness

14. Ensures safe transportation

15. Eases handling in emergency situations

---

Moreover, whether dealing with behavior issues or not, having our dogs in a crate frees us to attend to our other responsibilities without worrying about what they're up to. I know I find it difficult to concentrate on the demands of the day without the certainty of knowing my dogs are contained safely. But then, when it's time to be together, we're both ready and focused.

Because both scheduling and crating signal to the dog that we're taking charge, be ready to expect resistance. The dog will experience this change as pressure, but let's understand the real source of this pressure. It's not the crate that's the concern for the dog. It's our right to crate that the dog questions.

If we just adopted a rescue dog with problems, the dog has a lot of decompressing to do from their time in a shelter and from being in a new home. The dog is jittery. They're still stressed and aren't going to fall asleep quickly. They're not going to trust just like that.

By the same token, an existing dog who hasn't been crated will also resist the change and loss of past privileges. The resistance here is generally about trust in the human doing the crating and not necessarily about the confinement itself. You are disrupting the pattern that the dog is used to and enforcing a new paradigm that will take the dog time to adjust to.

Successful crating requires that the dog trusts the humans doing the crating, and this doesn't happen overnight. Different dogs will take to this differently, with some resisting and then agreeing (no-to-yes scenario) and others appearing to agree at first and then resisting (yes-to-no scenario). Let's look at the dynamic underlying this process and remember that riding out this initial resistance is an essential part of decompression.

## No-to-Yes Behavior

Like a tea kettle, dogs start to whistle under pressure. There are a range of protest behaviors such as barking, whining, scratching, and attempting to get out. These behaviors are very common.

I am sympathetic if you might be extremely bothered and stressed by a dog's barking. You might think the dog is in a great deal of distress. I get that you might feel guilty, sad, and upset. You could also be worried about disturbing the neighbors. (See insert.)

The calmer and more confident you are about crating the dog, the faster they will adjust. I can't emphasize enough how healthy it is to let dogs bark for some time and help them gain in the strength that comes with realizing your strength. When dogs bark in their crate, we are quick to think that they must be in deep distress, terrified, or traumatized and need to go out at once, going as far as labelling them with confinement anxiety. Yet, the barking is a healthy expression of past frustration, resentment at all the different things you tried to fix the situation, and a legitimate questioning of your right to crate them.

It is okay for our dogs to resist or question us; we don't want doormats for dogs. We want them sound, strong, and spirited. When dogs are being dogs, they will not accept everything readily. It's part of their predatory nature to resist, so we want to be okay with their resistance.

The barking also shows just how much is going on inside of that dog—something we'd never know about without applying that pressure. The pressure of crating dogs makes them more honest about how stable they really are inside; it shows the true level of agitation we're working with. How fast and how far should we be moving with a dog who won't settle?

It's also healthy and cathartic to allow dogs to express the frustrations they've had in life with or before us. As far as I am concerned, the crate is the safest way to let this all out once and for all. The entire process of resisting and then accepting, which I have been through with many dogs, reminds me of someone getting over an addiction. It doesn't necessarily look nice at the start, does it? Withdrawal symptoms can be violent—everything from heavy panting, barking, whining, whimpering, refusing to eat, to getting sick and soiling in the crate. That still does not mean we give up.

We want this decompression process to empty the dog of the anxieties and frustrations that are fueling their behavioral issues. Remember all the stress, angst, and mistrust we're going into this process with. Where does it say that change from such dysfunction is supposed to be smooth sailing? As I see it, better the dogs explode in the crate than with the neighbors' dogs or kids. Whichever way you shake it, the anxiety that's been building up all this time needs a place to go, and the crate is one of the safest ways we let our dogs bark out and release their frustrations.

I remember when I went back to Foundations with Maya, she was weirded out at first and barked a little.

"What's going on here?" she wondered.

With a little time, I could see her relax and ease into the new way of life. The stress started to wash out of her body. For a few weeks, she did nothing but sleep, her entire system adjusting to the drop in adrenaline. I, too, felt a change in the air between us. The tensions melted away, and it was wonderful.

## Yes-to-No Behavior

Sometimes it takes a while for the resistance to kick in. The dogs could be insecure and lacking in self-esteem to such a degree that they just go along with the crating at first, happy that someone's given them the chance to hole up. But then they start to come around and resist, and this is cause for celebration. "You have a voice," I'll say to the dog. "Let me hear you use it."

I once had a client with a rescued puppy mill mom who'd spent her life producing doodle-type puppies for scores of fans who were unsuspecting of the neglect and cruelty taking place behind the scenes. (We'll learn more about Katie in chapter 9.) When I began crating Katie, she was happy as a clam. She would have been glad to spend the rest of her days in her crate. But there was something about the larger outdoor kennel that pressured her, and she began barking. She realized she could express herself and that we would support her in that. She very soon took to the kennel and found herself at home in it.

These adjustments from yes-to-no and no-to-yes are changes we want to observe, as they offer confirmation that we're on the right track. When the barker settles and the polite wallflower starts to whine, this is progress and is very bonding.

---

# Crating Q&A

1. **Can we use a method of containment other than a crate?**

   Confining dogs in one big space, room, or x-pen is not the same as crating. Large spaces are not conducive to calmness like a properly sized crate is. As well, the idea of a small crate connected to a large exercise pen is also not the same as crating. Even the simple decision of going from a crate to an x-pen is more autonomy than dogs can handle at the beginning. Having the choice only confuses them and frustrates us. With that said, time in an exercise pen or in a room behind the baby gate can be added to the schedule as solo time in addition to time in the crate.

2. **What is the best type of crate to use?**

   Crates come in varieties including wire crates, plastic travel crates, fabric crates, as well as high-security crates. I recommend a plastic travel crate for car travel. For the house, I like the airy wire crates. If your dog is an escape artist, secure crates such as Zinger Wingers are recommended. If possible, use an outdoor kennel in addition to indoor crating. Outdoor kennels are outdoor enclosures that come in various shapes and sizes; mine happen to be 10 × 10 feet, which is as large as I would go.

3. **What is the right size crate to have?**
   The car crate can be a little snug in comparison with the house crate. For the house crate, I like for the dog to have more room and therefore recommend acquiring a crate one size larger than the size recommended for the breed.

4. **Where is the best place for the crate?**
   Work with the space you have to identify or create locations that are semiprivate and calm—for example, hallways, laundry rooms, dens, offices, basements, and guest bedrooms. It is fine to use different locations for day and night to ensure privacy.

5. **When is the right time to be crating?**
   Many people make the classic mistake of crating their dog only at night, when needed, or when away from home. What we want is a dog that is accustomed to being crated day or night and regardless of whether we're in or out of the house. During Stage 1, dogs will be in the crate often because they are decompressing; later, in Stage 3, they might choose to spend time in the crate or elsewhere but are still okay with being locked in the crate should that be required.

6. **How long is it okay to have the dog crated?**
   A Stage 1 schedule should include stretches of at least two to four hours to a maximum of six to seven hours in the crate. This is generally enough time for the dog to settle and sleep deeply. I work toward that with puppies as well because taking them out every two hours is detrimental to pups and robs them of the sleep they need. So with pups, I start off with three- to four-hour stretches.

7. **How do we reintroduce the crate after a long hiatus?**
   If a dog was crated as a puppy but hasn't seen the crate for a while, it may be

appropriate to reintroduce the crate gradually. In this case, I recommend we install the crate, furnish it with bedding, water, and toys, and start feeding the dog in there. Don't ask the dog to go in or make a big deal of the crate at the start. Once the dog appears to be comfortable, we can start closing the door and crating according to schedule.

8.  **Should we talk to the dog while crated?**
    The dog should be ignored completely when crated—not spoken to, not looked at, not praised for being quiet, and not corrected for being noisy. This truly helps the dog settle because it communicates that the crate is not just a physical barrier but also a communication barrier.

9.  **How do we outfit the crate?**
    Depending on the dog and the setting, it might be appropriate at times to cover the crate partially or fully with a blanket or towel and help the dog ease into calmness. I prefer for the crate to be partially covered as opposed to fully because we want the dog to have some vision of what's around, just as we want to be able to see what's going on inside the crate. I also recommend a comfortable mat that fits the crate floor fully or partially. Dogs can be given toys and chews that require minimal supervision, such as Kongs. Water should be provided as well, preferably with bowls tied to the wall of the crate.

10. **How do we deal with neighbors and our dog barking?**
    Whether we reside in an apartment or house, concerns with bothering neighbors are legit and require our consideration. It helps to identify crate locations that are as far removed from neighbors as possible. In addition, don't forget the effect of your own behavior; if you stay calm, it will help the dog settle. What I also find helpful and respectful is to inform the neighbors that we are working with our dog and are aware of the barking, which we know will subside.

11. **Why is it important to crate the dog during transport?**
    Think about the scenario where the dog is terribly excited to go somewhere, hops in the car, and then excitedly jumps from one window to another for

the duration of the ride, arriving at the destination already spent. This is not a state conducive to a successful outing—not to visit friends, attend a training session, or hike a trail. Instead, heading out with dogs contained and calm readies them for any activity and helps them internalize all the good they learned.

---

# Leashed at All Times

When dogs are not crated, they are on leash or a drag line at all times. A drag line is a long leash (10 feet or so) that the dogs drag as they move about; you don't necessarily need to be holding it or attaching it to anything, but you can grab it or step on it as needed.

At this point, we do not ask dogs to come or stay, we simply manage them using the leash, while encouraging them to heed and follow us when we're redirecting them away from things. But we're not asking, training, or having to get too close to the dogs.

Contrary to what some might think, this is securing for dogs—having a leash on means something to them. It's akin to an umbilical cord that tethers them to their safe zone and solidifies their understanding of the tranquil circle.

Remember that we are working toward complete freedom. We are working toward being able to have our dog loose no matter what. And that's why I'm so adamant that we be structured at the beginning: a dog who understands these concepts at a foundational level will never go tearing off to the other side of the park unexpectedly. If we are loosey-goosey at the start, it'll be a lifetime of having to watch the dog and keep a leash on.

## Exercise: *Handling The Long Line*

Many trainers use long lines (leashes that are 10- to 15-feet long) when they first start working with a dog. The long line gives the dog breathing room and relaxes the interaction. It teaches that the leash will not go tense and that we can have the dog on leash without it being a stressor. Any time the dog pulls, instead of instinctively trying to restrict the line, work on keeping it loose by calling the dog to you using food. (See exercise "Come Here.")

Depending on the dog you have, consider the pros and cons of using a collar, flat or a Martingale, versus a body harness (the regular, not the no-pull, variety). The choice will depend on the dog and the situation. I generally like working with harnesses with young dogs and moving up to a collar, provided we're able to keep our line as loose as possible. With strong and reactive dogs, the Martingale's safety makes it my go-to.

The bottom line is that you're maximizing safety while minimizing restriction, which means you work on keeping the dog engaged with you, handling the leash lightly and remembering that you have a living, breathing creature on your hands.

# Managing the Three Circles at Stage 1

At Stage 1, we set up understanding of the three circles. We need to ensure safety and to instill in the dog a strong sense that being with us and around us means being protected. Some of the following exercises offer variations to be done at the different levels of socialization, which are explored in greater depth in chapter 6.

## The Inner Circle

We want our dog to learn that being at our side, in our inner circle, is a safe and calm experience. This builds on that first level of socialization, primordial socialization, which is between only us and our dog. Throughout all the stages, working the inner circle means that we invite the dog into our space instead of going to the dog.

At Foundations, the dogs don't need to ask for permission to come in the inner circle; they're welcome in because we want them to understand that they can find safety near us any time. Think about all the things we're teaching our dogs here. A dog that learns to be calm at our side will be calm in all situations—

the vet's, the groomer's while we wait our turn, standing in line at dog-friendly stores, or waiting at the sports center or trial event. The list goes on.

With that said, gauge the attitude that the dog brings when they come to us without invitation. If the dog is pushy and obnoxious, I ignore them until they settle. If they're like puppy mill survivor Katie, downtrodden and asking for pity, I ignore them until I get a livelier attitude.

## Exercise: *Come Here*

During the scheduled time when your dog is out of the crate, introduce them to coming to you, starting with whistling and clapping, then using words such as "puppy," and eventually working your way up to the dog's name and/or the cues here or come here. The progression allows you to start from a more impersonal place and gradually work your way to the deeper intimacy associated with using the dog's name and the credibility to ask them to come.

As part of your recall games (see chapter 6) and throughout the day, ask your dog to come into your space. Step into your quiet area or working space, meander with your dog, and then call the dog to you. The dog comes and gets rewarded. Walk away from the dog and call the dog to you. The dog comes and gets rewarded.

During solo time (see chapter 6), call the dog to you from their solo time space (room or yard) and reward them for coming. The fact that the dog is contained and on their own at the start means they're more likely to come. Work on that for a while, building your primordial socialization. Use food and even toys if the dog is interested. Eventually introduce new environments (spatial socialization) and work on ensuring your dog's responsiveness with people, animals, and things at a distance (distal socialization), which we will discuss in upcoming chapters.

# Exercise: *Grounding*

The goal of the grounding exercise is for you and your dog to relax, with the dog next to you in your inner circle. You both catch your breath, get grounded, and find stillness in the here and now. You are calm, modeling calmness for the dog, and wait without words or actions for them to observe and do the same. Give the dog the time and space to process and relax instead of inducing an artificial state by asking them to lie down.

Hold the leash close enough that wandering around is not possible but not so tight as to prevent a natural movement toward relaxation, such as sitting or lying down. Don't talk much at all to the dog or pay attention to them; just work on your own state. Check in with your own body and mind. The aim is for the dog to eventually look up and check in with you, having been given enough time to do so of their own volition.

Trainers often say that focus is something to teach our dogs, asking them to respond to cues such as "watch me" or "eyes". My position is that if I've raised my dog right, my dog will naturally check in with me and pay attention to me without me having to ask. The idea is to let dogs think for themselves about what should be done.

## EARLY STAGE—PRIMORDIAL SOCIALIZATION

In the early stages, you're focused on just you and your dog, doing grounding exercises in your home and designated areas, without any other forces to contend with. At the start, the dog might not always welcome this closeness. Your relationship could be new, or it could be conflicted, so part of the challenge of the grounding exercise is having the dog hang out calmly next to us without pushing, sassing, retreating, or protesting. Food is a great way to help the dog settle because it is the number one comforter for dogs at this stage.

The moments in between activities are a good time to work with grounding. Say the dog is in the yard for some solo time. The dog is settled outside enough to be brought back inside for some mat time in the office before dinner. Step outside and call the dog to you, get a hold of their drag line as they come up, and praise them.

Hold the leash short in your hand and keep standing if your dog is excited and unsettled or sit on a chair or bench if they're more settled. Stand or sit calmly without paying attention to the dog, breathe and relax, and don't say anything. You will feel the dog relax. They do not need to fall asleep at your feet for your effort to be successful. Simply settling, sitting, looking up to you, or lying down are all indications that the dog has gone down a notch or two, and you can end the exercise.

### MID STAGE—SPATIAL SOCIALIZATION

With the dog significantly decompressed, expand to spatial socialization by grounding in new spaces. Say you're about to take the dog out. Spend a couple of minutes on the front porch, just taking things in before leaving.

If you happen to be headed to a new hiking destination, park, or working space, pause and wait for the dog to settle in the new place so that you can proceed with your dog clearheaded. This could be leaving the dog in their car crate for a few moments with the windows and doors open so that the dog can take things in gradually.

If you just got back from a strenuous session, again take a moment to ground by your car, on your porch, or by the door before going in. Continue to use food to help your dog settle and then increasingly as a reward for settling nicely and adjusting to the new space. Remember that things have a way of regressing in new spaces, so if we go to a new place and the dog is anxious, that's normal. Give the dog a moment and then see if a little food helps settle them in.

### LATER STAGE—DISTAL SOCIALIZATION

In the later stages, elevate the level of difficulty by introducing people, animals, or things at a distance, and work on having the dog calm at your side even with these stimuli, teaching the dog to settle and ignore things (distal socialization). The goal is for your dog to be calm, wherever you might be and whatever might be happening.

In the mid stage section, I mentioned hanging out on the front porch or front of the building, looking at things at a distance before heading off for a walk. If there are people, squirrels, or cars going by, this is great distal socialization. If you have multiple dogs, you can also ground inside the house with your new dog near you and the other dogs at a distance minding their business. These would be your longer-staying residents who need to be at Stage 3 for this to work. Remember that any time new levels of socialization are added, regression is to be expected. Use food to keep dogs grounded and calm next to you.

## The Tranquil Circle

Raising our dogs in a way that they learn to stay within the tranquil circle around us, that 10- to 15-foot radius, is one of the ways that we raise them toward freedom. If they know to always stay within a few feet of us, this minimizes our need to control and supervise them. Any time we are with our dogs when they're not crated, we want them at no more than that distance. In Stage 1, we enforce that with the long line.

### Exercise: *Mat Time*

Mat time teaches dogs to stay within the tranquil circle by giving them a physical object (a mat or blanket) to be on within the space. They eventually learn to park themselves nearby anytime you're not actively paying attention to them instead of being underfoot (i.e., in your inner circle) or leaving the space (i.e., busting your territorial line). You can apply the central idea of this exercise inside as well as outside, as you progress along the rungs of socialization.

In the early stages, once your dog has gotten the hang of the routine and is settling in the crate for decent amounts of time, if not all the time, this is a good occasion to start introducing the dog to being in the house with you in a restricted space. This is about having the dog with you in a controlled capacity.

For this exercise, choose a specific space inside the house with the leashed dog hanging out with you: the office while you work, the kitchen while cooking, or the living room while reading or watching television. At the start, pick a space where you're active and busy—the kitchen or laundry room as opposed to a TV room or office where you're likely to be stationary. Close off the space with gates or doors to prevent the dog from leaving. Make sure the space is cleared of anything you don't want the dog getting into.

If you have a dog who's having trouble relaxing in the space, they could be encouraged to do so by being given a chew toy as invitation to lie down on the mat. If they're still unable to settle, shorten the leash, bring the dog closer to you, ground with the dog and settle them down, and then take them to their crate.

Remember at Stage 1 we are not asking the dog to do anything, so if it isn't happening, the best thing to do is simply end the exercise. Don't attempt this exercise at a time where the dog might be too tired or too stimulated to settle. Maybe the dog can't really produce this just yet, and it means you try again in another day or two.

### EARLY STAGE—PRIMORDIAL SOCIALIZATION

Bring the dog to the designated space for the exercise, with a drag line (or a shorter leash if the space is snug). Block off the space with a barrier or baby gate so that you don't need to police your dog. There are no other people or animals around; it's just the two of you. Have the mat or dog bed in that space and go about your business. Again, don't say anything to the dog. If the dog moves to explore, let them and keep doing what you're doing, ignoring the dog completely. The dog can check things out until they find the mat and lie down. Call the dog gently to you if they appear distracted by things beyond the door. If the dog isn't settling, treats could be scattered on the bed and a chew toy could be placed on the mat to invite the dog there. The idea is for the dog to find the mat and lie down on their own, with a little help from us at the start.

### MID STAGE—SPATIAL SOCIALIZATION

Expand to other spaces around the house. Bring your dog and their mat to a blocked-off space, teaching the dog to "park" on the mat while remaining within that 10-foot radius. By having the dog on leash, you are keeping them within the tranquil circle, and they learn that they should stay in that space. By having a mat there without asking the dog to go to it, the dog will explore the space and eventually make their way onto the mat on their own. This allows the dog to figure out that it's probably the best thing to do with their own thinking as opposed to us asking, luring, or training. At Foundations, any time you have the dog with you in the house—i.e., not crated and not outside doing exercises—you have the dog in this format: blocked off, with a line on, and the mat nearby.

### LATER STAGE—DISTAL SOCIALIZATION

In the later stages, take this exercise outside, without a mat to help guide the dog, and with stimuli at a distance that you help the dog ignore. Take your dog to your park or designated working area. Play your games, work your long-line exercises, and then take a rest. Stand or sit with your dog on the long line, and let the dog explore the space until they settle. If they try to pull beyond the circle, shorten the leash to minimize movement and help them settle.

You could be hiking and decide to stop and sit down. Have the dog on leash and not able to go beyond the circle. The dog will explore the entire circle around you until they settle somewhere within the tranquil circle. Let the settling sink in with both of you in the tranquil circle and then proceed.

## The Territorial Circle

The territorial circle is defined by the outer boundary of the space we are in. When we are in any space with our dog, inside or outside, we prevent our dog from accessing, hanging out by, or patrolling that territorial line. Boundary lines inside and outside are ours only and are off-limits to the dogs, who do not go near the boundary line, much less cross to the other side. Beyond that line is another world. They know it and know whether we're allowing them near it. This is one of the foundations of raising dogs capable of being loose.

If we happen to be in the living room with our dog, why is the dog suddenly in the kitchen? If the dog is making those decisions inside, we can expect they will do the same outside. In the initial stages, this boundary must be enforced. We do not allow our dogs near doors, windows, gates, or fences. Dogs are not allowed near the territorial line.

When we cross from one space to another, even a change so simple as one room to another in the house, that is still a crossing of the territorial line. The mind me exercise that follows and later the territorial line exercise in Stage 2 help instill that understanding.

# Exercise: *Mind Me*

Mind me involves applying a grounding exercise at an entry/exit point, just as you're about to make a transition in and out of the space with your dog. This is about the dog "minding" you while you go from one place to another—for example, from the crate to the area where you'll be working or hanging out, from the crate to the yard, from the yard to the car, and so on.

This pause each time you're about to go through thresholds, gates, and doorways conveys to the dog that this movement is not a given. This includes whether you're both crossing a threshold—for example, both walking through a gate—or if you're bringing your dog out from a space such as a crate, from behind a baby gate, or from the yard to inside.

If you get into the habit of doing this with your dog at every door, you'll raise a dog that does not fly through doors or book it for a gate that's left open. They wait to be told and eventually simply check in with us to see that it's okay to proceed.

### EARLY STAGE—PRIMORDIAL SOCIALIZATION

Say you're going from crate to yard: leash the dog while still crated instead of allowing the dog to fly all over the place. Pause before you let them out, take a grounding moment and make sure your dog is calm. Make your way to the door and then pause again at the door, without saying anything. Just keep your leash short to keep the dog in your inner circle. Take a breath, let the dog shake and stretch, and praise lightly for that. Wait a moment—don't rush—and soon as the dog looks up, praise lightly and proceed. Remember to praise according to your dog's temperament; a softer and hesitant dog that takes a moment to look up should be met with heartier approval than an overly excited dog.

### MID STAGE—SPATIAL SOCIALIZATION

As you gradually expand your dog's world, there will be new opportunities to practice mind me with spatial socialization. Remember what happens, though, when you're in a new place—your dog will regress. So lower your expectations of anything your dog does well in a familiar place, including minding you. Breathe at the threshold all the same and give your dog the time to settle in that new place with you before you proceed. It does not need to be perfect but wait until you sense that your dog's anticipation has come down a little.

**LATER STAGE—DISTAL SOCIALIZATION**
At this level, we introduce distal socialization, working on mind me at thresholds, doors, and gates in the presence of people, animals, or stimulating things at a distance. These stimuli serve as distractions for the dog and require us to up our level of patience.

At Stage 1, managing space and boundaries is heavily regimented, consisting of regular crating, a schedule, and setting foundations for understanding the three circles through practicing inner circle exercises such as come here and grounding, tranquil circle exercises such as mat time, and territorial circle exercises such as mind me. We also progress through the levels of socialization, including primordial, spatial, and distal, which we will discuss more in-depth in the next chapter.

## CASE
# Chelsea the German Shepherd Puppy

Chelsea the German shepherd puppy was less than three months old when her owners, a young couple living with their in-laws, contacted me because they were concerned with her behavior. Their first message stated:

*I have a GSD, 11 weeks old. She has a chewing habit and has now started biting my hands and ankles. She's a little timid and somehow overly alarmed. Every time I take her out, she will yell or bark at strangers for no reason. She's also afraid of getting out of the car when we take her out. She pulls on her leash sometimes. I'm looking for professional training, which I hope can help her gain some basic manners so that I'm comfortable letting her walk around the house and taking her out for a walk.*

## The Issues

My clients were dealing with typical puppy issues such as grabbing, chewing, and getting into things. They also struggled with Chelsea's house-training. However, it was the pup's dismal lack of confidence, extreme timidity, and reactivity that they were rightfully worried about. Chelsea reacted to just about everything—sounds, people, and dogs that she would see outside or could hear from inside. Even with the space between homes and the relative peace and quiet afforded by their suburban neighborhood, Chelsea could not be outside in the yard without fiercely reacting to stimuli. Chelsea also scarfed down her food so quickly that she sometimes regurgitated it, which is often a symptom of a dog that's overly stimulated, stressed, and seeking comfort in food.

When we started working together, we began deconstructing Chelsea's way of life, going over everything they did with her from the moment they walked away with her from the breeder's property.

This story is very common: a young and serious couple are set on a particular breed, do their homework, locate a reputable breeder, and come home with their new friend. They are unable to contain their joy and excitement. Understandably thrilled to have their new pup, they doted on her and did more with her than what was appropriate at this stage, including not crating her properly. This, combined with the sensitive genetics of her pedigree, was enough to send Chelsea over the top.

## A New Way of Life

Still, we all considered this a lucky situation. Chelsea did not wait to let her people know that something was off. My clients were relieved to know they could go back to basics to fix things.

Because of how concerned they were with what they saw, they quickly adjusted their mindsets, going to a place of healthy, detached handling of their pup and modulating their emotions. They were reminded of the nature of puppies who are young, vulnerable, and ignorant. They understood that Chelsea wasn't to be disciplined in any form or fashion, only managed, redirected as needed, and praised. They realized that manners are not necessarily the first thing we work on; rather, they are the result of a healthy way of life. The owners fundamentally got the importance of managing the environment as opposed to trying to control the puppy, who has no self-control.

We tweaked the physical arrangements, tossing out the large x-pen connected to her crate, which let Chelsea choose to go in and out as she pleased. It took Chelsea a few days to adjust to the change in her containment, barking her little head off and showing us yet again that the experience of being contained in a crate is not the same as having in-out access.

Puppies and dogs like to keep their spaces clean, so crating the pup and alternating with periods where they are taken outside to do their business is how we house-train puppies. All it takes is a crate, a space outside, a schedule, and a little time and patience. Unlike the common advice of letting puppies out every two hours, we worked on a schedule that kept Chelsea crated for a minimum of three to four hours, allowing her the sleep and rest she badly needed. As expected, she settled beautifully and began showing improvements.

The schedule included crate time alternating with outings throughout the day. These outings included solo time when Chelsea would be by herself in the fenced-in yard, as my clients understood the importance of her learning to be by herself. They quickly noticed that Chelsea was less interested in what was happening in the neighborhood than in what her owners, who were inside, were up to.

During these sessions, which would last about an hour, she didn't scratch, paw, bark, or anything like that. She felt a little anxious but quickly adjusted, learning to take on the smells of the neighborhood on her own. Because things were being done correctly inside, gradually she started to lose interest in the noises of the neighborhood, and as soon as her people would step outside, she was glad to see them and engage with them.

In addition to solo time, the schedule also comprised outings where my clients played with Chelsea and worked on their exercises, including their grounding exercises, long-line exercises, and games with food and tugs. (See chapter 7.) They learned to remain neutral any time Chelsea would nip at them while praising her for working for food and biting on tugs.

They stayed on the property for the most part and restricted her handling to themselves, their in-laws stepping in only if needed. This allowed my clients to begin building the foundational socialization that is the prerequisite for all socialization. Chelsea's spatial socialization was restricted to the crate, the backyard alone or with her owners, and the gym room in the basement, their indoor training space.

As she began to settle down some, my clients set up a crate in their SUV and began taking Chelsea on car rides each time they went to run errands. She barked at things profusely at first, was ignored, and eventually came around to ignoring things in the car. With time, they began hanging out and working with Chelsea in their front yard, seeing people, dogs, and passing cars and trucks from the safety of their front porch and garden. Soon enough, we were able to designate a large park nearby where they could go on walks with space from people and their dogs, progressing Chelsea's socialization toward learning to ignore people and animals at a distance.

## Results

By the time we completed our course, Chelsea was well on her way to becoming a more confident and secure teen exhibiting increasingly the very soundness, strength, and spiritedness we want to cultivate in our dogs. Her body has grown beautifully and the ease in her psychology shows in the fluidity of her movements. The anxiety she exhibited at first has dissipated, and while she continues to be a sensitive dog, she now has the wits to think before she reacts.

Her reactivity to sounds has significantly lessened; she can be in the yard and not react to things. She can go for drives and take in the world relatively quietly. In the last session of our course together, after a barky introduction, Chelsea was able to join my girls Bruna and Nejra on a hike. My girls did a fine job of ignoring her, knowing she had to work past her insecurities. I said to the clients that this wasn't just Nejra and Bruna making it happen; this was all the work my clients had done managing Chelsea that made this possible. My clients were given the gift of knowing how to design a way of life that makes sense for where they and their dog were at in the process. They got the essence of this approach, which is about strengthening dogs by exposing them to things gradually.

# For Reflection

1.  Write down a list of what happens on an average day in your life, including work, school, gym sessions, or other obligations. How would you like to see your dog better integrated into your work and/or life?

2.  What are your thoughts and feelings about crating dogs, whether based on personal experience or messaging from the press, social media, or dog trainers? How might you reconsider these thoughts based on what you learned in this chapter?

3.  Decompression can be one of the most challenging parts of this process. As you begin decompression, what are you nervous about? How can you work on supporting your mindset to convey a sense of calm and authority to your dog?

4.  As you begin seeing the three circles throughout your home and outside environments, how has your understanding of space changed? How do you see your dog responding to or ignoring the three circles?

5.  As you begin the early-stage versions of the exercises in this chapter, what is the baseline for you and your dog? What does your dog struggle with, and what is easy for them? Recording this can be a wonderful way to track your dog's progress and accomplishments.

# CHAPTER 6

# Socialization at Stage 1

Do less sooner, so you're not doing more later.

—**RAY HUNT,** horseman and clinician

*O*ver a decade ago, I brought home Murphy on foster, and he ended up staying with me for 14 months—the longest I have fostered any dog. He was about two at the time, a shepherd-collie mix whose status was uncertain at the shelter where I volunteered. The shelter was in transition, and there were fears that the longtime residents, those who had not been adopted out successfully yet, might not survive the change. Murphy happened to be one of these dogs.

Murphy was extremely agitated and hard to handle at the shelter. He was terribly willful and strong, and he challenged the most able and patient staff and volunteers. When in his kennel, he jumped up and down, trying to escape. The first time he was adopted, he was returned promptly. The second time, the owners did their best but ultimately lacked the experience he needed. Before the building closed, he came home with me on weekends to get a little respite from shelter life. It helped him but wasn't enough to aid his dim adoption prospects. When the time came to get him out of the building, I didn't hesitate.

Few appreciate the toll that shelter life takes on dogs, even with the best intentions and efforts of the organization's staff and volunteers. One of the reasons why time in a shelter is so taxing is because of the hypersocialization that takes place. Dogs *are constantly exposed to many different people including rotating staff members, volunteers, dogwalkers with different attitudes and handling styles, and of course, members of the public checking out the dogs and visiting with them. And yet, what do people do when they bring home a shelter dog? They continue that process of hypersocialization with a dog who's already exhausted.*

*Decompressing Murphy was wonderful and not as challenging as I thought it would be. All this guy needed was a solid decompression and structure in the way of life. It was about six months before I felt Murphy was ready for adoption, but it took a lot longer to find the right adopter. When a Toronto police officer turned up one day wanting to adopt Murphy, I felt we might have finally found the one. I remember repeating to Murphy's new owner that if he ever encountered any issues at all, anything whatsoever, to bring Murphy back. If the new owner changed his mind in any way, at any time, and for any reason, he could return the dog promptly, knowing that Murphy would be staying for good this time.*

*Finally, the officer got a little annoyed at my repeating the same point and said to me, "That's never gonna happen."*

*The man sure kept his word. He followed my advice to decompress Murphy through the change and to take his time before doing or expecting too much. Despite having shared our home with Murphy for over a year, the fact that I'd been careful with how and how much he socialized with us kept him aware of his guest status. By the time he went to his forever home, he was eager to bond with his true family, and his new owner did not need much time to transition Murphy. Off they went on all sorts of hiking and camping adventures with friends both human and canine.*

The case of Murphy and many others I have worked with continue to demonstrate that we have a fundamentally flawed understanding of socialization. It is harmful and unnecessary to expose our new pups and dogs to excessive interactions with people and animals in their first few days, weeks, and months with us. This is not what's going to make them social and friendly. Murphy lacked nothing to be social, and he didn't need to be blasted with social experiences. What he needed was to feel safe.

At Stage 1, we are working with the idea of the den, where cubs have little to no access to the outside world. So here, we are instilling in dogs the capacity to be alone before socializing. Then we work with the first three levels of socialization: primordial, spatial, and distal. All three levels involve direct interactions with us only and no one else.

Primordial socialization is about exposing dogs to us as their primary handler and significant person, their safe base and refuge. No one else enters this space because you have to come to know your dog and let them come to know you first. If we started exposing our dog to other dogs when our bonds with them are weak—when their bonds with people are weak—there is a likelihood of overbonding with their own kind. How could they not? No matter how hard we try, we will never be a dog.

In addition, keep in mind that while we've been best friends with dogs for centuries, we've also hurt, neglected, and killed them. We've had them for dinner when times were scarce. There's tremendous abuse in this history. And this knowledge is also in the dog. The dogs know we can hurt them and, ultimately, have power over them. And so, how much are they really going to let loose? We must earn that trust.

# Before Socialization: Learning to Be Alone

The ideas of the den, or whelping box, represent a period of intense bonding between infants and mother as well as a time of isolation. By the same token, we have an obligation to teach our dogs to be alone and, better yet, to be so sound and strong as to welcome their alone time. I assure you that being alone is as natural and healthy for dogs as being social.

Most importantly, learning to be alone needs to come before a dog can access more time with us. The ultimate foundation of healthy and successful rearing is a dog who is independent rather than codependent. Learning to be gladly on their own is a wonderful trait to cultivate in our dogs.

## Exercise: *Solo Time*

Solo time is about nurturing in dogs the capacity to be by themselves while supervised. When I board or foster dogs or have my own dogs decompressed, they get solo time loose in my fenced-in yard or behind a baby gate in my office. My office and kitchen look out on the backyard, allowing me to monitor them from inside while occupied. I also prefer baby gates to shutting the door because the idea with solo time is that the dog can still witness some action in the home, while learning to accept not being a part of it. I can also indirectly observe what's happening while remaining occupied. Basically, solo time is scheduled alone and supervised time, which can be enjoyed in various places:

→　In an outdoor kennel or enclosure

→　In a protected backyard or closed-off deck

→　On a safe balcony

→　Behind a baby gate in a separate room

→　In an exercise pen inside or outside

If no such space is available, use your designated quiet area for training and exercise for solo time as well. Simply incorporate some downtime into your exercises and disconnect from your dog as if they were in a backyard alone. Again, it's essential that the level of stimulation be conducive to that. Applying the logic of the three circles, you have the dog on the long line, and they can walk around us along that length.

Just as with being crated or confined, dogs may resist solo time, which can take the form of scratching at the door, barking and whining, or being quietly glued to the door. Ignore all these behaviors and take note of the ups and downs in progress. Try to wait for the dog to settle before calling it quits. Observe changes in the dog's capacity to go from protesting being alone to relaxing, taking in the sights and sounds, and enjoying the space.

If you're working in a fenced yard and the dog is hanging out near the fence line, open the window and call them off. They don't need to come back inside, and they don't need to leave the yard; they simply need to get off the boundary line. If they remain amped up, patrolling the fence, and barking, consider whether the dog could use more physical exercise, more time in the crate, or both, and pull back a little on the solo time. The goal is to work to a place where the dog hangs out close to the house instead of anxiously running along the boundary line.

# Primordial Socialization

The first and most important level of socialization is what I refer to as primordial socialization, which occurs between the dog and the primary handler and members of the immediate family.

Choosing and sticking to one or two primary handlers to begin with is important. In a duo such as a couple or pair of roommates, take turns—but only if you can be 100% on the same page. If your family is large and you're all over the place, designate a primary handler at the start, and the others can be participants who eventually become handlers. Both dogs and wolves appreciate the idea of an extended family, and they relate differently to different members. But to start from a place of stability, we need to minimize the cooks in the kitchen.

At primordial socialization, the dog experiences close and daily interactions with the primary handler(s), including these situations:

→ Initial interactions at shelter, foster home, or breeder

→ Daily management

→ Daily handling

→ Feeding

→ Vetting

→ Medicating

→ Grooming

→ Transporting

→ Exercising

→ Training

At this point, socialization does not include interactions with the other animals in the house, nor does it include interactions with people or animals outside the house. This allows for imprinting and bonding between us and our dog. We are forging our relationship within a simple environment. The dog is being socialized with us and getting used to us.

When we have a healthy relationship foundation, dogs trust that the people, animals, and things to which they're being exposed are safe. When we have a budding bond with our dogs—relationship material—they understandably become more open to the challenges and experiences we show them.

This primordial socialization and temporary delay of the other levels of socialization minimize the likelihood of the dog having negative reactions to things. Premature exposure can result in negative reactions, not because those things are inherently negative to the dog, but simply because the dog does not yet trust the humans showing the dog those things. We need to mean something to our dog before we start socializing in the outside world. That's why it's essential we keep it low key at the start and allow for simple and successful one-on-one interaction and primordial socialization to happen without competing sources of attention.

Once achieved, the benefits of primordial socialization last for as long as our life with our dog endures. So don't take this stage lightly! Stay here as long as necessary; it's never just a few days, as people seem to think. Give the dog time to truly see that you are the center of their world. Your attitude also matters: dogs come around faster and begin to show readiness for more when you are detached and not in a hurry.

Keep in mind that many people around you aren't necessarily going to understand the approach you're taking. You might face opposition, even outright criticism. At best, expect some bewilderment bordering on guilt-tripping as to why you're not out there socializing your pup with everything under the sun. Be prepared and stand your ground without entering philosophical debates. Time will tell the tale. Your dog will ultimately show that you did the job right.

## Activity: *On The Grooming Table*

Grooming is an essential activity and part of our way of life with dogs. Grooming first fulfills an important health and wellness function, ridding the coat of falling fur and helping keep the skin breathing and stimulated. Of course, some aspects of grooming can be quite uncomfortable for dogs, including nail trims, anal gland expressions, and ear cleanings. Other parts, such as brushing, can be soothing and bonding, and that is where we start.

Once your dog has decompressed some and is adjusting to you and your schedule, set a time for a grooming session. Identify an elevated surface either inside or outside. An elevated surface is helpful in keeping you standing tall. The dog is also more conscious of having to stand still on that elevated surface, lest the dog fall, easing your grooming task. Lure the dog with a treat or place the dog on that surface and take a moment to ground with your dog on the grooming table before you do anything.

Once the dog has settled and stops trying to get off, start stroking the dog in long strokes using your hand, stroking as if you were brushing. Punctuate your strokes with treats. Start with a few minutes at a time and work your way toward longer sessions. Keep it simple at the start and avoid sensitive body parts, but eventually progress toward touching parts that could be a little uncomfortable including the face, feet, and tail. I recommend transitioning to using brushes by introducing a grooming glove first. Sessions should always start short, no more than a few minutes at a time so that you can end with the dog still in a receptive state.

Down the road, introduce the care that's less comfortable—for example, ear cleaning, nail cutting, and anal gland expression. Unless you are proficient at these aspects of care, I don't recommend you attempt them on your own. Hire a professional who can assist you in getting the work done correctly while you ensure that the experience is as stress-free as possible.

## Exercise: *Recall Games*

Building on the come here exercise discussed in chapter 5, recall games are a fun way of engaging the family in primordial socialization by building bonds around games that both dogs and people enjoy. Of course, we have to begin with dogs in the right mindset. Just recently, I attempted this exercise with a new client, and when the dog realized that there was no one holding the leash, he took the opportunity to bound around us, glad he was out of reach.

Remember that one of the principles of the three circles is the idea of calling the dog into our space instead of going to the dog. Games of recall are a fun way of continuing to instill the idea of dogs coming to us when called. They are a terrific way of getting our dog exercised, running, and exerting some energy. These are games that can be played by us and our dog as a pair, and if there is more than one handler, the humans can pair up and engage in a game of dual recall, sending the dog from one person to another. One more tip is to start with sounds such as whistles or general words such as "bud" or "pup" before moving to personalizing the interaction by using the dog's name.

### SIMPLE RECALL

Arrive at the yard or working space and give the dog, on a long line, a chance to walk around and check things out before you start. The goal is to create opportunities for recall. For example, call the dog, show them the treat, toss it in bowling-ball fashion a few feet away to start (no longer than the length of your line), and let the dog get it. Then call the dog back in only to send them back out again with another treat toss. (See exercise "Treat Toss.") You can also show the dog treats and lure them in with your hand. (See exercise "Hand Lure.") Walk or run away from the dog and call them in. You can also meander around the quiet area and call the dog to you.

### DUAL RECALL

If you happen to be a pair or couple, you can have loads of fun recalling the dog from one person to the other using a form of restrained recall—basically holding the dog, calling, and releasing it.

→ Person A holds the dog in a way that aims the dog toward person B.

→ Person B approaches the dog and shows the dog the treat.

→ Person B backs up and calls the dog.

→ Person A releases the dog to run to person B.

→ Person B receives the dog, treats the dog, and then aims the dog back to person A.

→ Person A approaches the dog and shows the dog the treat.

→ Person A backs up and calls the dog.

→ Person B releases the dog to run to person A.

**VARIATIONS**

There are many ways of building on this exercise:

→ When person A releases the dog to person B, person B could start walking (which can progress to running) away with the dog following until eventually stopping to reward the dog.

→ When person A releases the dog to person B, person B could be hiding with the dog looking until eventually finding person B and receiving the reward.

Remember that the dog is always on a line at the start and that you're using food and toys to lavishly reward the dog, engaging in this exercise with joy and enthusiasm. You are also working with the primordial, spatial, and distal levels:

→ Start these exercises in quiet and familiar spaces without distraction (primordial).

→ Eventually experiment with recall games in new spaces (spatial) while keeping in mind the regression that comes in new spaces. Become more familiar with a space before attempting recall games.

→ Toward the later parts of Foundations, you want to be able to practice these fun games with people, animals, and things at a distance (distal).

# Spatial Socialization

With a basis of primordial socialization, we can expand to different spaces. Spatial socialization is about experiencing different spaces and environments without engaging or participating. So at Stage 1 this means solely adjusting to changes in spaces and settings. The following are examples of spatial socialization inside the home:

→ Adjusting to the new home

→ Adjusting to the crate

→ Getting used to the yard, garage, or designated solo time and working spaces

→ Dealing with construction work at the house (the dog cannot see the workers but can sense the change of environment created by their presence)

→ People visiting (the dog cannot see the visitors but can sense the change of environment created by their presence)

→ When any of the humans are absent

→ When any of the humans are not behaving as they normally would (for example, being ill or injured)

Spatial socialization also happens outside the home. The dog experiences different environments simply by going to different places and witnessing these spaces without socializing with people or doing anything in these spaces, as with the following examples:

→ Taking our dog with us on errands, occasionally leaving the dog behind (crated or tethered in the vehicle, weather permitting)

→ Taking our dog on car rides

→ Taking our dog to our working spaces

→ Visiting a new place

Simply being in a new space is an exercise in socialization, and that alone requires adjustment. Because being in a new place can cause dogs to regress, we allow our dogs to adjust to that environment change without any other levels of socialization added on top. For example, seeing things from a distance and while safely crated prepares the dog to eventually participate in new environments as well as to understand differences in what's permitted in one environment versus the next.

To begin, we get the dog used to a small set of environments. This allows the dog to adjust to new environments more quickly down the road. At the start, we specify the spaces where the dog is active. For example, inside the house we would specify that we will only have the dog in these locations:

→   In the crate

→   In the room or space where the crate is

→   In the office

→   In the kitchen

At this point, all these spaces are closed off with doors or gates when the dog is in them. I also recommend creating a larger indoor space where you can be more active with your dog if possible, such as one of these areas:

→   A garage

→   A finished or unfinished basement

→   A spare room

Outside the house, there are also a limited number of spaces for spatial socialization:

→   Building hallways and stairwells

→   Building basements and garages

→   A quiet park nearby

→   A sports center where you have access to a private space or fenced area

→   A quiet alleyway in the neighborhood

→   A private backyard

## Activity: *Identify Stage 1 Locations*

Identify a quiet area where you can work with your dog with minimal distractions and interruptions. This is essential at the start—remember the idea that intimacy is not built in a crowd and that having a quiet place where you can do your exercises is critical.

If you have the room, that space can be your driveway, backyard, front yard, or a big enough basement. If you live in an apartment building, there is a lot you can do with hallways, stairwells, and garages. There could be quiet spaces in the neighborhood that are workable. The place does not need to be pretty; it just needs to be relatively free from social distractions.

Make a list of the specific indoor and outdoor places and locations that you will be restricting your dog to during Stage 1, including the following:

→   Contained spaces inside: crates in the house, day and night locations

→   Inside areas: inside areas for solo time and mat time

→   Outside areas: backyard, deck, parks, or rental spaces for exercise, solo time, and outings

# Distal Socialization

Distal socialization means witnessing things at a distance and learning to ignore these things. This form of socialization goes by many names—for example, "passive socialization." Sam Malatesta referred to this as "indirect socialization,"[10] while Denise Fenzi calls this "exposure without interaction."[11]

---

10   Sam Malatesta and Souha Ezzedeen, "One with Dog: Sam Malatesta's Whelping Box Approach to Rearing and Training Dogs," (unpublished manuscript, Canadian Intellectual Property Office: Copyright Registration #1130736, 2016), 27.

11   Denise Fenzi, "Understanding High-Drive Dogs: When the Abnormal Is Absolutely Normal," Virtual conference session, Aggression in Dogs Conference, 2020.

To teach dogs to ignore people, dogs, and other things they may see moving in any environment, we model the attitude that we are not paying attention to those things, so the dog doesn't need to either. We note and move on; we do not pay undue attention, react, or engage. Distal socialization can include the following:

→  Seeing people at a distance inside/outside the home

→  Seeing animals at a distance inside/outside the home

→  Seeing cars, trucks, and traffic

→  Walking at a distance from construction sites

For me, this is one of the most important aspects of socialization—raising dogs that are generally indifferent to things, people, or animals unless I direct their attention toward those things. Isn't this alone a huge deal? Think about it: you're out for walks, and your dog doesn't care who else is out! You're in an obedience training class, and the dog is happy to pay attention to you and no one else! This kind of socialization also reinforces the intimacy of our growing bond by not allowing others to interfere with and hinder our bond.

You might struggle with this, coming across people who ask if they can say hi to the dog or if their dog can greet yours, or even people who don't ask. This is a test for you! How strong is your determination to keep these crucial boundaries and maintain that inner circle around you and your dog?

Of course, there will be times when our boundaries are violated. People come close despite our preference that they didn't. Other dogs invade our space without our permission. When this happens, do not make a big deal of the situation. Simply walk away without anger at the invading parties, without asking the dog to do anything. (You being angry reduces your credibility in the eyes of your dog.) We will get into this more later with oppositional socialization, but for now, focus on redirecting your dog away with treats or walking them away from the situation.

The important thing is to not turn incidents like these into emotional events, as this is a sure way of teaching dogs that chaos ensues each time someone intrudes on our space. Getting upset reduces our power and presence in the moment, undermining our credibility with our dog. By walking away and ignoring things, I am communicating to my dog that the "visit" will not continue because I did not allow it. If my dogs know that I will take the situation under control, they remain calm. So, we've got other dogs coming; I block them. We've got people wanting to touch the dog; I say no. The dog is like, "She's got this."

## Exercise: *Going For Car Rides*

One of my preferred ways to expose dogs to new places and various stimuli at a safe distance is to take dogs on car rides in their crate. Provided the weather is conducive (meaning not too hot and not too cold to leave dogs in the car), I frequently take my dogs—new or seasoned—on errands to the grocery store, car wash, gas station, and dry cleaners. The dogs see and hear things, all while safely crated in the car.

With this exercise, the dogs can see the world from a distance without being asked to engage in any way. This simple exercise provides primordial, spatial, and distal socialization. The dogs can bark all they want in the vehicle, and we don't need to say anything. Let them realize this is a waste of energy. When of sound mind, dogs regulate their effort and conserve their energy. We can work this exercise in levels:

→ Begin with simply going for a car ride and trying to go long enough until the dog has settled. Notice the difference between stop-and-go city driving versus cruising along on a highway.

→ Progress to parking the car and stepping out for quick errands, leaving the dog behind. Remember: we don't talk to dogs when they're crated, so don't say anything when you step out and don't acknowledge the dog when you return.

→ Progress to parking the car and opening the door or hatch so that the dog can see more and smell more. You can hang out by the dog's crate as the two of you take things in, but don't acknowledge the dog or respond to any stimuli.

→ If possible, then find a situation where you can park the car, open the door or hatch, and leave. Not long ago, a client sent me a picture of her dog crated in the back of their SUV with the hatch open and the dog looking into the restaurant patio where the owner enjoyed a meal—a perfect example of distal socialization.

→ Progress to parking somewhere you won't be interrupted and taking the dog out of the crate. Simply hang out by the vehicle, grounding the dog as you both look at things from a distance.

→ Another tip for when coming back from car rides? Park the car and leave the dog crated in the car. Go inside and take care of business, and then return to fetch the dog, who will probably have settled a little more from the ride before being brought inside.

## Exercise: *Having People Over At Stage 1*

One of the things many of us enjoy is having friends and family visit, and this simple pleasure is compromised by dogs with behavioral issues.

In the very early part of this process, when we're still in decompression, try to keep things as quiet around the house as possible. This means minimizing or eliminating new people coming into the house. A few weeks into the new routine with everyone getting the hang of things, we can progress to having people over.

Ideally, you want visitors who support your rearing efforts. They understand and respect your wishes on how the dog should be handled during those visits. They can carry on with fun and conversation even if they hear your dog barking their head off, and they will respect the fact that they should not approach the crate or try to engage the dog. Always brief your visitors in advance on your expectations for their level of interaction with the dog.

### EARLY STAGE—SPATIAL SOCIALIZATION

In the early stages of Foundations, have the dog crated in their usual crate area, away from the visitors. You will have dealt with the dog—they have been exercised, fed, and left with some chew toys in their crate. Before the visitors come, be sure to brief them so they know not to talk to, approach, or acknowledge the dog. When they arrive, let your dog deal with the change of environment that this creates. Your dog can smell and sense the action happening, and that is plenty to deal with at the start. Your dog might bark or not; regardless, the dog is to be ignored. The dog remains in the crate and will not be meeting visitors yet.

### MID STAGE—DISTAL SOCIALIZATION

In the later stages, start off the same way—with the dog squared away in the crate and the visitors coming in. Enjoy your visitors and wait for the dog to settle some. Once the dog has settled, let them out on their leash, walking the dog at a distance from the visitors to the yard or outside for a quick bathroom break. Return the dog to the crate without any interaction or acknowledgment from the visitors, only a chance to walk by and ignore them.

### LATER STAGE—DISTAL TO PROXIMAL SOCIALIZATION

In the later stages, follow the same routine. But this time when the dog comes out of the crate, bring the dog to the space where you have your guests, and ask your guests to carry on ignoring the dog. Ground with the dog. In essence, you are asking your dog to ignore the visitors as well from enough distance. Take as much space near or far from the visitors that helps your dog settle. Once the dog has settled some, taking treats from you and ignoring the visitors, end the exercise and return the dog to their crate. Go back to your guests and enjoy the rest of your evening!

## Exercise: *Engaging With Other Dogs At Stage 1*

It is wonderful to see dogs hanging out and playing with other dogs. But this is another pleasure that's compromised when our dogs have behavioral issues.

The early days of Foundations are not a time for our dogs to interact fully and freely with dog friends or even their human owners. However, just as with people visiting, this will be a time to prepare our dogs to meet other dogs. I have a hard-and-fast rule when it comes to other dogs: they cannot meet, and they certainly cannot play until they learn to ignore.

This of course assumes that our dogs' (future) friends have the same skills that we are trying to instill. Work with your dog-owning friends and see if this gradual socialization is something they can get behind. If none of your friends are willing, share a copy of this book with them, and hopefully they'll come around so you can all raise your dogs consistently, and they can enjoy enduring and healthy friendships.

## EARLY STAGE—SPATIAL SOCIALIZATION

In the early stages of meeting other dogs, have the dog crated in their usual crate area. You will have dealt with the dog—they have been exercised, fed, and left with some chew toys in their crate. Have your friends come over with their dog on leash and let your dog deal with the change of environment that this creates. Your dog cannot see the visitors but can smell and sense the human and dog action happening, and that is plenty to deal with at the start. Your dog might bark or not; regardless, the dog is to be ignored. They will remain in the crate and will not be meeting anyone yet. At the same time, the people visiting with their dogs need to do their own work of grounding their dogs in your home, getting them also settled in and ready for the future dog-on-dog interactions.

## MID STAGE—DISTAL SOCIALIZATION

In the later stages, start off the same way—the dog squared away in the crate and the visitors coming in with their dog on leash. Enjoy your visitors and wait for the dog to settle some. You can use food or something like a Kong chew to help the dog deal. Once the dog has settled, let them out on their leash, and walk the dog at a distance from the visitors (with their leashed dog) to the yard or outside for a quick bathroom break. Return the dog to the crate without any interaction or acknowledgment from the visitors. Your visitors also work on keeping their own dogs grounded through the experience.

## LATER STAGE—DISTAL TO PROXIMAL SOCIALIZATION

In the later stages, follow the same routine. But this time when the dog comes out of the crate, bring the dog to the space where you have your guests with their dog. Our guests are paying attention to their dog, and we are paying attention to our dog. The dogs are at sufficient distance from each other and are asked to ignore each other. Essentially, you are each in your tranquil circles, about 10 feet away from each other—enough space that it is doable for your dogs to ignore each other. The humans can talk to each other while keeping in mind that this raises the level of engagement to interactional, which could ramp up the dogs. Again, you can use treats to help ground the dogs.

This is basically a grounding exercise at a distance from another human-dog team who are also grounding. End the exercise with the dogs paying attention to their people and not minding each other.

Progress to taking the dogs for walks at a distance from each other and again asking the dogs to ignore each other and focus on you and their natural surroundings instead. Sometimes starting with grounding at a distance from another dog in a public park and then going for walks, together but also at a distance, is a better place to start than in someone's backyard.

In closing, socialization at Stage 1 is about instilling the capacity to be alone and building rapport between handler and dog in the myriad of activities involved in living with dogs. This is what I call "primordial socialization." With an emerging closeness between human and dog, socialization is expanded to new environments (spatial) and gradually introduces stimuli at a distance (distal), which we ask our dogs to ignore and focus on us instead.

**CASE**
# Stella the Mastiff-Mix Rescue

Stella's people, a young couple with their hearts in the right place but little experience with dogs, came to us alarmed at the growing challenges they were experiencing managing their big girl. At a little under a year old and 110 pounds—and counting—Stella was terribly hard to handle. She'd bite the leash and drag her people out of the apartment, through the corridors of their condo building, into busy elevators, and out into the crowded streets of downtown Toronto. In their words, they felt "overwhelmed and out of [their] depth" with their "ungovernable" dog, whom they knew was incredibly sweet at the core.

## The Issues

When leashed, Stella would grab the leash and sometimes her owner's arms. With Stella's power and their insufficient experience, my clients were unsure what to make of her mouthing. One of them construed it as aggression, while the other knew there was more going on there. Stella also paced around the apartment constantly, not settling down, licking her owners' faces, which the owners confused for affection instead of the appeasing behavior of a stressed-out dog.

Like many rescue dogs, Stella was not given the decompression that a young dog that had been bounced around needed. Stella's time wasn't structured; she wasn't crated consistently, nor was she on a schedule.

Compounding the issue was that my clients were not on the same page vis-à-vis Stella. The woman felt bad for her, while the man felt resentful. He never really wanted a dog, and now he not only had to contend with a dog around but a badly behaved one. While he was encouraged to hear that Stella had, in fact, a fantastic temperament, it still took him some time to get over his interpretations and fears that her behavior was aggressive. Eventually, he, too, came to see the stable, solid, and kind nature of Stella, who just needed to be understood.

My clients were also under the impression that socialization meant allowing anyone to check out Stella and letting her "say hi" to people. They thought this was good because they'd read so much online about the importance of socializing dogs, particularly rescues like Stella. They had allowed Stella to check out dogs and people and vice versa, and Stella's anxiety bubbled up as did her poor leash etiquette.

## A New Way of Life

The first thing we went to work on was bringing into alignment the views, attitudes, and handling behaviors of my clients. Neither one of their attitudes could stay; her coddling and feeling sorry had to go, as did his resentment. We also worked on developing a better understanding of the differences between healthy socialization and the unfettered greeting and touching of dogs that people call "socialization." It meant appreciating that successful socialization required that Stella trust them first.

We also went to work at the practical level, structuring Stella's daily life, crating her consistently, governing her social interactions, and handling her size kindly, safely, and effectively. This did not involve the use of any tools that are commonly used for large and strong dogs: no choke chains, prong collars, e-collars, or head halters. Rather, it involved coaching my clients on handling with power and poise in a way that helped the dog settle. For example, while out walking, my client would minimize direct contact between her and other people and dogs by turning into Stella. Or if Stella pulled in one direction, rather than try to stop her from pulling, the client would walk in the opposite direction.

Stella's new schedule included physical activity away from people and exercises to begin harnessing her food drive, which she had in abundance. When they could, my clients drove to more spacious and quiet parks nearby. Otherwise, the halls and stairwells of their building gave them plenty of space to work Stella to satisfaction.

With their new understanding of socialization, my clients set boundaries around Stella and made decisions about her interactions instead of letting her (or the public) decide. Stella boarded with me several times, enjoying my outdoor kennels. These successful handler transfers only served to boost Stella's confidence in herself and in her handlers, solidifying her transformation.

# Results

As a breed and breed group, mastiffs are generally laid-back animals who are calm by nature. They were originally meant to just look scary sitting there in all their majesty. It wasn't long before Stella responded positively to the change in handling and attitude. I knew the moment I met her how stable and sweet she was; only she wasn't sure at first if she could let herself be that way.

Not long ago, these clients had the opportunity to move out of the city, and while out on a walk one day, they received a fantastic compliment from a stranger. The person said she could see how "good-natured and bonded" Stella was and that it was "nice to see someone who is well suited to having a dog have one." I believe this to be one of the nicest compliments ever paid to a client.

Stella has become a lot calmer and respectful of her handlers. She hangs out while mom does the dishes, while dad works at his desk, or by herself in the fresh air of her new yard. For their part, her owners have come to see that there was no aggression, only a dog who needed understanding and whose way of life needed to change.

# For Reflection

1.  What has been your experience socializing your current or any past dogs? How did the dog(s) handle this kind of socialization, and what kinds of behavioral issues might be sourced back to it?

2.  Take a moment to write down interactions or activities with your dog that fall under primordial socialization. How can you continue to develop this primary level of socialization?

3.  How does your dog currently deal with being in new places? How about with seeing people, animals, and things at a distance? Pinpoint any areas you and your dog might be struggling with when it comes to spatial and distal socialization.

4.  A difficult part of Foundations is that other people may not understand or

respect the process you are working through. Brainstorm some ways you might calmly handle friends or strangers who attempt to bypass you and breach your dog's inner circle.

5.  What is one surprising and wonderful thing that you've learned about your dog since beginning this process?

# CHAPTER 7

# Drive Development at Stage 1

When I first get a dog, I let it get its head back.

—**KATHY WARNER,** farmer, herding instructor, and cofounder of Tee Creek Dog Training

*M*uch as I enjoy being able to help people fix their issues, I also relish the opportunity to prevent issues from taking hold, by getting people started off right, sparing them and their dogs a lifetime of frustration and stress, not to mention expense. The initial message from this client outlined all the things he was busy doing with his new mini goldendoodle puppy Neptune, including house-training, crate training, and teaching him his name and a few basic cues. His goals were "good obedience, recall, comfortable with the crate, basic commands, walking, and most of all developing a meaningful bond."

This was clearly an enthusiastic client, and working with him and his puppy has been nothing short of fun. He quickly understood the Way of Life method, and we went to work on Neptune's schedule, including crate time alternating with outings for exercise and exposure. We worked on channeling Neptune's energy and drive, which had been frustrating my client. Like many owners, my client saw nipping as a bad behavior to be curbed as opposed to a wonderful, natural drive to be channeled. People tend to have a hard time when puppies start to nip at them. This is when *they'll call trainers and ask whether they should be firm and start correcting the behavior. They wonder whether the nipping is cause for concern and means the pup is aggressive.*

*My client quickly came to realize that all this nipping was a terrific opportunity to redirect the pup toward a correct object to bite on, turning it into a game that boosts the dog's confidence. Neptune had loads of food and play drive and needed help engaging these drives. He was always ready for a meal and responsive to treats, even in new places and even if the treats weren't the highest value.*

*But his most ardent love was tugging on toys, and once we found the right toys for a pup his age, providing tugging action that was appropriately challenging, it was a different story. My client found a way to engage his playful pup in a way that built up the dog's drive and self-esteem, tired him out, and made him think that his owner was the most wonderful human around.*

*My client also learned to look at his pup's behavior in context, in other words, evaluating the situation for whether Neptune needed more play or whether he'd in fact had enough and it was time to put him away. Was he a little hungry, tired, sleepy, or overstimulated? If so, my client ended the session and returned the pup to his crate or playpen with his meal and toys.*

*My client's understanding of the importance of channeling these perfectly natural drives is in fact one of the reasons why he can enjoy his puppy as much as he has. The pup is challenged correctly, managed thoughtfully, and related to in a healthy way. He is allowed to be a pup. He is permitted a childhood. And because of that, we can only look forward with certainty at the sound, strong, and spirited adult he will make.*

The final but no less critical pillar in our way of life is the development of canine drives through exercise, training, and sport. Remember that one of our main goals in the family hierarchy is to strengthen our dogs and mature them up the hierarchy. One of the ways we mature dogs is by revving up their drives. At Stage 1, we are concerned primarily with food drive and secondarily with prey drive.

When cubs and pups are born, they're not interested in chasing after things or pouncing on each other as much as they're interested in food. Their potentially powerful defensive drives are also dormant. The initial rearing stages focus on food as a source of survival and comfort during a stressful time of change. The mother dog wants to see her pups driven. The mother wolf even more so. Similarly, it is our job to rev up that food drive.

Feeding is an exercise in bonding. In human relationships, the sharing of a meal is deeply meaningful and can foster bonds that facilitate communication and collaboration. Think about what happens when couples regularly go on dinner date nights, when families gather around a meal, or when a large group of coworkers comes together for a holiday celebration. Think about the enjoyment and relationship renewal that is made possible by enjoying food.

When dogs are truly responsive to food, it becomes much easier for them to ignore things and be redirected away from sources of stimulation or stress. But this won't work if the dog isn't interested. So we begin by building that food drive. In the case of Katie, whom you'll be reading about in chapter 9, strenuous physical exercise helped wake up her dormant food drive, in turn helping us energize and challenge her with working for food. As her desire for food became better established and we could count on her finishing her meals, her motivation for toys and balls began to emerge—this is a great example of how the drives are layered.

Everything we do at Stage 1 supports the development of dogs' food and prey drives. By decompressing and creating foundations of simplicity, structure, and success, we instill a deep sense of safety that makes it possible for the dog to let loose their desire for things and express their appetite for food and play. It might not appear related at first, but the careful management of space and boundaries at the onset (crating, following a schedule, and so on) contributes to revving up drive.

In addition, tiring out the dog reasonably at this stage also contributes to food drive. Don't underestimate the "exercising" effect of social exposure, which can be taxing and tiring for dogs, hence the need to return dogs to their crates for rest and recuperation.

# Food Drive

Food drive is a dog's very first sense of enthusiasm and motivation for a goal. When wolf cubs are newborn, the mother is not teaching them hunting skills. The mother is feeding them, building their food drive. Later as cubs grow and start participating in hunts, it is their hunger and thinning bodies that tell them it's time to work. The young wolves become charged and electrified, ready for the danger inherent in any hunt.

In working with dogs with behavioral issues, I find some extremely motivated by food, some possessive over food, and others with low food drive. It really depends on several factors, including breed, background, personality, and of course, way of life.

Note that weight and desire for food aren't always correlated. We can have lean dogs refuse food. Revving up their food drive could involve making sure they are physically exerted to open their appetite. We can have dogs who are overweight with huge amounts of food drive. Consult with your vet on ways to trim down your dog, while keeping in mind that vets see so many cases of obesity that your somewhat-pudgy dog could be considered of correct weight while your lean dog could be considered skinny!

Essentially, food drive means that food matters more than anything else at any given moment. Food drive is more than mere interest in food; it involves a willingness to eat anywhere, anytime, and even if under some duress. A dog who is intently food driven will eat even if fed, even if full, and even if the food isn't particularly appealing or "high value." Food drive helps dogs find comfort in food in the stressful situations that we're asking our dogs to deal with. Essentially, food provides comfort until our dogs find comfort in us.

When a dog wants food badly, it gives us a way into a relationship with the dog because food is something we can control. Building soundness with food drive is about giving the dog a reason to be happy, to feel alive, and to partake in the joys of life. It is such a shame that so many trainers consider the use of food to be bribery and that many owners out there think their dogs ought to behave without food rewards. I think of bribery as payment for actions that a party does not wish to engage in. Meanwhile, our dogs do want to please us, just not right away. Food, as an offering of love and means of survival for a dog, is where we start.

We also want our dogs lean and at a working weight not only because it's good for their bodies but because it's good for their minds. When dogs are fit and at a correct weight, they feel better, and this helps bring about a certain positive attitude. It makes them more driven, engaged, and juiced up for work. We want to see their tummies tucked in, their waists defined, and no flesh wobbling around.

To build up food drive and work toward that healthy weight, managing food intake is essential. Feeding is a part of the dog's schedule, remember? Feed the right amount of food at a set number of meals that happen at a scheduled time. I do not recommend hand-feeding or allowing dogs to free feed (grazing on food that's left out all the time). Take away food that has not been consumed promptly.

It's important with those dogs on "hunger strike" that we vibe an attitude of not caring whether they eat or not. We're working on getting them to eat, of course, but we're not fretting about whether they eat or not. That only makes them worry more because they sense our concern. I have seen many owners who stress about their dog not eating and go so far as hand-feeding, which only causes further refusal. Your dog will not starve to death. Give them time because food drive is not just about survival; it is about a zest for life.

With those dogs that can be possessive around food, be conscious of how you manage this in training and in feeding situations. In training situations, handle food calmly and help settle the dog's anxious desire for that food before treating. When feeding meals, feed dogs in the privacy of their crates where they can eat in peace.

Speaking of possession over food, there are many things we do that create this potentially dangerous tendency—for example, when we hand-feed our dogs, thinking this will prevent resource guarding. Also, when we feed our dogs in the open, as opposed to in the privacy of their crates, and touch or talk to them while they're eating, we're teaching them to tense up around food. Depending on what else could be going on, this could progress to resource guarding.

As I see it, food is the one thing in the pet dog's life that we can guarantee they're getting pleasure out of. It matters that we let dogs enjoy their meals without interruption. It matters that we feed fresh and species-appropriate foods, which not only help dogs physically but psychologically as well.

# Prey Drive

While food drive is a juvenile drive, prey drive is an adolescent or emerging-adult drive. Prey drive includes a variety of related drives including the drive to sniff things out (hunt drive) or chase after things (offensive drive). We develop and harness prey drive through games of chase, retrieve, and tug, as we progress with Foundations and move into Exposure.

When food drive awakens, it is only a matter of time before prey drive follows. Often dogs display a preference for prey drive activities, such as ball play and tugging, from the start. This is wonderful, and we can work on both food and prey drives in tandem. However, let's be sure that we have a strong enough food drive, even if it means favoring food at the start before we optimize prey drive.

There are wide variations in dogs' degree of prey drive, and just as with food, there are situations where a dog might be possessive over toys. If that is the case, I back off using toys for some time and let decompression and Foundations take some of the edge off. That's why the layered process is so powerful: we get to back off certain experiences, return to basics and clean things up, and then move forward again.

When healthily harnessed, prey drive is such a wonderful power to nurture in dogs. Sadly, many consider prey drive problematic, seeking to curb it instead of channeling it correctly. Others might confuse anxiety for prey drive. Say we have a dog in a certain sport acting over-the-top excited; yes, this could be drive, but it could also be agitation under the pressure. I remember being at a ring sport trial once where one of the award winners' dogs broke from his sit-stay to attack the other finalist's dog. This was blamed on drive, but I would call this agitation, overstimulation, or poor drive management at the very least, because real drive is laser focused and backed by clear thought.

## **Exercise:** *Using The Long Line*

Before hitting the busy sidewalks, begin your leash work in an indoor or outdoor space that's quiet, such as a basement, backyard, or other quiet or private area you can access. Instead of the conventional four- to six-foot walking leash, work with your 10- to 15-foot long line.

Remember to ground and relax with your dog upon arrival, and then give the dog a moment to check out the premises. You're not yet in a place where you can just get to work immediately.

At this stage, you will have worked on building food drive and have a dog that is keen to work for food. Retain loose handling of the long line and keep the loop of the line resting around your wrist, freeing your hands and helping you forget that the line is even there.

As you progress with these exercises, remember the three levels of socialization that we're working with at Stage 1: primordial, spatial, and distal. Therefore, begin by practicing in the privacy of your working space or quiet area, building your bond and connection without distraction or interruption (primordial). Eventually, move to another space and attempt your exercises there (spatial), keeping in mind that both human and dog have a way of regressing in new spaces. Eventually, work up the capacity of doing these exercises with people, animals, and things at a distance (distal).

All the following and other long-line exercises that involve the dog chasing after food, following our hand for food, and following us for food help us build not only food drive but also prey drive because we have the dog chasing after and going for food.

### *Exercise 1: Treat Toss*

Call your dog and show them that you have a treat. Toss it underhanded, which helps the dog see where it landed, about three to four feet away. Once the dog gets the treat, simply by virtue of the mechanic of having been sent out, they will likely quickly come back for more. If not, whistle or call the dog to come back, use the leash to pull the dog ever so slightly and show them that you have another treat waiting, or walk in the opposite way and draw them to you. As soon as they come back and look at you, toss the treat in the opposite direction. This gets the dog bounding for food, working both food and prey drives. Even dogs that aren't prey motivated or don't care for toys yet will still "chase" after treats.

→   Start on a surface where the dog can see the treat easily (carpet, hard flooring, asphalt, rubber garage mats, etc.), and don't toss it far.

→   Progress to tossing the treat further out, while remaining within line length.

→   Progress to working on grass where the dog must now smell for the treat.

→   Progress to tossing the treat further out on grass.

## Exercise 2: Hand Lure

With this exercise, you're teaching the dog that following you means they get treats. Call the dog to your side and show them you have a treat in the palm of your hand. Keeping your hand at the dog's eye level, walk away, luring your dog with the treat in your hand. When the dog follows your hand, treat the dog, and start again, going in the opposite direction. Progress to doing this exercise while running and taking sudden turns.

## Exercise 3: This Way

This way is an extension of hand lure, but in this case, you do not keep a treat in your hand while walking. Imagine an invisible 20–30-foot line on the ground, and start walking straight on that line, calling the dog to you and having them walk with you a little before you stop and reward. Start walking again, this time in the opposite direction, again calling the dog to follow. "This way!" is the wording I like to use to have the dogs follow.

Progress to walking along that invisible line on the ground without saying anything and rewarding the dog plenty when they follow. So, we're not exciting the dog with treat tosses and hand lures; we're simply walking in opposite directions within a restricted space and praising the dog for choosing to follow us without the incentive of a game but with the reward of food and praise.

When the dog follows and is happy doing so, reward with praise, smiles, food, and/or pats—whatever works in the early going. If the dog gets a little sidetracked, walk in a different direction, and work on keeping the dog engaged with you. (This is why you need a quiet space to start!) Depending on the kind of dog we're dealing with, if they get distracted, call and encourage the dog toward you, or let slight tension on the line prompt the dog to follow.

## Exercise 4: Loose-Leash Walking

All these exercises are preparing for walking on a loose leash and engaging in one of the most rewarding activities: being able to walk our dogs anywhere with them close and attentive—eventually without a leash at all where we're able. Loose leash means the dog is attached to us by a leash, but it is hanging loose, and the dog is walking closely and aligned with us, without it being a militaristic heel.

The this way exercise begins building this capacity, and eventually, as you're walking up and down that invisible line with your dog following you attentively, you start shortening the leash and working toward loose-leash walking. Keep those initial attempts short and successful, and alternate a little loose-leash walking with pauses, treat tosses, hand lures, and games of tug. (See next exercise.)

## Exercise: Tug-Of-War

Tugging continues to be a misunderstood and underutilized game, but it is an essential way to build up dogs and increase their confidence. Tugging can strengthen your bond while at the same time challenging it because the game appears to pit you against your dog—that is, until the dog understands that the game is about letting them win for good effort. There are many excellent instructors and resources for proper tug play that extend beyond the scope of this book, but here are a few points to keep in mind.

→ The game is about boosting the dog's confidence and not about you winning. Let your dog win after a measured amount of effort, which boosts confidence and lets them feel on top of the world.

→ Keep the game energetic and interesting. One thing that helps me do that is thinking of the toy as a prey animal fighting for its life. It is hard to catch and does not give up easily, and we can mimic this primal reality in the game, applying a fair level of difficulty.

→ The choice of toy matters, and tugs come in infinite varieties of material and degree of toughness. Start soft and easy with flirt poles and rags and work your way up to tougher toys.

# Exercise

Making sure that the dog is getting enough physical exercise is one of the most important things to do at Stage 1. Exercise feels good and helps dogs in just about any scenario. Physical tiredness and exertion spur interest in food, which in turn juices up the dog to work for more food. This growing motivation develops prey drive, meaning the strength to play with toys. Tiredness and exertion also make for deep rest and for appreciating the crate as a place of recovery.

Depending on what we enjoy doing, we might look at hiking, jogging, running, swimming, or walking with our dogs as a means of physical exercise. We ensure that we are doing those successfully—away from sources of fear or reactivity—and that we're going to only a few places to start.

For my clients who have reactive or very fearful dogs that present a real challenge in public places, I recommend locating sporting centers with indoor or outdoor spaces that can be rented and used in privacy. I also often recommend a canine indoor pool where the dog gets to swim with instructors—though always away from other people, animals, and things—which includes the soothing and therapeutic effects of swimming.

In my case, I have a large fenced-in yard and a dog training studio in my basement. While I like to hike with a new dog or take them to a park with plenty of space around, I don't do these things right away. Instead, I keep them to the house and yard for a couple of weeks until I start to see signs of decompression and the dog is more comfortable being handled.

My personal favorite thing to do with dogs is hiking, which I consider one of the best means of exercise and socialization. An entire book could be written about the benefits of hiking for dogs and their people! These include physical benefits, as hiking across different terrains challenges and strengthens our and our dogs' bodies. In addition, dogs are incredibly physical creatures whose psychology and mental well-being are greatly affected by their degree of physical strength and fitness. Being light and strong on their feet boosts their confidence while being heavy and sluggish harms their self-esteem much more than we realize.

The sensory stimulation derived from hiking is also tremendously satisfying for both person and dog. While our pleasure tends to be more visual, it's easy to see how much the dogs get a kick out of picking up messages from just about all their senses.

Psychologically, hiking is stimulating, bonding, and healing because it takes us both, human and dog, home to our wild roots and to our untamed selves. This goes back to my core philosophy about letting dogs simply be dogs again, and there's nothing quite like a hike to aid in that. There's much talk these days about our collective nature deficit disorder and that prescribing more time in nature is the medicine we need. By being out in nature, our minds are invigorated and refreshed, our stresses are eased, and whatever traumas we carry lift away, offering a new sense of perspective, awe, and appreciation for nature and life, as we experience it with and through our dog.

## Exercise: *Tire The Dog Out*

The purpose of this exercise is to tire the dog, not exhaust the dog. We need to find that ideal level of exercise that challenges the dog without making them wired and anxious due to excess exhaustion. This can cause the dog to feel uncomfortably vulnerable at this stage.

Endless Chuckit! tosses across large fields are not what we're aiming for; remember, we're keeping our dogs within our circles and on leash. I also don't recommend walking on city sidewalks as a start. Sidewalks do not provide the space and privacy that we are looking for at Foundations, nor is it always possible for us to walk our dogs on long lines in a way that relaxes them and frees their movements.

To tire the dog out at Foundations requires a good amount of space and your 10-foot line. The first few times you try it, a large park or grassy area that is secluded or a quiet parking lot are great, but you can also graduate to doing this on a hiking trail and eventually to exercising in busy parks and sidewalks.

If you arrive at the spot in your car, take some time to ground with your dog crated in the car. Wait for the dog to settle some, then open the crate. If you're arriving on foot, ground with your dog at the boundary of the space. Remember the mind me exercise, where you are again waiting for the dog to settle some before letting it into a new space.

Then, hang out with your dog in your inner circle. Breathe and relax together to take in the space. This is a good habit to get into. Take your time if this is a new space and be of the attitude that you are prepared to go back home if the dog doesn't settle well enough to proceed.

Once you feel you and your dog are settled, and the dog has checked in with you by looking up to you and seeking your face, you can proceed. Start walking, jogging, or hiking while giving your dog good length on the line. If you are in a park or parking lot with lots of open space, walk parallel to each other instead of the dog walking ahead. The idea here is to relax the dog and to have plenty of space between yourself and the dog, which you can't have on a narrow trail or on a sidewalk.

Give your dog length on the line but ensure that your line is loose and that the dog is not using the full length and pulling ahead. Like the this way exercise, simply go in the other direction until the dog follows and the line is loose again. Then turn back the other way, going a bit further out this time. Repeat, gradually proceeding further ahead each time you change directions.

Get in the mindset that at Stage 1, you don't need to go far; you just need to go well. The dog is dealing with plenty already, so the space of physical exercise can stay simple. On a trail, I will circle a short trail several times instead of going farther. In a park, I will select a space, mark its boundaries, and walk up, down, and diagonally in that defined space.

The length of time exercising also matters. You want to reach that sweet spot where the dog is tired, and you can see that in their demeanor, but not so tired that they become wired, anxious, and challenging on the way back. This ends the exercise on a less-than-optimal note. Tire the dog without exhausting the dog and build on that.

Remember the three levels of socialization that we're working with at Stage 1: primordial, spatial, and distal. Therefore, practice your physical activities in specific spaces first without distraction or interruption (primordial). Eventually, move to new spaces (spatial) and with some action in the distance (distal).

# Training

People are often surprised when I say that their dogs having commands such as sit, stay, or wait is all well and good, but it's not what's going to give them a dog free of behavior issues. The three traits I want to cultivate do not include the word "obedient." My aim is that they be sound, strong, and spirited, and that's what makes them want to listen and behave for me.

At Stage 1, our training is largely informal, relying on disciplined management of the dog's movements. When we see the dog figuring things out correctly, we let them know it. We "capture" behavior as it occurs and praise it instead of cueing or asking. Both the mat time and mind me exercises in chapter 5 are great examples of this. There is no disciplining. Heck, we barely know the dog, so how can we expect to train effectively? If you're applying Foundations correctly, dogs can't help but succeed.

At Stage 1, we are working on energizing the dog's enthusiasm for life through developing the dog's drives. One of the ways we build drive at the start is by "letting dogs be dogs" and backing off the traditional forms of training with their relentless cue-reinforce sequences. This is not the time for obedience commands. Try to stay quiet and let the dog observe and think.

No formal training doesn't mean that the dog isn't learning, though. The dog is learning a lot by way of safety, predictability, and success thanks to the structure and simplicity that we're creating.

At this stage, we are encouraging our dogs' creativity, their capacity to think without our constant conditioning and programming, which boosts not only the dog's intelligence but their self-esteem as well. A thoughtful dog is the opposite of a reactive, insecure dog. In these early days, I tell my clients, "Stop talking. Stop commanding. Let that dog think." And then what happens when we embark upon Stage 2 and start formalizing training? The dogs are eager to hear what we have to say. The dogs are happy to listen because we started with silence and did not bombard them. They are clearheaded and learn easily.

You can find many ways to let the dog think during the day. For example, at feeding time, I want the dog to go in the crate on their own for their food, so I'll open the crate, bowl in hand, and wait to put the bowl down until the dog figures out to go in the crate first. Or, if we're about to let the dog out from the crate, and the dog is excited to come out, we open the door slightly and let the dog think about settling down before we let them out, again without saying much.

Sometimes the dog just can't deliver, and we need to "manhandle." Two examples come to mind: My fosters and boarders usually crate in my studio basement, which is reached via a narrow stairwell. This stairwell can worry some dogs, and instead of asking them to brave it, I will carry them down (to the extent that I can lift them!), and eventually they'll be able to make it on their own. The second example is with a dog I was boarding that didn't know to jump in the car crate. Eventually, she figured it out after I'd lifted her in a few times.

Foundations is about micromanaging precisely so that you don't have to discipline as neither the dog nor the relationship can handle discipline at this point. You're conservative with what you're allowing and not allowing because you don't want to be correcting your dog at this stage. Instead, it's all "Good boy!" and "Good girl!" at Foundations. It is your job to structure the way of life such that these are the only words we can say. You're setting them up for success in every instance; that is the level of discipline required on your part.

Imagine the boost in self-esteem and spirit that comes when that's all a dog hears from you.

I remember a client with a new puppy asking me once, "Do I put the shoes away, or do I discipline him for going toward the shoes?" I say, put the shoes away because we manage babies—we don't discipline them. We work on foundations from the start, and if the pup never knows that shoes are something he can play with, he'll never play with shoes as a grown-up. When we have foundations, we're able to introduce a more formal approach to training, including attending structured group classes. Teaching various commands can be tons of fun and is a great way to use a dog's natural drives, but we need to prepare the dog first.

The following do something exercise is a fun exercise to work with at Foundations because just as the name indicates, it's about letting the dogs just "do something"—anything they choose. I love this exercise and learned it many years ago in a freestyle class. "Freestyle" means dancing with dogs, sometimes performing elaborate moves apart or in unison. These complex moves often start with a very simple request: "Do something."

It's fascinating to see how many of my client dogs that have been trained too much and too soon will struggle with this, which at its core is very simple. All they need to do is something, anything, to get rewarded, but they will sit there frozen in front of the closed hand, waiting to be commanded. When one of my clients who had been struggling with this exercise messaged me to tell me that her dog had finally come around, volunteering all sorts of things including barking, play bowing, lying down, and so on, we knew it was much more than the dog doing those things. We knew the dog was finally thinking for himself, figuring out different ways of getting rewarded.

## Exercise: *Do Something*

Hold a treat in your hand, and let the dog see that you have it. Close your hand with the treat in it and hold it to your heart. Look at the dog and try to stay quiet. If nothing happens, say "Do something"—not because the dog necessarily knows what this means but as a way of getting the dog going.

The dog wants the treat but isn't quite sure what to do to have it, and so the dog will volunteer body movements and come up with moves. In that moment, anything the dog volunteers is good. They sit? Wow, great job! They tap their feet? Beautiful! They lie down? Good work!

If the dog volunteers a behavior you'd prefer not to reward, like jumping up, hold the treat until the dog jumps off you. If the dog continues to volunteer the same thing repeatedly, hold back on the treat, and give the dog the chance to think of something else and then end the exercise on a good note.

At Stage 1, you're working with primordial, spatial, and distal socialization. Therefore, start the exercise in your quiet area, with just the two of you and no distractions (primordial). Now, try this in a new space, after having given the dog some time to adjust to the new space (spatial). Eventually, take your exercise to spaces with some action available at a distance, which we're asking the dog to ignore and to engage in the exercise with us instead (distal).

# Sport

Dogs come with scores of instincts bred into them, sometimes for thousands of years. For example, terriers were made to locate and kill vermin. Hound dogs are hunters that get a total high from tracking scents. Their gundog colleagues were also used in hunting to retrieve and carry birds or other game. Herding dogs were bred to manage all kinds of livestock, performing one of the most universal functions known to man.

But now, most dogs lead lives that are quite different. Not only do they not work, but many of them are given lavish lives and have their every need met. This has turned the tables in many ways that are not necessarily good for the dog. At the same time, it has given rise to countless sports that dogs of all kinds can partake in. (See insert.)

Some dog owners are die-hard devotees of a particular sport or discipline. I think most pet owners don't quite know about the possibility of engaging in games with their dog or have dogs with issues that preclude them from pursuing sport.

I have participated in canine sport for almost as long as I have shared my life with dogs. I've tried every sport imaginable including obedience, agility, freestyle, flyball, protection, herding, tracking, scent detection, and barn hunt. In the last decade, herding has been my primary interest. In the last few years, I've also picked up training and trialing in scent detection.

In the early going, I sought sport thinking it would help heal Maya by giving her an outlet for her energy. But while sport enhances bonds, it cannot fix problems and might even make them worse.

If you're not into a sport, I highly encourage it. Every breed and personality have things that they like. Research an activity or sport that you and your dog can enjoy. If you have a dog in a certain breed category, research the types of activities that these dogs were bred to perform and the sports in which they can practice their skills and give free expression to their natural inclinations. If you have a mixed breed, you might consider genetic testing to find out more about the dog's inherited tendencies. It also never hurts to just go out and try a sport! Keep in mind that within any sport or discipline, you will likely encounter very different ways that instructors teach the sport.

At Stage 1, though, we are not "asking" for things. We need to avoid situations where we could get into conflicts because our bond can't really handle the stress just yet. This happens a lot in sport situations because both handler and dog are under the natural stress that comes with learning something new. Structured sport classes have a lot of moving pieces and are not the place for a dog just beginning Foundations.

Therefore, if you're completely new to a sport but want to give it a try, start by getting yourself introduced to it. Check out different schools, talk to different instructors, and attend a class or two—all without your dog. A good instructor will allow you to check out the premises without and then with your dog as a way of getting you both acquainted with the environment and equipment.

As you progress with Foundations and depending on the situation, I encourage private lessons as a way of dipping into the sport before engaging more fully at Stage 2. At Stage 1, our introduction to our sport is light and informal, primarily about getting the dog adjusted to the space where the sport activity takes place without engaging with people and animals or performing in any way.

If you're a veteran of a sport, consider the quality of your interaction during the sport activity. Does the dog perform clean and well, or are you arguing? If the dog performs well, continue your sport in a space where the dog can only perform well and not practice any of the problematic behaviors that brought you to this book. If on the other hand, you fight and argue trying to accomplish the task at hand, then back off the sport entirely, clean up your bond, and get back to it later.

## Select Canine Sports

There are canine sports in all areas of interest, giving dogs a chance to practice some of their natural skills and instincts while bonding with their handlers. Here are a few you might consider:

→ **Obedience** is among the most popular sports, which give you a chance to solidify your obedience, adding the well-known distance, duration, and distraction levels to common cues such as sit, stay, stand, wait, heel, and lie down.

→ **Rally obedience,** or Rally-O, is a fun way of practicing obedience, giving handlers and dogs obstacles with cues at each obstacle that are a little more elaborate than found in traditional obedience such as 360-degree rotations and combinations of different moves.

→ **Agility** is both accessible and popular. Dogs run a course of obstacles with their handlers guiding them, including bar jumps, A-frames, tables, and teeter-totters, building courage in dogs and bonding in a shared, exhilarating experience.

→ **Barn hunt** is a more recent sport where dogs work at locating rats in straw structures, as would be found in farms. Live rats are placed in safe containers, and dogs climb on the structures and go under tunnels looking for the rats.

→ **Sheep herding** involves dogs driving, holding, and organizing livestock animals such as cows, sheep, and ducks.

→ **Dock diving**, also known as dock jumping, is a sport where dogs jump from a raised platform or dock to retrieve a toy thrown into the pool below.

→ **Sprinter trials** involve dogs running a 100-meter sprint. They are scored based on their height and finish time to determine their speed.

→ **Lure coursing** involves dogs chasing after a mechanized lure across courses, simulating chasing live prey.

→ **Tracking** is a scent-oriented discipline where handlers lay foot tracks for the dogs to follow, tracking food to start and eventually alerting to objects along the track, with tracks increasing in difficulty by aging and weather elements at play.

→ **Scent detection** is another sport where dogs learn to alert on specific scents. Scents can be hidden in containers and in indoor or outdoor areas for the dogs to find and alert their handlers to.

→ **Protection sports**, informally known as bite sports, include IGP (German acronym for International Working Dog Trial Regulations; previously known as Schutzhund), Mondio, Protection Sports Association (PSA), and other disciplines involving combinations of obedience, tracking, and protection/apprehension trials.

---

Drive development at Stage 1 involves building food drive primarily and prey drive secondarily and practicing long-line exercises across primordial, spatial, and distal levels of socialization. We emphasize tiring the dog out through strenuous exercise and games such as tug-of-war. We're getting slowly acquainted with a sport to pursue with greater intensity at Stage 2, which I discuss next.

## CASE
# Eddy the Australian Shepherd

Eddy the Australian shepherd was a well-trained dog, in the sense that he was obedient, knew a long list of commands, and was active in several sports including agility, Frisbee, and Rally-O. Being a bright and driven Aussie, he excelled at all these activities.

Outside the sporting ring, he led a rich and active lifestyle with his energetic and dedicated mom who took him on frequent walks, hikes, and swims at their local indoor pool. During the week when she worked, she had a dogwalker take Eddy out. She also fed him a wholesome diet, holistically managing a mild case of food allergies.

## The Issues

Still, Eddy was reactive to just about anything—critters on their walks, people near and far, dogs near and far, and noises outside the house, to name a few. He was insecure and lacked "confidence in the world," as his owner put it.

Smart as he was, he lacked the capacity to consider the various stimuli in his environment in a thoughtful manner and modulate his response. Going to new places, trying to swim, and participating in other activities were scary to him. In sport, he was easily distracted and reacted to things outside the arena. He was talented but also inconsistent. In his day-to-day dealings with his owner, he took it upon himself to bark his needs at her, herd her around the apartment, bark at things outside the apartment, or hide behind the couch. On their walks, he pulled and, of course, reacted to things.

My client was at a loss. She's a smart, studious, and serious dog owner who thought she'd done everything right with her Aussie, who was also her first dog. She understood that Australian shepherds are a work-oriented and intelligent breed that needed to be challenged, but she could tell something was amiss. As an empath, she sensed her dog's unease and lack of trust, which made her question whether he had a good life. My client wasn't having any of it and sought help from many trainers. She was told repeatedly that she could only "manage" the reactivity because it would never go away. She was finally referred to me and our work together began.

In coaching together, my client learned that a dog's optimal way of life involves more than obedience and sport. She learned that sometimes we can have too much of a good thing, which in this case was too much obedience, too much "programming" of the dog, which had stripped Eddy of his natural intelligence. My client got to see that Eddy's extensive vocabulary, while helpful in a lot of ways, had undermined his capacity to think for himself, weakened his instincts, and fed into his insecurity and reactivity.

We can also have too much stimulation in sport, even for an Aussie. Stimulation turns to agitation as opposed to stability when we don't have the right kind of relationship and way of life to balance things out. As an example, Eddy was loose all the time—no schedule and no crating, no downtime or real rest from all the learning and stimulation. Like many people, my client had dispensed with crating as soon as Eddy was house-trained. She realized now how "lost" he must have felt. No wonder he hid behind the couch, looking for a break and a little privacy. She understood that herding breeds thrive on law and order. Absent her decision-making, he decided for himself by hiding inside and chasing after things outside.

As our work progressed, my client and I went even deeper into our coaching and worked at the level of the codependent relationship she had with her dog, which was the core issue underlying all the other symptoms. She was single and introverted, and the dog was her world. She realized how much she'd relied on him for her emotional needs. She came to see that this was an unfair burden for a dog to carry and how it had caused him to lose confidence in himself as a dog.

## A New Way of Life

To help her dog, my client realized that she needed to make both psychological as well as physical changes. She needed to become a more whole and grounded person and was prepared to relinquish even her strong feelings for her dog. We talked about her pursuing other activities that didn't involve the dog. If she liked dogs so much, she could perhaps volunteer at a shelter.

We also introduced a greater degree of structure in Eddy's way of life, including crating, which he resisted fiercely at first. This lead-or-be-led herding dog wasn't going to relinquish control that fast. He gave my client and the neighbors an earful until he was able to trust her with the change and feel good about it.

As he began settling down in the crate more, we started to give him alone time. My client lives in an apartment but happens to have a safe balcony. Still, she was concerned about putting him out there before being able to trust that he could be quiet. One would think that Eddy would cause trouble and bark. Instead, with a toy to help him, he was able to settle by himself outside, sitting by the door.

We also restructured the physical activities Eddy was taking part in. We suspended Rally-O because we wanted to get off formal obedience and start deprogramming him so he would be more of a dog and less of a performer. The structured Frisbee sport was also cut out, but we retained his agility practice by going to a place where there would be no distractions and where they could play Frisbee alone.

Socialization was also rolled back. My client used to take Eddy to her mother's, where there were several other poorly behaved dogs. The family dynamic could turn negative and got played out on Eddy, as the family argued over how he ought to be treated, and sure enough, he felt the tension.

I tell my clients all the time to not argue in front of the dog because dogs can tell when they're the subject of discord. This gives the dog more influence over humans than is healthy for either dogs or humans. My client was dedicated enough to suspend Eddy's visits to her mother. She became the kind of person who could tell her mother, with whom she also had a codependent relationship, that Eddy would be staying home.

## Results

The change in the dog has been remarkable—and in the human even more so. My client had started off wanting her dog to be a "super dog" and worked him hard with that ambition in mind. They both paid a price for putting performance ahead of stability and bond. As the way of life had to change, the relationship changed, and the individuals in that relationship changed. My client started to feel better simply by taking charge of Eddy and getting off the codependency train. He could feel her growing independence from him, and he was gradually decompressing from the pressure of being everything for his human.

There is much more independence and leadership on the part of his owner. The fear she felt handling his reactions and the sorrow she felt witnessing his lack of confidence are gone. We have a more assured handler working to grow herself and her canine partner in soundness and strength. As a result, she's better able to handle his outbursts, which has further raised his trust in her; he knows she will handle any situation.

One of Eddy's very first improvements was that he started to swim. That happened within a week of my client crating him and taking charge of him. He quickly became a skilled swimmer, happy to swim at their indoor dog pool and in any of the many lakes and ponds around.

Within about a year of diligent work, it was clear that Eddy and my client were cruising nicely toward Exposure. One of the first Stage 2 successes was Eddy having a meet and greet with the landlord, which my client had never dared before lest Eddy react and sour her relations with him. More recently, Eddy experienced his very first in-home canine massage to help ease the stress of his agility schedule. Eddy was quickly comfortable with his new masseuse and a few moments later, was able to completely relax and enjoy his massage.

Eddy and my client have also resumed trialing in agility, earning their very first qualifying score almost immediately and, a mere few weeks later, his first title. They worked inside and outside the arena to be able to return to the sport they both loved, feeling more connected and secure in their relationship. Now, training has its place; it is no longer the way of life but an aspect of it. My client goes in with an entirely different mindset, prioritizing fun with her dog and her partnership with him over any points to be earned. The relationship these two now enjoy is the goal, and any ribbons on top are but a bonus.

## For Reflection

1.  How would you describe your dog's food drive? Are they a picky eater, or do they have a strong interest in food?

2.  What do you feed your dog? How would you describe your dog's weight and body condition?

3.  How would you describe your dog's prey drive? What are your dog's favorite games and toys?

4.  What is your approach to exercise? What are your preferred ways of giving your dogs a good workout?

5.  What kinds of sport have you tried with your dog, and how was the experience? If you haven't tried any sports yet, which kinds interest you or sound like they might be suited to your dog?

STAGE 2: EXPOSURE

# GROWING AND CHALLENGING OUR BOND

# CHAPTER 8

# Relationship, Mission, and Mindset at Stage 2

Familial security...forms a basis from which the individual can work out gradually, forming new skills and interests in other fields. Where familial security is lacking, the individual is handicapped by the lack of what might be called a secure base from which to work.

—**MARY SALTER AINSWORTH,** developmental psychologist

*S*haron looked at me as if I'd lost my mind. "You're doing what with this dog, dear?" she asked.

*The late Dr. Sharon Kopinak was our holistic vet of many years—someone I looked up to, respected, and cherished dearly. In her 70s at the time of this conversation, she'd graduated decades earlier from the Ontario Veterinary College at the University of Guelph, one of North America's most prestigious veterinary programs, which few women attended at the time.*

*Since then, and true to her Indigenous roots, Sharon emphasized holistic medicine and prescribed herbs and foods as part of her healing practice. She had an extraordinary feel for animals, able to vet the most recalcitrant of patients. And here she was smitten by my new dog, Nejra.*

*Sensing profound disapproval, I hesitated before I said, "I adopted her from that tiny shelter because I couldn't stand the idea of her not going to a good home. Thing is, I am not sure I am it, so I've been asking around …"*

*"You've been doing what?" she repeated. "Why aren't you that good home?!" she exclaimed. "This is not a dog I would give away so easily!"*

*In all the years I'd known Sharon, and the various dogs I'd brought to her, I'd never heard her speak so glowingly of a dog. I was a little intimidated because Nejra was my first Belgian Malinois, and while she wasn't nearly as intense as the average Malinois, she was still a force to reckon with.*

*I'll never forget the day I first saw Nejra (named Scarlett at the time), as the shelter assistant walked me to her glass-walled enclosure in the back of the hall. She'd been spotted roaming the farmlands, was captured by local animal control, and brought to the shelter where she was found to be pregnant, giving birth soon after to two puppies that were swiftly adopted. But still she sat there, waiting for her turn.*

*I remember feeling a little faint the first time I met her intense amber eyes. They radiated intelligence but also kindness. The shelter's notice emphasized that her "new home MUST have a fenced yard as she likes to run a lot and explore!" It also stated that she "must be the only dog" as she wasn't found to be particularly good with other dogs. I was transparent with the shelter officer I spoke with, stating that I already had dogs.*

*The officer asked if I could bring all of them for a meet and greet, but I responded firmly but kindly that I could not do that, as that's not how I did things. I explained that a sure way of setting these dogs up to not like each other was to subject them to such abrupt introductions. The officer could tell I knew what I was doing and asked me how soon I might be able to collect her.*

*Because of the upheavals in her life, Nejra was insecure and flighty at the start but came around rather quickly, aided by the Way of Life method and an exceptionally easygoing temperament. After going through the stages, Nejra and my other dogs have all adjusted fine to being together. She has a sunny personality and a certain magic with other dogs, proving to be the opposite of what she was originally described as at the shelter. She is a great example that we don't really know dogs until they're in healthy relationships, raised to be sound, strong, and spirited.*

By the time we're ready to begin exposing our dog more and upping the ante in all aspects of way of life, we will have established solid foundations. The dog has been decompressed whether we are transitioning a new dog or resetting a relationship with an existing dog. At this point, we feel a little more like a team instead of a pair of strangers or a warring couple. We can tell that the dog is juiced up and ready for more. The dog likes us enough and is comfortable with us.

It's only with that kind of mindset and attitude in the dog that we can begin serious Exposure, going beyond our bubble. In doing so, we are challenging the bond created at Stage 1 because we're doing more and asking more. This tests and strengthens our bond because every time we expose our dogs successfully, they come back feeling better about themselves and better about their bond with us. They're being introduced to new things effectively because they have us to rely on.

Building healthy foundations takes time, but we can see the results of our effort in how relatively easy exposure at Stage 2 becomes. If our dogs trust us, they will trust what we expose them to. It's that simple.

## The Adolescent Stage

When the wolf cubs are big enough to leave the den, they're now able to travel with the pack. They relocate to rendezvous sites to begin the education that is necessary for them to participate fully in family life. Similarly, when puppies turn approximately four to six months, the teen period starts to kick in. Of course, there are wide breed and background variations in how fast this maturation process occurs.

Regardless of the chronological age of the dog, at Stage 1, we see our dogs as young pups to be kept safe and managed carefully. At Stage 2, our aim is to develop them through adolescence. As someone who has volunteered with rescues and shelters, I know that many dogs are relinquished when the teens kick in. This is not because the teen stage is necessarily as terrible as we like to believe, but because it is when pups come out of the infantile innocence of puppyhood that they begin showing us the mistakes we made in the early stages through the behavioral issues they manifest.

If we did our work correctly at Foundations, our dog is now more confident and trusting. But remember that adolescence is an in-between state characterized by infantile as well as adult behaviors. The adolescent veers back and forth from child to adult until firmly established in adulthood. We will be dealing with normal fluctuations between adolescent fears and adult boldness, between the instinct to seek safety and the impulse toward growth and individuation. It is up to us to bring a balance of support with direction to see our dogs through this growth phase.

# Relationship

At this point, our dogs should see us as a safe base, meaning they should feel emboldened to venture out into the world and secure enough that they can seek us out in times of trouble or uncertainty. Because we've had our time together at Foundations, we're now more of a role model for the dog.

At the same time, the intimacy and simplicity of Foundations can present a risk of overbonding, either from the dog toward us or from us toward the dog or both. This manifests as the dog being obsessed with their person, unable to function without them. The same goes for the person who depends on their dog for pleasure and gratification. This is neither healthy for us as individuals nor good for our relationship. This is an intimate journey and a natural process for the dogs, creating the deep attachments that we want. But we want to avoid codependent relationships. More than once, I have suggested that clients develop interests and activities that do not concern their dogs as a way of establishing a greater degree of healthy independence.

While the bond has been established, keep in mind that it is still new. The bond has not been challenged or tested yet, and therefore it is still a fragile bond. Let's also keep in mind that we have a young dog on our hands. This is an adolescence stage with an adolescent bond. Real bonds come with maturity, and maturation takes time.

At this point, reflect on the family hierarchy. Is the dog more confident and mature? Where are they sitting in the hierarchy? Where are you sitting? If we're going to lead our dog into the chaotic world out there, we better have that relationship material and take our role of leader to heart. Therefore, by the time we're ready for Exposure we have our pups turning into more assertive teens. The cubs are now yearlings. The dynamic, inevitably, must change.

# Mission

The mission at Stage 2 is to build on the relationship established at Stage 1 by challenging and thus strengthening our bonds. Now, it's not just the two of us anymore. When we start to do more and ask more, we will inevitably hit roadblocks, but guess what? We have relationship material to help us through.

So we're going out there, and the dog is going to see things that could be uncomfortable. The dog might have reactions of all kinds, from trying to withdraw or get away from a situation to trying to confront it by barking or engaging. The intensity of the dog's responses and how quickly the dog recovers and responds to our redirecting should give us a good idea of the quality of our foundations at this time. We are testing the idea that if we have good foundations with our dog, we should be able to say, "Don't worry about it; come here," and our dog will respond in kind.

If we have real material with our dog, it should be enough for us to remind a dog to pay attention to us without having to teach a command like leave it or watch me. If we have to repeatedly ask our dog for their attention in a situation, that's a lack of foundations. When we have foundations, we have relevance to our dog. The dog cares what we think and looks to us for insight on how to react to any situation.

A dog with foundations is easy to redirect. The dog is listening and cares for our approval. Therefore, if I disapprove of reactivity or fear, the dog will want to work through it because the dog wants my approval. Isn't that what we do for the ones we love? We counter weaknesses and work to improve our strengths.

Stage 2 is where school begins; it was all preschool until now. Learning is stressful and vulnerability inducing and will therefore challenge the bonds we set up. The strength of our foundations is exposed, and with it the strengths and weaknesses in our bond. So, these are our missions at this stage:

1.  Formalizing our dog's education

2.  Strengthening drives

3.  Expanding socialization

4.  Beginning the process of freeing the dog

5.  Introducing firm and fair discipline

# 1.  Formalizing Our Dog's Education

At first, we focused on setting dogs up to succeed and ensuring they heard nothing but praise. We relied on capturing good behavior and rewarding it. Now we begin to formalize education, which means introducing verbal cues. In other words, we start to "ask" things of our dog.

This could include introducing the dog to a formal class environment to pursue obedience training in a group setting. This is also the time you can start a structured sport or activity.

# 2.  Strengthening Drives

Stage 1 was about building strong food drive and introducing prey drive while monitoring the dog's development and interests.

While food drive is a juvenile drive, prey drive is a maturing, adolescent, or emerging-adult drive. Therefore at Stage 2, we strengthen prey drive. We develop the dog's interest in toys and games, trying different things to see what sticks. Of course not all dogs will exhibit the same interest and drive intensity. But it's important to cultivate that prey drive even in dogs that are soft and don't appear interested. Prey drive is natural to all dogs, so we want to channel that drive as much as the dog lets us. As you work it, prey drive will increase, which is crucial since each drive feeds into the next. Without a minimum of prey drive, we won't have a healthy pack drive, meaning a dog's motivation to please out of love and belonging.

For example, my own dog Kizzy is a rather soft and aloof dog. Over the years, I kept working to get her to a place where she would tug and play ball. Now she thoroughly enjoys these games, engaging with me in a way I never thought possible and according to her level of intensity. Only when we started to interact at that level did I start to feel that Kizzy and I had a close bond and that she became stronger, more outgoing, and social.

So if we want deep bonds, we want strong dogs. And one way to strengthen the dog is to engage the dog at that prey level, conscious of the power that lies in layering the development of our dogs' drives.

## 3.  Expanding Socialization

At Stage 1, our dog did not have direct interactions with any people or animals outside of our immediate circle. In Stage 2, we continue to strengthen primordial, spatial, and distal socialization. Consistent and successful socialization each day strengthens these relationship foundations.

As the dog is ready, we will take them places and teach them to ignore things that are closer to us (proximal socialization). We eventually begin engaging and interacting with other people and animals (interactional socialization).

## 4.  Beginning the Process of Freeing the Dog

In the later stages of Stage 2, we begin to work on what I call "freeing the dog." As we accumulate successful exposures, ensuring the maintenance of drives across spaces and situations, we begin loosening up the schedule and introducing challenging exercises such as the tie-out (see chapter 11), off-leash work, and transferring the dog to another handler.

## 5.  Introducing Firm and Fair Discipline

As we progress into Exposure, our dogs start to see more. They start to do more closer to and with other people and animals. There will be a greater likelihood of the dog making mistakes, but because we have foundations, we can easily redirect our dog. This also means that depending on the dog, the quality of our bond, and any relevant circumstantial factors, we might need to discipline our dog.

## What Is Discipline?

Just like every aspect of living with dogs, there are varied opinions on discipline. You may see professional trainers using harsh treatment or corrective tools, but harsh physical discipline is unacceptable on many levels.

On the flip side, you may have been scared away from any kind of discipline because of the pervasive focus on positive reinforcement. Many of us are afraid to apply any kind of discipline for fear of being labeled as supporters of dominance theory at best and as abusers at worse.

Although in the mainstream discipline or correction is synonymous with punishment, that is not the case here. Simply put, I consider a correction to be a gentle reminder and realignment of the dog in a better direction. It means being firmer in my expectations and correcting without anger, physical force, or coercive tools.

When we have foundations, discipline, if ever required, does not need to be harsh to be effective. Now, it matters to our dogs that we are not pleased, and they are eager to fix things. Also at this stage, dogs are becoming motivated by healthy attachment and respect (pack drive), and we have credibility to discipline, meaning they'll see the correction as legit, and it won't hurt their feelings.

Let me be clear that the most effective form of discipline is simply us carrying ourselves with authority. It's all about attitude. As Sharon, my vet and an accomplished horsewoman, used to say, "Walk like you have a whip in your boot." Nothing needs to be done *to* the dog, but plenty is being done *for* the dog. Dogs are smart: if they know that you could correct them if needed, you won't have to. But many dogs know their people don't really have that capacity. When we're soft, we harden the dog, unknowingly creating an even greater need for correction.

So what does this discipline look like? I grab the dog's attention, simply calling the dog to me by saying their name or asking them to come. Sometimes

I grunt, as if I am clearing my throat—"ahem!" Sometimes, a simple "hey, hey!" with a sharper tone or a snapping of my fingers will do.

## Correction in the Canine World

Perhaps you've heard that the mother dog corrects her puppies and that therefore we have the right to correct puppies. Or that wolves aggress on each other and seek to dominate one another, and therefore, we have the right to do the same. These ideas reflect a misunderstanding and misinformation about how mother dogs and wolf packs discipline.

Here's the scoop: The mother dog's approach toward behavior she does not like is to ignore and walk away from it. She doesn't correct; rather, she asks the pups to step up their game. She ignores behavior she doesn't like and praises that which she does. At about five weeks, pups may start trying to one-up each other. The mother dog may offer mild discipline by separating the pups. The corrections are not about punishment; they are about keeping the peace and protecting softer puppies from bolder ones.

Often people will leave puppies with their mother beyond weaning, and in these cases, they may observe the mother nipping at the pups, which is often misconstrued as a kind of natural discipline. Quite the contrary—this is an unnatural situation for a mother dog; we are asking her to continue to raise that pup when it's no longer her job but ours! Her corrections are a way of saying, "Go away already." So let's ask ourselves what we're really teaching our own dogs when we correct them harshly.

Wolves do not correct their young ones either—at least not in the violent ways you might be imagining. Wolves supervise their cubs vigilantly, interfere with where they go, round them back in, and block them from going where they shouldn't. This is management and not punishment or discipline per se. Sometimes, adult wolves trying to catch some shut eye will shake puppies off, curl their lips, or simply walk away from them.

The first real corrections, or what would be construed as discipline, occur way beyond the den, when at around four or five months old, the cubs are ready to eat real food instead of food regurgitated by the adults. In response to their continued demands for regurgitated food, the adults will pin these cubs down, asking them to grow up and take their seats at the adult dining table. It takes several weeks before the cubs understand the lesson and transition to joining the others at the carcass. Just like with the mother dog, corrections happen when cubs are maturing, and the corrections are only meant to mature them even more.

I am certainly not asking you to pin your dog down or anything inhumane (and ineffective) like that, but I am asking you to consider that firm and fair discipline—and the right mindset around it—ought to be part of your rearing toolbox. "Firm" means you mean it. "Fair" means you've earned the right to discipline and the dog knows better. Part of maturing our dogs up the family hierarchy means reminding them of certain rules, especially as we start to do and see more.

If you're concerned about the fairness, ethics, and humanness involved in correcting dogs in any form or fashion, as we all should be, let's do our Foundations and Exposure work right so we don't have to correct. The stricter we are with Foundations, the less of a disciplinarian we will need to be later.

# Mindset

The main issue people run into during Exposure is that it shows us the cracks in our Foundations work. Sometimes, we might need to go back to some basics, clean stuff up, and progress again. Therefore, we are still an objective observer, a student of this method and of our dog—making headway, praising, checking, evaluating, and then deciding whether to continue or to step back, if needed. Let's observe, take notes, and proceed, stay put, or step back accordingly.

As far as the dog goes, their mindset is going through a big adjustment, from infancy to a growing teen. We must support our dog, knowing that there may be some regression as the dog works through their new position and new expectations. We are asking the dog to mature, and therefore we need to mature as well, for them, for us, and for our relationship. Otherwise, we're asking the dog to change while we remain the same.

We are also more actively working and training the dog and stepping up our psychological game because we're doing things involving greater pressure like socializing closer to others, interacting with others, participating in group activities, dealing with the pressure of obedience and sport classes, while handling our dog with poise through it all.

# Moving to the Next Stage

As with Stage 1, there is no set period to spend in Exposure that means you'll be ready to graduate. It will take the time that it takes. Rather, we carefully observe and watch our dog for signs of increasing comfort with Exposure. So, we are looking for a dog that is open to challenges and experiences. The nature of our bond is such that the dogs are incentivized to learn and grow, knowing they have us as their safe base.

Once we embark on expanding the dog's world through exposures of various kinds, we help them succeed while gauging their reactions to things, their ability to maintain interest in food, toys, and us across situations. This gives us feedback on whether we have done our work right or whether we need to go back to the den a little bit longer.

As you do more and go more places, a dog with sufficient foundations will deal well. This allows us to integrate our dog more fully into our home and our lives. Then, the dog understands that the better they deal with life, the more freedom they enjoy and the more of a place they have in our hearts.

On a physical, observable level, we have dogs at the correct weight, in fit body condition, and with strong and reliable food drives. We have dogs displaying healthy prey drives, growing in pack drives, and handling firm and fair discipline. We have dogs that are crate-capable at home, in the vehicle, and in boarding situations. While they are still on a schedule of sorts, they can handle variations in schedule and are gradually more integrated in our homes. The dogs deal well with environmental changes, ignore people and animals near and far, and can politely engage with people and animals. Our dogs can tolerate a certain amount of oppositional socialization, which we work to minimize and regulate. Through formal training and sport, their skill sets are growing, and we begin practicing the capacity to be off leash.

At Exposure, our mission is to formalize our dog's education, strengthen drives, expand socialization, begin the process of freeing the dog, and introduce firm and fair discipline. At Stage 2, our dog is maturing into a teen, and our relationship is by the same token entering its adolescent stage where there will be much experimentation and learning. Again, regardless of age or background, we relate to our dogs as teens who still need to be guided but are given more freedom and handled with a firmer stance. We expose more and shift back to simplicity to allow recovery and then go back out in the world again, allowing cyclical decompressions from the significant growth and change being experienced.

## For Reflection

1.  How has your role and attitude toward your dog changed since beginning this process?

2.  Summarize and recognize your accomplishments with your dog to date. Identify the challenges and growth opportunities that still lie ahead.

3.  At Stage 2, we are asked to think of our dogs as adolescents or teenagers. How does seeing your dog this way change your perception of the dog? How does it change your practical approach to dealing with your dog?

4.  What has been your experience with disciplining dogs? Were those forms of discipline effective in the long term? What is different about this approach to discipline?

5.  Which aspects of Stage 2 feel accessible to you, and which ones are you excited about? Which aspects feel challenging? What are you apprehensive or nervous about?

CHAPTER 9

# Managing Space
# and Boundaries at Stage 2

Let me not pray to be sheltered from dangers but to be fearless in facing them.

—**RABINDRANATH TAGORE,** Indian poet and mystic

*Jackson, a mixed-breed dog, was brought into a local shelter as a teen pup, around six months old. He was promptly fostered by my client and eventually placed in a home. The years went by, and a few months into the COVID pandemic, my client, who'd continued volunteering at that same shelter, found out that Jackson had been returned. He was in the back hall and in rather rough psychological shape. It turns out he'd severely bitten his owner, who'd brought him back promptly, after three years of living with him.*

*My client immediately asked to foster Jackson again, and a few months later, she officially adopted him. She knew enough to take things easy with him at the start, but gradually Jackson was given more freedoms than was perhaps appropriate so soon in their relationship. It was the height of the pandemic, and my client, like many of us, felt isolated and sought in her pet the company she so needed. The main freedom that caused issues was that Jackson was allowed to go in and out of his crate as he pleased.*

*There is a time and place for choice. Jackson was generally easygoing, but he was also insecure and reactive, particularly to the many sounds in downtown Toronto—*

*garbage trucks, construction sounds, fireworks, and thunderstorms, to name a few. He would respond to these noises by rushing to his crate in a fearful fit. By giving Jackson permission to deal with his fears as he chose, his insecurity heightened. Giving dogs agency and choice is not helpful when they are immature and incapable of making sound decisions, when the dogs act from a place of fear rather than a place of soundness and strength.*

*While it's good for the dog to know the crate is a space of safety, this inadvertently created a situation where the crate became a place of high arousal and increased defensiveness for Jackson. The crate was his armor, and he felt he could express himself more loudly in there. Then, realizing that he could let loose safely behind that barrier became something he did behind any barrier.*

*A few months of this and eventually Jackson developed what is referred to as "barrier frustration aggression," making it challenging for my client to close him in the crate and even put him behind a baby gate. At being locked in, he would bark ragefully, sending my client shaking and shivering.*

*Among other things, she has now gone back to regulating Jackson's access to his crate and taking better charge of him during fear episodes, which has led to a calmer dog. This is a perfect example of why it is essential to control space at the start and to delay the giving of choice, particularly with dogs displaying issues of any kind.*

Managing space and boundaries is a crucial aspect of way of life throughout all the stages. Our mission at Stage 2 is to strengthen the bond we established in Stage 1 through exposures, helping us weather challenges together that bring us even closer.

## Scheduling and Crating

At Stage 2, we are still on a schedule. But the schedule is bound to change and may not be as predictable as it once was. We continue to use the crate extensively, but the dog is also out more. Mat time sessions are longer. Outings are longer and more eventful. As we progress, we can switch a block of time when the dog would have been in the crate to having them out with us in an enclosed space in mat time format. (Check out the sample schedule that follows for an idea of what the day might look like.)

At the same time, recovery from exposure is key. The new stimuli, changes to the schedule, stresses of learning, and depleting effects of overcoming new experiences all mean that we should continue giving our dogs long periods in the crate to help them recover.

Say you're going to take pictures with Santa at the local humane society. Your dog's never done this before, but they behave decently, aided by your poised and confident handling. Because this was a new and certainly taxing experience, you come back home and give the dog plenty of rest in the crate. Or, say you just participated in your first group agility class with lots of action happening. Again, the dog will likely be taxed. A little extra time in the crate that day and for a few days after helps dogs decompress from new experiences.

The focus is on building up successful exposures while not overwhelming the dog. Then, the dog begins getting more time with us inside the house as a reward for having done well with these new experiences outside. Dog behaves outside equals dog gets more inside. Therefore, there is growing inclusion at this stage.

## Activity: *Writing Up A Schedule*

Just as you did at Stage 1 to draft your Foundations schedule, come together with your family to draft your Exposure schedule. Think about how you can start changing things up, given all the progress you've made. Again, design the schedule accounting for work, family, and community obligations. Choose a weekly rest day to keep things low key. Make sure everyone has a copy and discuss any changes in advance. Include these events in your schedule:

→ **Crate time:** You can still aim for two- to six-hour stretches in the crate, but you can now substitute crate blocks with mat time.

→ **Solo time:** Continue to provide alone time in a backyard, on a balcony, in an x-pen, or behind a baby gate.

→  **Outings:** Continue to provide three to five outings daily, while becoming more flexible and working toward longer outings.

→  **Meals:** Continue to feed according to your dog's age and health at a specific time in privacy, whether in or out of their crate.

To get you started, here's a sample schedule that you can use at Stage 2. Adjust as needed.

## Sample Stage 2 Schedule—Day 1

**OUTING 1: 7:30 AM—9:30 AM**
Wake up and take out of crate
Walk in yard/quiet area for pee break
Long walk or hike + exercises
Backyard for solo time
Return to crate with breakfast

**OUTING 2: 1:00 PM—5:30 PM**
Take out of crate
Walk in yard/quiet area for pee break
Backyard for solo time
Mat time in kitchen with chew toys
Return to crate with dinner

**OUTING 3: 7:30 PM—10:30 PM**
Take out of crate
Solo time in yard/quiet area
Mat time in family room with chew toys
Walk in yard/quiet area for pee break
Return to crate for the night

## Sample Stage 2 Schedule—Day 2

**OUTING 1: 7:30 AM—8:00 AM**
Wake up and take out of crate

Walk in yard/quiet area for pee break
Backyard for solo time
Return to crate with breakfast

**OUTING 2: NOON—4:00 PM**
Take out of crate
Walk in yard/quiet area for pee break
Long walk or hike + exercises
Car ride
Mat time in office with chew toys
Return to crate with early dinner

**OUTING 3: 6:00 PM—9:00 PM**
Take out of crate
Solo time in yard/quiet area
Mat time in living room with chew toys
Return to crate

**OUTING 4: 11:00 PM—11:30 PM**
Take out of crate
Walk in yard/quiet area for pee break
Return to crate for the night

# Use of the Leash

Remember that the leash is not just about managing dogs and keeping everyone safe, but it is also about the dog feeling safe and connected to us. With Foundations firmly in place, we are starting to see that for a sound, strong, and spirited dog, it is not the leash that's keeping the dog there.

At Stage 2, we begin the process of freeing the dog—we're not freeing the dog yet but preparing them for it. When we are inside, we may or may not need to have a drag line on our dog depending on the situation. When outside, we are progressing from the dog being on leash, to being on a drag line (dropped leash), to being completely off leash.

Our aim is to work toward dogs who are as free as possible. Perhaps the dog has become excellent at hanging out in the kitchen while we cook or sleeping on their mat while we work at our desk in our home office. Perhaps the dog has become better at respecting house boundaries. The dog doesn't bump into our space nor do they go to windows and doors. Based on that, we might decide to reduce using or removing the leash inside.

As well, depending on how well the dog is dealing with maturation and taking things in stride outside while maintaining focus and drive, we become ready to introduce a little dropped-leash work, progressing to completely off-leash work.

# The Three Circles at Stage 2

By now, the dog should be aware of the three circles, and we show the dog that we are as well. The dog knows the boundary within which they need to stay when they're with us in any space. The dog knows the safety and privilege of the space right next to us. The dog knows there is such a thing as a territorial boundary. While we will always continue to govern space, the need to enforce boundaries eventually fades away.

## The Inner Circle

At Stage 2, our dog has learned that being at our side is a safe and calm experience. If the dog had initially resisted being this close, they are now more comfortable being there. The dog feels safe and worthy of being in our inner circle.

We can ground our dog when it's just the two of us and when we're in our designated working spaces (primordial), when exploring new spaces (spatial), and when there's some action in the distance that the dog is able to ignore (distal).

# **Exercise:** *Grounding*

Remember that the goal of grounding is for your dog to relax at your side, in your inner circle, no matter what. In this exercise, both handler and dog take a moment to breathe, get grounded, and ensure that you're connected.

The speed and ease with which your dog settles at your side is an indication of the health of your foundations. You should have a dog that sits calmly at your side in the spaces and with the levels of socialization you've been working with so far.

At Stage 2, continue moving up the rungs of socialization, adding on proximal, interactional, and oppositional. As part of the transition toward maturation and freedom, start with your dog on leash, progressing to a dragging or dropped leash.

## EARLY STAGE—DISTAL SOCIALIZATION

In the early period of Stage 2, continue working on the distal level of socialization, meaning you and your dog can hang together calmly with things happening at a distance. You could be at home looking out from your porch, sitting in your parked car in a busy supermarket parking lot, or on a hiking trail, seeing people and their dogs at a distance.

## MID STAGE—PROXIMAL & INTERACTIONAL SOCIALIZATION

Getting your dog calm at your side with action at a distance is one thing, but it's a whole other ball game with people, animals, and things that are in our space. If someone is right next to you, they're in your tranquil circle, which isn't so tranquil anymore now! Much of Stage 2 is working on grounding your dog when things are close and still asking the dog to ignore those things.

With success at ignoring things in proximity, introduce interactional socialization, meaning practice having your dog grounded and calm at your side while you interact with other people, animals, and things. Importantly, we are the only ones doing the interacting in the beginning. The dog needs to stay calm and continue to ignore.

## LATER STAGE—OPPOSITIONAL SOCIALIZATION

In the later stages, you will have prepared a dog who can stay calm at your side even as you deal with contentious situations. I think about a friend who was mugged with her rescue dog Cody at her side—clearly a confrontational and invasive situation that was extremely stressful for her. Yet Cody remained calm, allowing her to safely diffuse a potentially deadly situation.

Hopefully you won't have to deal with a mugging, but another oppositional situation that could be more common is an unleashed dog that bombards you while walking or hiking. People often don't think twice about invading a dog's space and petting it. Modern life is chock full of examples of oppositional socialization like this.

We can't always stage oppositional socialization to prepare our dogs for it, but should it happen, a dog that's been grounded through all the other levels of socialization will remain calm, confident that you will deal with the situation.

Moreover, introducing greater independence means we are gradually transitioning the dog toward agency and freedom. This begins with us being comfortable asking our dog to leave our inner circle. This also means our dog is okay being told to leave. When I ask a dog to leave, all I'm saying is "Leave my inner circle and remain in the tranquil circle."

Part of the dog's maturation is it having better manners with our inner space, learning to observe whether it's all right to come in, knowing that the dog sometimes needs to ask to come, and being certain that it's safe to seek us out in emergencies. There are many reasons why we want to teach respect for our personal space; think of instances like settling our account at the cashier, dealing with a delivery person at the door, carrying and interacting with a child, dealing with another dog, grooming our cat—the list goes on! We want our dogs evaluating whether it's all right to come in, asking to come in, and being fine if they're asked to leave.

## Exercise: *Come Here, Get Out*

At Stage 2, introduce your dog to the get out request, and make a game out of it using recall games. (See chapter 6.)

Step into your quiet area or working space, meander with your dog, and then call the dog to you, "Here!" The dog comes and gets rewarded with a treat. Toss a treat a few feet away and give your chosen command; get out, out, let's go, and get out of here all work well. After the dog gets the treat, quickly call it back in, also for reward.

The dog will stay within your tranquil circle; you are simply calling the dog in and out of the inner circle and making a game of it. Show the dog it's okay to be sent out because it is only a mere moment before you'll be calling them back in.

# The Tranquil Circle

Dogs who know to stay within that tranquil line, almost by instinct, are dogs who can be loose because they stay close. Importantly, dogs do this because they want to—being near us is their safe and cherished space, and they are not compelled to seek out experiences or things outside of that space.

So, at Stage 2, we are working with a dog who doesn't need to be asked to stay within the tranquil line. We continue to work with the mat time exercise inside as well as outside, moving along the rungs of socialization and progressing to where mat time can be practiced wherever we happen to be.

## Exercise: *Mat Time*

Mat time as practiced at Stage 1 (see chapter 5) is about instilling in the dog the habit that when the dog is in a space with us, and absent any other direction, they find a place within the tranquil circle to park themselves and rest.

At Stage 2, we begin working toward this happening anywhere. We move up the rungs of socialization toward proximal, interactional, and oppositional. Attempt the exercise with the dog on a drag line and without a line, with the space closed off or with doors open, and with or without a mat. Does the dog realize that the best thing to do, absent instruction and with you clearly engaged elsewhere, is to find their place within the tranquil circle around you?

### EARLY STAGE—DISTAL SOCIALIZATION

In the early period of Stage 2, continue practicing at the distal level of socialization, meaning your dog finds their place in your orbit and settles in your tranquil circle even with stimuli at a distance.

After a walk or exercise, designate an outdoor place where you'll attempt mat time. Instead of bringing the dog to you with grounding, keep your 10-foot line loose, and sit if the dog is calmer; stand if otherwise, and shorten your line a tad. Ignore your dog and pay attention to other things while of course remaining aware of your dog. Breathe, settle, and wait for the dog to do the same.

### MID STAGE—PROXIMAL AND INTERACTIONAL SOCIALIZATION

As the dog settles into this exercise and performs consistently, begin introducing proximal socialization where stimuli are considerably closer, still asking the dog to find their place, relax, and ignore things.

Interactional socialization follows this, with the dog remaining unbothered in the tranquil circle while you interact with other people, animals, and things.

### LATER STAGE—OPPOSITIONAL SOCIALIZATION

As we progress through Stage 2, strengthening the dog's capacity to find a spot in the tranquil circle around us no matter what might be going on, the dog will eventually be able to ignore even oppositional socialization happening.

I think of my dog Kizzy, whom I had around at my last pre-pandemic holiday party. In the middle of a very busy house with people drinking and eating, many interacting with me and others reaching out to touch her, she had the wherewithal to find parking spots for herself, staying out of trouble, engaging lightly with people, and staying in my orbit.

## The Territorial Circle

At Stage 1, we stopped and took our time at entryways, breathing and relaxing before proceeding across boundary lines (the mind me exercise from chapter 5). At Stage 2, we continue to regulate our dogs around the territorial circle, the outermost boundary of whatever space we are in, minimizing them from getting too close to these boundaries.

When your dog is ready for Stage 2, you shouldn't have to actively do the mind me exercise. You should have a dog who doesn't cross thresholds without you. The dog almost automatically gives you a little space and waits for you to okay moving from one space to another. This behavior is one of the building blocks of a dog who's reliable off leash.

At this stage, we also work on enforcing boundaries a little more. For example, if I put the dogs out in the yard and open the door to get back in, that doesn't mean I wish to be followed unless I ask. If I am walking up to the sidewalk to speak to my neighbor, that doesn't mean they need to follow. Respecting territorial boundaries means dogs cannot cross from one space to another, inside or outside, and regardless of our own movements across boundary lines.

The territorial line approach (TLA) exercise that follows is a more elaborate, broken-down, and deconstructed form of mind me. The goal is to teach our dogs to instinctively hang behind us as we both approach a territorial boundary. They leave it up to us to scope things out and signal to them to follow along with us. Here are a few examples:

→ We're hiking in the woods and hear traffic; this signals that a road is approaching and that a new territory is near. Our dogs will circle back behind us and let us lead the way.

→ We're walking on the sidewalk and approach a crosswalk. Our dogs will circle back behind us and wait for us to decide which way we're going.

→ Our space is invaded by a loose dog coming into our space. Our dogs will circle back behind us and let us handle the invader because, by definition, a stranger belongs in another territory.

→ We're at a store cashing out and interacting with the cashier. Our dogs will hang back and not interfere.

→ We're on the sidewalk shooting the breeze with the neighbor. Our dogs will not come to check out the neighbor unless invited.

→ We're taking the garbage out to the curb. Our dogs will not follow all the way to the curb; the dog will hang back in the driveway, waiting.

## Exercise: *Territorial Line Approach*

There are many ways of staging a TLA exercise. Let's start with an easy way of teaching this exercise, beginning with just you and your dog in your yard, training space, or quiet working area (primordial socialization).

→   Place a bowl with some treats or a toy on the ground.

→   With your dog on a short but loose line, walk several steps away from the object.

→   Now stop with you and your dog facing the object.

→   Ask your dog to sit or handle the dog to help them sit.

→   Take one step toward the object with your dog still sitting.

→   Encourage the dog to join you on the next step.

→   If the dog follows you before you encourage it, start again.

The closer you get, the more you work toward your dog staying seated and not coming with you unless you encourage it. Once the dog begins letting you take a step without coming alongside you, you know the dog is starting to get it. Essentially, you work your way toward your dog letting you proceed all the way to the treats or toy without coming with you. When this happens, pick up the food and give it to the dog or toss the toy toward the dog.

### Variations

Another way to stage this exercise is to work toward a door or gate, whether inside or outside, closed to start and then open for added difficulty. Again, we start several feet away from the door or gate, but we are aiming ourselves and our dogs in that direction. We take one step, asking the dog to sit. Another step and another, asking or helping the dog into a sit each time. Eventually, you want to be able to leave the dog behind you, as you walk toward the door. If the dog hangs back, waiting for you, return to them with lots of praise and end the exercise.

Next, you can practice the exercise around different parts of the house and in familiar places before trying new places (spatial socialization), first without stimuli at a distance and then with some (distal socialization).

You can also make this exercise a lot more challenging and a lot more fun by working with another person:

→ Begin by starting 10 or so feet away from the other person, with your dog on a short but loose line.

→ Start walking toward each other one step at a time. The dog takes one step with you and then the next.

→ Ideally, you get close enough to that other person, which signals to the dog that we're approaching a territorial line.

→ The dog hangs back, and you can step closer to the person, talk to the person, shake hands and hug, all while the dog is hanging back.

→ End the interaction and return to your dog.

You can attempt this variation again with a person and their dog that is also working the territorial line exercise toward us. This can feel oppositional for both dogs who are stepping closer to one another. The idea is for both handlers to meet with each one of their dogs hanging behind.

When you work with someone alone or with their dog on this exercise, you introduce proximal socialization. Remember as well that part of our mission at Stage 2 is to begin the process of freeing the dog. Therefore, start practicing with the dog on leash, working up to the dog dragging the line, and then working completely off leash.

Amazingly enough, this exercise is so powerful that you only need to do it a few times in different places and formats for the dog to get it. The dog innately understands that for them to join us in the new territory, they have to be called in. What you'll also see with this exercise is that the dog will start to hang back a lot sooner, giving you plenty of room to proceed and deal with whatever needs to be dealt with at the territorial boundary.

In closing, socialization at Stage 2 is about continuing to strengthen the capacity to be alone while enhancing rapport between handler and dog (primordial socialization). With foundations developed at Stage 1, the Exposure stage expands socialization beyond new environments (spatial) and stimuli at a distance (distal) to include proximal, interactional, and oppositional levels of socialization.

## CASE
# Katie the Doodle Puppy Mill Mom

Katie the goldendoodle was a retired-at-last puppy mill mom of about seven years old. She'd spent much of her life producing litter after litter of doodle puppies for a public that was willing to pay ridiculous sums of money for such dogs, not knowing the real price being paid by the animals and those who rescue them.

The effects of having her body used for commerce and her mind and heart conveniently overlooked showed in Katie's eyes, demeanor, the scars on her body, and stubborn ear and anal gland infections. The message from her owners read:

*She has a lovely temperament and is beginning to trust (a little), but we believe (and the vet agrees) that she may be a little depressed. She was used for breeding for her sad seven years, and we are hoping to provide her with a better life. We just want her to be happy!! She is still pretty skittish and, understandably, hesitant and not comfortable around new people.*

*So far, she has not shown much interest in any dogs on our walks. (Again, this may be part of her depression, coming here after never having lived in a house.) She is house-trained (that wasn't as hard with her as we expected) but is unfortunately NOT food motivated yet. (We have a hard time, still, getting her to eat on a schedule or, some days, to eat much at all!)*

## The Issues

With a dog like this, we're not dealing with reactivity, resource guarding, or even separation anxiety. She's a little startled by all the sounds and sights that her limited life didn't prepare her for but tends to recover quickly. Yet these aren't the primary concerns. Rather, our challenge with this girl is to take her back to a time of innocence and to restore her to the joy and mischief that are inherent in any dog.

She was frozen in time and dissociated from her new reality. She was lifeless and happy to remain unseen and unheard. She was indeed depressed, lacking in self-esteem, and not displaying enthusiasm for anything. My clients had her for several months, doing what they thought was right, before she came to board with us. What started as a two-week boarding was extended to a month, which allowed us to decompress Katie and instill a real change, one that's continued since she's gone back home, where the clients have continued working on the stages with zeal.

Clearly, Katie had landed in her new situation with baggage that her owners did not create. They were not the ones who'd used her all these years, oblivious to her as a sentient being. But simply being rescued from a bad situation and being loved does nothing for dogs like these.

Katie had been in her home for about three months and had yet to smile. She was integrated without proper foundations or exposure. Instead of this being encouraging for Katie, it depressed her even more because she wasn't given the incentive to get over her past. In her eyes, what was there to work for?

# A New Way of Life

My work with Katie involved several aspects, crucial among which was physical exercise. Prior to boarding, Katie's owners had taken her on walks regularly but never pushed Katie to walk briskly or trot, allowing her to shuffle at the speed that her weak body allowed. Of course, years in a puppy mill took their toll, and she could barely walk without running out of steam, having so little muscle tone. Through neighborhood walks and hikes, I exercised her more strenuously over time. By the time she was ready to go home, she'd lost six pounds and was stronger, plus she clearly enjoyed the physical and psychological benefits of physical exertion that included eating fully and resting deeply.

As with any dog, Katie spent copious amounts of time in the crate, which was easy for her. But when I put her in the larger outdoor kennel, she started to bark. The crate wasn't a challenge, but the outdoor kennel was. I welcomed her barking, as so far she'd been mute. In no time, she conquered the challenge of the outdoor kennel and enjoyed it till the end of her stay with me, frequently seeking it out whenever she was outside.

Another critical aspect of our work was revving up Katie's desire for food. Dogs that are depressed like Katie are not necessarily gobbling food down, and yet food is such an important tool in our feel-better toolbox. So we took several avenues to rev up her food drive including physically exerting her and waking up her senses to different smells. I had her with me while I cooked in the kitchen and put all the dogs' meals together. Making her smell things and even just being around the dogs that were excited about dinner helped wake up her senses. Even though she was on a restricted diet, we were able to add a few fresh foods to make her kibble more appealing.

Though normally I don't include boarder and foster dogs with my other dogs except in short spurts, in this case, I felt Katie needed the presence of other sound and healthy dogs. My dogs gave Katie plenty of room and offered an attitude of polite indifference. This did wonders to motivate her to feel better so that she could be accepted.

It was Bob who was most influential for her because she genuinely liked him, drawn to his swagger and confidence, while he was the most dismissive of her. "Look, lady," he seemed to say, "toughen up and I'll talk to you."

The attitude of these sound dogs informed my own. Who better, after all, to teach us about dogs than dogs? That's the underlying logic of this entire approach. And yet, questioning and changing our own attitudes can be difficult because we want to practice the normal human tendency of protecting and loving, thinking that we can love dogs out of that state when what they really need is detachment.

We need to be careful about the affection and inclusion given to a dog that is this low in self-esteem and confidence. All my dogs were aware of the dark place Katie was in, but they did not treat her any differently, nor did they reduce their own joy and serenity. Katie had to give us "proof of life" to get attention, affection, and inclusion.

## Results

As a result of these efforts, we saw many improvements, including an almost immediate willingness to go to the bathroom with us around, which she'd never done with her owners before. This was later followed by a willingness to eat and drink in our presence.

Outside, Katie had started off by hiding in the garden, but her hiding area got closer and closer to the house, until she no longer needed that hiding space and could just hang out at a distance from the others.

She began to show interest in food, finishing her meals and taking treats, and closer to the end, she showed interest in toys as well. A maturing prey drive was kicking in when we saw her inviting Bob to a game of chasing the squirrels and pigeons. Normally, I'm not a fan of my animals harassing wildlife, but Katie needed permission to be a dog again. When she starts feeling better and being a bit of a brat by going after squirrels more routinely, then we can start introducing a bit more civility.

The change was palpable and visible in her body language through smiles, a relaxed body, and tail wagging, all proof that we'd done our job and turned the page. Of course, all the physical interventions and practical changes in the way of life helped. But I know without a doubt that the biggest change was careful management of feelings around her, including affection toward her. She understood that she needed to have more pep in her step to be worthy of affection and inclusion.

# For Reflection

1.  What does your schedule with your dog look like now? How has it changed since Stage 1? How would you like to see your dog better integrated into your work and/or life?

2.  How is your understanding of the importance of crating evolving? How has your experience crating your dog been so far?

3.  Decompression after new exposures is a crucial part of this stage. What are the signs that your dog is becoming overstimulated or overtired? What are the signs that your dog is recovered and ready for more?

4.  As your dog's understanding of the three circles grows, how do you see your dog responding to or ignoring the three circles? What kinds of situations are easy, and which ones are difficult for them?

5.  As you begin the early-stage versions of the exercises in this chapter, what is the baseline for you and your dog? What are the signs that your dog perhaps needs more time with the Foundations exercises or is ready for more Exposure?

# CHAPTER 10

# Socialization at Stage 2

It is not because things are difficult that we do not dare, it is because we do not dare that things are difficult.

**—LUCIUS ANNAEUS SENECA,** Stoic philosopher

*D*esiree, a puppy mill mom rescued from Newfoundland, was a pug who reacted to people, dogs, and children. My client realized she must have done things a little too fast with Desi, as she liked calling her, and proceeded to go back to basics. She wanted to be able to take Desi with her to visit her daughter and grandchildren, who were four and six years old. These children were too young to be expected to have discipline around dogs. So, Desi came to board with me for a few weeks.

*Of course, boarding dogs allows them to be looked after when their people need to travel or deal with personal matters. However, boarding is also an opportunity to challenge dogs and the bonds they've developed with their owners. Before boarding, dogs should be comfortable crated and be stable enough to be transferred to another handler in an unfamiliar environment.*

*When I board dogs, I do with them what I tell people to do with a new dog or a dog they're just getting started with—decompression. Because this dog is new here, we go back to Stage 1 with that dog instead of thinking we can pick up where the owners left off. This means extended periods crated, some solo time, and not much* exposure to anyone or anything for a few days. This allows me to accurately evaluate the dogs and coach their owners better, as I can see how the dogs take to the challenge.

Moreover, the structured and challenging manner of boarding this way also helps stabilize and strengthen client dogs because it ensures that the handler transference is safe and successful. Once over the stressful experience, back home, and rested, clients tell me their dogs appear to have taken a jump in maturity, which was exactly the case for Desi. Her reactivity to people and dogs eased considerably because of boarding this way and my client felt encouraged about trying to have her around the children.

She worked up a plan of taking Desi for visits to her daughter's house and, initially, worked solely on getting Desi adjusted to the new space without engaging with the kids. She went for short visits, keeping the dog crated or leashed up—in other words, carefully managed.

Over time, Desiree began to adjust and could be trusted with finding her way to the mat in the tranquil circle with the kids around. The experience not only boosted her self-confidence but also made her feel included and part of the family. In turn, I could see that rise in self-esteem when she boarded with us again because she was even better with the dogs this time. It was almost like boarding with us was nothing after she'd successfully dealt with the out-of-town visits and two rambunctious children! With the right foundations in place, we shouldn't be afraid to push and challenge our dogs. Otherwise, we will never know what they're really capable of.

From the start, I have emphasized the importance of dogs being alone and appreciating their alone time. Learning to be by oneself, whether in dogs or humans, is a hallmark of maturity and steadiness. I view appreciating one's own company as essential to mental health. When I have my dogs outside, I love to see them enjoying themselves quietly and serenely, not needing to come inside and not needing to cause trouble outside.

At Stage 2, we continue to work on giving dogs alone time, in the crate and secure outside locations. We continue strengthening the first three levels of socialization—primordial, spatial, and distal—progressing toward the higher rungs of proximal, interactional, and oppositional. We steadily progress with our dog from accepting a change of environment (spatial), to ignoring people and dogs at a distance (distal), to continuing to focus on us even with people and dogs near (proximal). We also work toward allowing the dogs to interact with people and dogs directly (interactional and oppositional).

# Primordial, Spatial, and Distal Socialization

Primordial socialization is everything we, as the primary handlers, are doing with our dogs—every interaction and the spirit we bring to it, every day and how we manage it, and every situation and how we deal with it. All these experiences factor into our dog's understanding of who we are and what we signify for the dog as a source of safety. This will make all the difference in the world when we're ready for the higher levels of socialization.

With spatial socialization, we are exploring different environments as opposed to simply being exposed to different environments. We are now engaging in these environments. For example, at Stage 1, we had one or two designated hiking places. Now we go hiking in new places. We keep in mind the need to introduce gradually (i.e., grounding at the start, going successful and short, instead of far), but the introductions also go a little faster in the sense that the dogs adjust to new spaces more readily.

Each new environment brings a certain amount of stress. Any time we have stress, we are bound to have a regression in behavior, such as hesitation or fear. Think about how you feel in a strange place versus a familiar place. Consider the difference it would make to your experience to have a trusted friend in that new place versus not having anyone with you or, worse yet, someone you don't trust.

Changes of environment also happen when there's a change in the household. If we are dealing with work stress or medical issues or if a new human or animal comes into the house, that is a change of environment where we can expect the dog to regress.

Therefore, we go back to basics a little in new spaces and environments— if the dog had nice behavior in one area, this does not mean that they will have the same behavior in another. However, looking to us for guidance and responding to food and attention help the dog ride out the adjustment. If the dog weathers these changes well, it is a testament to the dog maturing and stabilizing under our care.

Grounding should be a habit for you by now, and sometimes it takes only a mere moment and sometimes longer. When you're in a new place, settle the dog and ground before proceeding. Say I just got back from a hike. Before I let the dogs in the yard, I take them out of the car, and we hang out there for a few minutes. I get everyone calm before going inside. What we are trying to instill in our dogs is that we will not move to another space unless we have calm in the present space.

One way that I like to easily change the environment is by propping doors and gates open. Automatically that changes the picture because the dog has a way out. Dogs that haven't been through Foundations see this as an invitation and will go flying through it. But at Stage 2, we are able to operate as normal with doors open—the dogs ignoring what is outside the current territory. We teach dogs that we don't go outside just because it's open; they need permission before traveling to a new environment.

Finally, the distal level of socialization is about ignoring people, animals, and things at a safe distance. One powerful way of teaching dogs to ignore things is for us to mentally ignore them. Take note of things, file them in your picture of the situation, and keep your focus on what we want your dog to focus on: the walk, hike, or other activity. When you're walking down the street and paying attention to things like incoming people, dogs, and other sources of potential stress, the dog is going to pay attention to these as well.

## Proximal Socialization

At a herding class once, I happened to be talking to a classmate in between our turns. She had her dog with her, and mine was crated in the car. She and I were talking, and her dog kept pulling in my direction, wanting to check me out, and making it difficult for us to talk. I finally suggested she officially send him over to check me out.

At the next turn, I met my friend again. This time I was with Kizzy, while my friend was dogless. We picked up our conversation and not once did Kizzy pull toward my friend. Instead, after a few moments, Kizzy sat and waited without being told, garnering praise from my classmate who noted the self-initiated thoughtful behavior. I can assure you that when dogs are pulling toward people, it is not because they're dying to say hi unless this is something you've encouraged in the name of "socialization." Rather, dogs pull toward others as a redirection of the stress felt within their relationships with us. If all were well between us, why would they be looking for a stranger's attention? At a minimum, they pull toward others in proximity because we've not worked them well enough at the more basic levels of socialization leading up to proximal.

Proximal socialization raises our dogs to ignore people, animals, and things that are close by. While we kept things at a healthy distance in Stage 1, we're now coming closer at Stage 2, while still expecting our dogs to ignore stimuli, which will be understandably more difficult.

After time practicing with both us and our dog ignoring proximal stimuli, we can then begin practicing having the dog ignore stimuli that we are engaging with. The level of difficulty is raised because it signals that the external thing is relevant to us. The dog wants to check out what's interesting us, but still, we're asking the dog to ignore because we should be able to have real-life (and virtual) conversations without our dog butting in.

As we expand our dog's world at Stage 2, we make it a point to seek out experiences that involve closer proximity, including vet and groomer visits, taking public transportation, and going to busier places. We use any of the drives available—food, prey, and emerging pack drive (see chapter 11)—to remind our dogs to ignore those things.

## Activity: *Waiting At The Vet's Office*

Vet visits provide good opportunities for spatial, distal, proximal, and interactional socialization. Treat these aspects of your dog's life like any other training exercise—bring your training mojo and treat pouch and have an image in your mind of what a successful visit to the vet looks like.

You will likely be waiting your turn sitting next to or across from someone with their pet, possibly a dog or a cat in a carrier. Perhaps they are smiling at your dog and making eye contact, perhaps even trying to engage your dog while bypassing you. (Sound familiar?) There's also activity at the vet clinic—people moving around, restless animals, conversations. Model ignoring all these happenings for your dog, and work on maintaining your inner circle amid the busyness.

This is essentially a grounding exercise in a relatively busy place, where at times you might engage in conversation, having to split your attention from the dog. Work on having a part of you focused on the person you're talking to with the other part still aware of and "on" your dog. Dogs can tell when our attention is divided, so convey to your dog that while you're talking to someone, you're also still with them.

At the same time, if the dog is having a hard time with that higher level of socialization, ask yourself whether this is a good time for you to be interacting with others. I find the less I interact with others, the less they will ask to interact with my dog, and this is what I want when we're working at the proximal level.

At Stage 2, we're strengthening prey drive and allowing for pack drive to emerge, which means we start to rely more on praise and approval as a reward instead of food. As always, though, be prepared for regression in behavior when new levels of socialization are added. This means that you can continue to use food to ease the experience when necessary.

## Activity: *Taking Public Transportation*

Another potentially fun and challenging activity to expose our dogs to the proximal level of socialization is to take public transportation with our dogs. Many cities around the world permit dogs on public transportation, often during certain hours when there is less traffic. If this is an option for you, give it a try!

In using public transportation, you could be standing in a crowd waiting to get on the bus or train. Once aboard, you and your dog could be sitting or standing next to all kinds of people. The vehicles are noisy, and loud voices blare out information through speakers.

Start by getting your dog accustomed to being near buses and trains, such as by walking through the commuter crowds but not yet getting on the bus or train. Do that a few times before actually getting on for a short ride to start. Later, attempt a longer ride, giving your dog time to stress and get over it.

Go on excursions like these with a spirit of adventure. Carry yourself with confidence and poise, as if taking public transportation is the most pleasant, least stressful thing in the world, and project that onto your dog. See if food helps your dog settle, but if they are nervous and don't want any treats, handle the dog with poise, keeping them calm and still, while detaching psychologically from their state of apprehension. In other words, you're aware of the dog's state but not feeding into it by dwelling on it.

## Activity: *Milling Crowds*

Another way of experimenting with proximal socialization is to visit crowded parts of where we live—shopping malls, busy touristy spots, downtown streets, and so on. We begin by grounding in our starting spot and then going for short walks around the busy place, modeling for our dog that we are ignoring the milling crowds around us. We can also run or hike closer to people and in busier locations. The idea is to see whether the dog can sustain hanging out and working around a group of people, whether these people are stationary or moving around.

# Interactional Socialization

When our dogs demonstrate to us their capacity to deal with environment changes (spatial) and to ignore things, people, and animals at a distance (distal) as well as nearby (proximal), this becomes a good time to introduce our dogs to interactions with people and dogs (interactional). We are upping the socialization challenge because now we're asking dogs to engage with elements that thus far, we'd emphasized they should ignore.

At the interactional level, the dog engages and interacts physically and psychologically with people and animals inside and outside the home. This is where our dog meets people and gets a few pats. This is where our dog gets to check out the cat. This is where our dog greets and engages with another dog.

**Exercise:** *Having People Over At Stage 2*

At Stage 2, carry on with the exercise of having people over, which you started at Stage 1 (see chapter 6). Make sure the dog is leashed up, at the very least on a drag line. So far, you have asked your dog to deal with having people over at the spatial level (adjusting to the change of environment created by having people over), distal level (ignoring your guests at a distance), and proximal level (ignoring your guests who happen to be right there).

You will also be adding interactional socialization, where the dog will be able to approach and have brief interactions with your guests. Brief your guests and outline the way you want the interaction to go. They should always check in with you and follow your lead on how to deal with the dog.

### EARLY STAGE—PRIMORDIAL, SPATIAL, AND DISTAL TO PROXIMAL SOCIALIZATION

In the early stages of Exposure, focus first on strengthening the work done on the first three levels of socialization, especially optimizing your dog's capacity to handle proximal socialization. With everything you've done so far, it should not be too difficult for your dog to ignore things—you've imprinted yourself as the focus of their attention, they want the food you have, and you've taught them to ignore things as a default position.

### MID STAGE—PROXIMAL AND INTERACTIONAL SOCIALIZATION

In the later stages of Exposure, introduce interactional socialization. After giving the dog the time to (1) adjust to the new environment, (2) ignore the person at a distance, and (3) ignore the person in proximity, you can "send" your dog to say hello to the person and then call the dog back to their secure base.

Before bringing the dog out, brief your guests on how you want them to behave. When the dog approaches them, they should let the dog sniff them, offer a treat with an open palm, and give some praise and a few pats. We want to keep touching to a minimum and avoid a lot of enthusiasm and loudness, even if they think your dog is the cutest thing to walk the earth.

Begin with your dog grounding next to you on leash. Ask your guest to come a little closer and speak softly to your dog but wait for your dog to acknowledge you first—the dog must ask for permission to leave the inner circle. Then send the dog to greet your visitors with a command, such as go say hi. Let the dog approach the guest for a treat and short interaction, and then call back the dog to you.

This way, we regulate the interaction, and the dog can tell that the meeting has occurred on our terms. This is the essence of exposing successfully. You don't need to do this too frequently at the start. Just try a few meet and greets that end on a high note and return the dog to their crate to rest and reflect on their experience.

### LATER STAGE—INTERACTIONAL SOCIALIZATION

In the later stages, you can have the dog out near your guests for longer periods of time, whether interacting with them or simply hanging out. You can also start with the dog on a drag line once the dog has had successful meetings on leash.

# Oppositional Socialization

In the later stages of Exposure, we start to evaluate whether our dog can accept the more oppositional forms of socialization, which involve interactions that could be experienced as uncomfortable, invasive, intrusive, or confrontational— for example, when people or animals invade our inner circle or when children pull dogs' ears and tails or interrupt them while they're eating or sleeping. Environments can also be uncomfortable. I like to challenge my dogs at the oppositional level by walking near potentially stressful spaces—for example, construction sites, school yards during recess, and dog parks.

# Vet Visits and Grooming

Veterinary examinations and grooming can also be invasive for dogs. At the vet, dogs will need a physical exam, which may include a bright light shining in their eyes and their mouth being opened. They may need shots or to have their anal glands expressed. At the groomers, dogs are bathed and shampooed, propped up on a table and restricted by a harness, surrounded by other groomers and their dogs, and touched all over their body.

Note that up until this time, we will have done everything to protect our dog's space. We have also been adamant about keeping our dog at our side before sending them out—on our terms—to meet and greet people. Having done that, the dog becomes increasingly capable of handling the invasive experiences that are common in their existence with us humans. We have maturing and strong dogs who are sound enough to take things in stride and are ready for the challenge.

Basically, the more relationship material we have with our dogs, the better they deal with oppositional socialization. A big part of that relationship material is whether we socialized gradually before reaching oppositional. When the dogs know we've kept them safe all along, the sense of being invaded is taken with a great deal more stride.

I think about my dog Bruna, who spent about a year being examined by various doctors and specialists as we went about trying to figure the cause of her medical issues. Had it not been for our bond and the strength she'd gained because of feeling so safe, I know the many tests and vet visits, at the height of the pandemic when I could not be with her, would have taken their toll.

**Activity:** *Let's Go To The Vet!*

To the extent that you can manage, take your dog to visit the vet while working through the rungs of socialization:

→   Start from a place of having a minimum rapport with your dog (primordial socialization).

→ Progress to exposing your dog to the vet clinic without any interactions (spatial socialization).

→ Move up to being at the clinic while ignoring people and animals at a distance (distal socialization).

→ Progress to sitting in the clinic in proximity to other people and animals, while having your dog ignore these other people and animals (proximal socialization).

You may or may not be able to expose your dog to your vet with this degree of approximations—it's unfortunate that we think of visiting the vet as doing it all at once, going there, meeting people, interacting with people, and being touched by people—all in one visit. But if you have a dog without pressing professional grooming or medical needs, wait before asking the dog to deal with intrusive handling, touching, and examining. Again, every case is different, but if you need to take the dog to the vet a lot, dial down other socializations since they're already having to deal with strange people poking and prodding them while the dog barely knows us. I know without a doubt that if we raise our dogs the way I outline here, including exposing our dogs along the rungs of socialization, vet visits would be a lot easier on all involved.

Ideally, you would follow this gradual manner of exposure, and you will have had as much time as possible with your dogs before exposing them to the invasiveness of vet visits. It might not always be realistic to wait this long for such important aspects of care, but let's at least be aware of how the experience is lived by the dog. I should also note that the vets and vet techs also play a role, and I have seen wide variations in the skills and attitudes of vet staff in handling dogs when they are uncomfortable.

## Socializing with Other Dogs

Sometimes, there might be aspects of engagement between dogs that feel confrontational, especially at the start when the two dogs are figuring themselves out. But here's the thing: when they have experienced being in the same space together (spatial socialization), at a distance from each other (distal socialization), and then in proximity (proximal socialization), they have, in many ways, already met. This means that once we're ready to take it to the interactional level, things are likely to go smoothly.

The capacity to ignore other dogs that is stressed at Stage 1 is a prerequisite for meeting and interacting with them. I believe a dog that is not obsessed with other dogs makes a better play partner and canine friend. Remember that play between dogs will include invasive and confrontational aspects, and thus we want stable dogs going in. So that dogs can interact constructively, each dog should be already enjoying decent relationship foundations with their person—as in the dog is responsive to you. This allows for safe engagement without leashes on.

At Stage 2, we allow dogs to meet, to go for closer walks and hikes together, and eventually to play and engage. We also have dogs that are relatively sound and strong and that make good playmates and models for other dogs.

Many people think it's okay to introduce new dogs and let them play together immediately. I get asked a lot about whether dogs who have been socialized gradually can meet dogs who haven't been. To the extent possible, try to get your friends on board with a gradual introduction just as I describe here. If they're not on board (which may be worth having a conversation with them about), you can still take some chances and monitor the play closely. Move about so the playing dogs are somewhat distracted by your presence and give them occasional breaks.

Here's the thing: when you raise your dogs following the stages, they should be able to take on new dogs and diffuse any arising tensions. The dogs don't have an axe to grind; they're not out looking for trouble. These dogs will shut down attempts to misbehave and will walk away. It's also our job to regulate, protect, and interfere if necessary, continuing to exude a presence of safety and authority in our dogs' eyes.

Not too long ago, I felt that two of my friends ought to introduce their dogs and see if the two could eventually play as both lacked a proper playmate. The dogs included Mary, a two-year-old Malinois–cattle dog mix rescue with a relatively easygoing and social temperament, and Jonathan, a ridgeback mix with a more nervous disposition.

Neither one of my friends had a yard where the dogs could play, so I suggested they begin by taking separate walks in the park where they would eventually meet. They started by taking their dogs for walks on their own in the designated park, which was accessible to both of them. They progressed to walking their dogs there together but at a good distance from each other. While Jonathan was happy to ignore other dogs, Mary needed to learn to ignore Jonathan as they walked closer and closer to each other. They took these walks a few times over the course of several weeks, gradually walking the dogs closer.

When the dogs were relaxed around each other, primarily focused on their handlers, and able to sniff the same spot without engaging, I felt it was time to bring them to my backyard. We met in the park by the house to start, giving the dogs the chance to meet again and exercise a little. We then moved to my backyard, on leash first and then loose. Not much happened the first time because the dogs needed to adjust to that new space. The next few times, we allowed the dogs to play with each other while we remained standing, taking walks around the yard.

Gradually, Mary and Jonathan have increased the level of intensity of their play while also learning to just hang out. Interestingly, Jonathan's relationship with Mary seems to have spilled over onto Mary's owner, as he has also developed a liking for them. Both of my friends have reported that this gradual introduction, culminating in healthy play, has benefited the dogs in other avenues—Jonathan is a little more confident while Mary is less obsessed with dogs on the street.

## Exercise: *Engaging With Other Dogs At Stage 2*

Our goal at Stage 2 is to bring our dog closer to other dogs (proximal), eventually allowing them to meet (interactional) and engage (oppositional).

### EARLY STAGE—PROXIMAL SOCIALIZATION

Begin by strengthening the proximal level of socialization, working on your dog ignoring other dogs nearby. Just like Mary in the preceding story, some dogs who want to engage with other dogs might find the proximity challenging, but you have credibility in your dog's eyes and are fostering emerging pack drive. You certainly can use food to keep your dog focused on you but start seeing how much your words matter at this point. The dogs eventually learn to go for walks or hikes at proximity while generally ignoring each other, focusing on their surroundings and their owners.

## MID STAGE—INTERACTIONAL SOCIALIZATION

As you start to work toward the dogs' meeting, start engaging with the human on the other human-dog team. This raises the level of engagement to interactional, which will ramp up the dogs. Start allowing the dogs closer and closer to each other, linger a little, let them meet naturally, and then proceed with your walk. If you're ready to let the dogs play, take them where they can play safely— preferably an enclosed space. Go back to the beginning, grounding with your dog in the new space and asking the dogs to ignore each other first.

## LATER STAGE—INTERACTIONAL AND OPPOSITIONAL SOCIALIZATION

When the dogs have succeeded at ignoring each other at proximity, you're ready to cut them loose in your play space. Start the session by grounding for a moment and then letting the dogs off their leashes. Gauge their play—my friends had to encourage Jonathan and Mary at times, and you can certainly do that. Since the introductions have been so gradual, the play will likely be successful. If the dogs are very excited to play, allow some of that, and let them figure out how to dance with each other. Make sure at first you're standing up and walking around the yard—this serves as a source of distraction for the dogs so that they tone down their play if it's getting rough.

Play itself isn't something we can teach dogs; we can only raise them to be clearheaded and stable so they don't take out whatever frustrations they might have on the other dog. If we have enough rapport and good foundations, we should be able to call off our dogs, give them short breaks, and let them engage again.

Soon you'll be able to trust that the two dogs have figured out a way to play with each other, and you can relax and let them do their thing, while still stepping in as needed to give them breaks. Note that hanging out by smelling the air and taking in the sights and sounds together is just as good a form of socializing with other dogs as anything else.

Try not to exhaust the dogs as tiredness can make them less able to regulate their behavior and play constructively. End things after a short session to conclude on a high note. Back at home, put your dog away so they can reflect on their positive experience.

# Handler Transference

Another crucial form of oppositional socialization that is introduced later in Stage 2 is handler transference. This process can include letting another person hold onto our dog while we are nearby, or if we leave the space for a few minutes, transferring our dog to another handler for exercises (see chapter 11), or a full-on boarding experience.

Transferring our dogs to other capable handlers helps the dogs strengthen and grow in confidence, knowing they can be away from home and handled by other people. Overcoming their feelings of vulnerability hugely boosts the dogs' inner strength. And, if their new handler does things the same way we do, it also strengthens our bond.

Think about the value of having dogs who transfer well. They don't panic at the groomer's; they handle being vetted—something that became that much more important during the pandemic when many of us had to wait outside while our dog was seen by the doctor. These oppositional forms of socialization are likely to feel less invasive and uncomfortable when our dogs have the benefit of foundations and lots of practice at exposure. Think about going on vacation and being able to take your dogs with you to experience new things successfully, like hotel rooms, new hiking areas, or other people's homes. Think about being able to go on vacation and leaving your dogs behind, knowing they will handle the boarding just fine. These are all part of a richer and happier life for us and our dogs.

## Activity: *The Boarding Experience*

For this activity, you want to think about boarding with a trusted friend, family member, or professional who will reinforce the work that you have been doing. This could mean having someone stay in your home and look after your dog, boarding your dog at someone's home, or taking the dog to a boarding facility that gives you a say over how things are done.

Choose this person or facility carefully. Essentially, they must approach boarding as decompression and follow the strict strategies outlined in Stage 1. Decompression includes a predictable schedule, time in the crate, solo time, and exercise. It does not involve socialization beyond the distal level. The person boarding for you should understand that boarding is not about giving your dog unstructured, free-for-all time while you're gone but rather ensuring that the experience is simple, successful, and not stressful. Understand that no matter their behavior, when dogs are allowed to do what they want in a new place without you, it does not exactly feel like success. It feels like stress we created for them.

The goal of boarding should be to stabilize and strengthen the dog through dealing with the vulnerability involved in being separated from their owner and handled by someone else. How your dog responds to the situation speaks to their foundations. If you hand off your dog to someone for boarding, some apprehension is to be expected, but ideally, your dog will have developed enough trust in you to trust the person you're handing them to. If you hand your dog off to someone and they don't recover fairly quickly, reflect on your foundations and where there could be holes that made the boarding experience more challenging. What could be the physical or psychological aspects in the way of life that have the dog struggling in this situation?

In closing, socialization at Stage 2 is about continuing to instill the capacity to be alone and continuing to strengthen the rapport between handler and dog (primordial socialization). With Foundations established, Exposure continues with spatial as well as distal socialization in new locations and activities, then progresses toward proximal, interactional, and oppositional.

## CASE
# Molly the Cockapoo

A couple came to me concerned with a range of issues displayed by their four-year-old cockapoo, Molly, including anxiety, reactivity, and noise sensitivity. These issues had become increasingly hard to deal with as the owners attempted to balance managing Molly's behavior with the needs of their two very young children. Molly liked the kids and was excellent with them, thankfully, but much else was problematic. Their initial message stated:

*She's really bad on leash and is constantly barking in the house at every little sound. She barks and jumps at visitors. Since we've had Molly, we have moved to a busier street with people and dogs walking by and have had two children under two.*

## The Issues

Molly was reactive to the noises that are typical of a home, especially one with children—TV sights and sounds, rings and whistles from various kitchen appliances, and kids playing and screaming. At the kids' feeding time, Molly crowded them, licking their faces, eating stuff off the ground, and being a general nuisance.

When my clients had bought their home, they imagined how much Molly would enjoy looking outside. But now, she barked ceaselessly at the door and out their living room bay window. Molly's noise was so bad it would wake the kids and garnered an anonymous note from a neighbor. Molly also reacted to people and dogs on the streets, pulled on the leash, and despite her petite size, was impossible to walk alone, much less alongside the stroller. There was also a minor bite history in Molly's past when she had been boarded with family, as both my clients as well as those who boarded her had underestimated her stress.

Out of all these issues, Molly's reactions to the many sounds and noises of the household were their biggest predicament. Though her breed is known for sound sensitivity, I hope you know by now that breed explanations are not enough. With this issue as any other, we question the way of life first. My clients had worked with a trainer who used a counterconditioning approach, and just as I expected, the behavior modification strategy made Molly that much more aware of, and obsessed with, these sounds.

Looking closely at Molly's situation, I noted again the usual culprits. The man and the woman in the relationship had different views and attitudes about Molly—the woman coddled Molly like one of the kids. The man was irritated with her. Molly had the run of the house and no structure to speak of—no crates, no schedules, no baby gates. As is common, the owners had crated her until she was house-trained and then the crate went into the garage.

Molly was also insufficiently exercised and had no downtime nor solo time. She was with the humans all the time and clearly had had enough. Through no fault of their own, my clients had a limited understanding of what it meant to socialize dogs in healthy ways. As such, Molly had been around two other dogs who hadn't been particularly nice to her, but my clients still felt it was good for Molly's socialization to be around them.

## A New Way of Life

Our job with Molly was to bring down the agitation by reframing the attitude of her owners, regulating her access to things such as doors and windows, structuring her time, supervising her more carefully, and challenging her innate talents.

First and foremost, we worked on the psychology of her people. Neither her coddling nor his impatience were going to work. If anything, Molly needed as much patience as they showed the two infants they were raising. In a way, the heavy crating and strict scheduling we do at the beginning gives the humans time and space to come around from their own attitudes, at which point it's easier to see the contribution these attitudes have had to the issues they're experiencing.

At the start, Molly was crated heavily, and not only was she able to gain some distance from the chaos, but she was finally able to catch the rest she badly needed. We also exercised her more. We started to socialize her in a proper way, which meant rolling back direct interactions with dogs and people, going back to primordial socialization, and working our way up.

Barking at windows is a common issue among many dog owners. With the three circles in mind, when we allow dogs to patrol the edges of a space, we're charging up their inner territorial nature, which makes them feel they need to police that space. In addition to any underlying stress building up because of a messy way of life, we then see them reactive near these boundaries. Dogs are not cats; they do not need windows looking out into the world for entertainment. They need to be taken out into the world, stimulated, and brought back home and regulated until a certain level of maturity is reached. I only allow my senior dogs, who are finished and integrated, to look out the window if they so choose.

A dog who's stressed because they're not handled properly inside is bound to redirect that stress onto something else, such as by barking at dogs and people when out and about. Dogs change when they're taken from one familiar space (inside) to an unfamiliar space (outside). With that change, underlying stress shows up more honestly, and the dog finds something to beat up on. Ultimately, a dog who is composed will deal with things differently than one who isn't. A calm dog is a thoughtful dog who is better able to modulate emotions and judge what's worth reacting to and what's not. I ask my clients to look at these issues as symptoms and to reflect on why their dog is so easily triggered.

## Results

With the changes we introduced, Molly settled down a great deal and everyone in the family was happier, the two kids included. I was thrilled to see how quickly Molly relaxed, as if to say, "Thank god, they get it now!" We also found that this little dog had a lot of spunk to her. She had a lot of interest in working and training, and she clearly didn't want to be just a pet.

When the crate was reintroduced, Molly was clearly glad to see it, which my clients said was "eye-opening." When her mom worked out in the basement, Molly would go by herself into her crate, which had been placed there. She became better able to deal with the various sounds of the house and take in stride the children's ruckus. She and her mom looked forward to the end of the day for their girls' night out, leaving dad and the kids at home to head out for a run or walk.

Molly also welcomed being given her own bed, which after practicing mat time, she used any time she was uncertain of what was expected of her. She also learned to stay there while the kids enjoyed their meal if she happened to not be crated. Because she was comfortable crated, she boarded with me easily, enjoying exposure to my dogs as part of our work.

When the family moved again, Molly adjusted seamlessly. She learned to find her way to her mat immediately in the new home. Molly could also be alone outside quietly, soaking in the sun and enjoying herself in the fenced-in yard. She'd become the sound, strong, and spirited little dog she was all along.

# For Reflection

1. How is your primordial socialization with your dog continuing to evolve? Take a moment to write down any new interactions or activities falling under primordial socialization.

2. In which ways could you go about spatial and distal socialization with your dog at Stage 2? Write down the new spaces inside the home and outside the home you will be exposing your dog to, such as new rooms, hiking or exercise spots, and more crowded areas.

3. In which ways could you incorporate opportunities for proximal, interactional, and oppositional socialization in your outings with your dog? Write down some new activities you can try with your dog, such as a new sport, taking your dog to work, meeting extended family members, meeting friends and other dogs, or taking trips.

4. It is normal for a dog to regress as they are challenged with new experiences. In what areas are you seeing your dog struggle? What parts of Foundations might need strengthening based on this?

5. What is one surprising and wonderful thing that you've learned about your dog since transitioning into Stage 2?

# CHAPTER 11

# Drive Development at Stage 2

Excellence requires that you not be satisfied.

—**MICHAEL ELLIS,** founder of the Michael Ellis School for Dog Trainers

*M*y client, an avid hiker and camper, recently took her dog Max, a one-year-old cockapoo, on his very first camping trip. We'd prepared for it for months and were thrilled that Max had mostly behaved, enjoyed himself, and come back feeling like a million bucks.

Things weren't always so positive for Max and his people, however. As new dog owners, Max's guardians, an active brother-sister duo living with their senior parents, had come to me seeking solutions to Max's reactivity. There was hardly a thing that didn't trigger Max, including but not limited to noises from the neighboring yard, people and dogs on the streets, and any fast-moving things like joggers, bikes, mopeds, and so on.

Sometimes Max would be triggered by nothing that our human eyes could see or our human ears could hear. Once activated, Max would stay in that heightened state, and my clients were at a loss on how to help him get his brain back. They sought help from traditional trainers who taught commands such as sit or leave it as *a way of dealing with his reactivity. Because it failed to account for the true cause of the dog's anxious behavior—his way of life—this training approach went nowhere.*

*When we began working together, we addressed Max's way of life, instituting a structured schedule, crating, and activities meant to engage him physically and mentally. We worked on getting everyone in the family on the same page. All these changes were challenging at first, particularly in terms of convincing my clients' elderly parents to quit spoiling Max and to get over their need to have him around all the time.*

*Max resisted fiercely—barking and fussing in the crate. He continued reacting to people and dogs on the street and on hiking trails and had a hard time settling when loose in the house. It was a few months of this, but my clients stuck it out. They could see remarkable improvements in Max appearing here and there, which kept them focused and optimistic.*

*One of the most important factors for Max was the level of physical exercise and mental challenge that he required. He was always at his best after big hikes and camping trips. Tugging, playing ball, and other prey games were essential for his stability. The case of Max and other cockapoos I have dealt with suggests that this "designer breed" can at times be more than what people have bargained for in getting a small dog. These dogs can have a lot of spunk and drive that need to be channeled correctly in their way of life.*

*Max and his people are in a much better place now. He is excellent in his crate, settles down nicely when loose in the house, and is much less reactive to things on the street. There's no doubt in my mind that their next camping trip will be another success, given the care and commitment that his people have put forth by establishing foundations and channeling his drives.*

Drives will always be an important part of a dog's life. This is their bread and butter, the thing that revs them up, fuels them, and gets them excited for opportunities like play, training, sport, and exercise. During Exposure, we first continue to develop food and prey drive. This paves the way for pack and defensive drives, which come naturally with maturation. We continue to use exercise, training, and sport to build these drives, introducing greater formality in training and beginning to work in a dropped-leash capacity, with the goal being the ability to work fully off leash at Stage 3.

# Food Drive

If we did our work correctly at Stage 1, we should have dogs with a solid or, at the very least, promising food drive. For dogs with behavioral issues, this means that the desire for food is strong enough to want to take the food even if afraid or wanting to react to something. They will not pass on the opportunity to eat. This level of drive helps dogs physically be able to sustain new experiences at Stage 2. As they mature and work their way out of youth and into adolescence, this also leads to the higher-order desires of prey, pack, and defense.

# Prey Drive

At this stage, our dogs should start to show healthy levels of prey drive in accordance with their breed, personality, and temperament. This drive varies greatly among dogs and expresses itself very differently, including by chasing after things, tracking things, and rounding things up, to name just a few examples.

Now, we have the level of relationship that really allows us to play. It's not that we haven't been playing with our dogs all this time, but now we are in a place where we can really engage each other on a similar level, in the same way that we cannot play with children as we can play with teens or as we can play with grown-ups.

Play is powerful—it not only channels dogs physically, mentally, and psychologically, but it also strengthens our bonds and relationships. Our relationship can handle the challenges to our bond created by these games. When that deep, primal prey drive is harnessed appropriately, it becomes an incredibly bonding thing, paving the way for the emergence of pack drive.

There are many ways of initiating play, such as running toward and chasing the dog, running away from the dog, tapping the ground or legs, play bowing, picking up toys, teasing dogs with toys, and so on. We are looking for activities that encourage chasing, grabbing, and tugging. There are countless ways of playing with dogs and many good books with instructions.

Tugging and retrieving are great prey-driven games to play with our dogs. As you strengthen your dog's prey drive and interest in playing tug, begin incorporating tugging exercises, such as the prey cycle exercise that follows.

Another great thing to teach your dog is to practice going from stimulation to calmness and back up to stimulation—the on-off switch. To do this, intersperse short pauses into your tugging and obedience games, and conclude the entire session with a grounding exercise before you move to the next item on your schedule.

Some dogs enjoy tugging more than retrieving (and vice versa), others enjoy both, and yet others appear to show interest in neither. I know from Kizzy and other dogs, though, that all dogs enjoy prey games and exercises, so if they don't respond to toys, you can try food. With the treat toss exercise, for example, they can chase after treats.

The magical thing about this process is that we really get to see dogs' true personality and discover what they really enjoy. Because they feel safe with us and trust whatever we share, we can count on their sincere efforts to go along with us and be honest about what they like and don't like.

## Exercise: *Using The Long Line*

Continue to work your skill at handling the long line, especially when you get tangled. Tangling up is inevitable, but it is also an opportunity for training. Instead of fixing it for the dog, loosen up the line and give the dog the chance to think about their own body and getting themselves out of the line.

Whether working on treat toss, hand lure, or this way (see chapter 7), at Stage 2 the focus is expanding toward proximal, interactional, and oppositional socialization. Begin challenging these long-line exercises in spaces that are new and busier spaces (spatial), at a distance from people and animals (distal), moving closer and closer to people and animals (proximal), and potentially in the way of intrusions (oppositional).

At Stage 2 we also begin introducing drag-line work. This means you are attempting these exercises with the dog dragging the line instead of it hanging on your wrist. We are working our way toward having no leash on the dog as you play these games, which we'll talk more about in Stage 3.

## Exercise: *Prey Cycle*

The prey cycle exercise is one I learned after spending a short stint at a working dog club. This exercise requires that we have some experience already tugging with our dogs and that they love the game. It requires you use a tug toy attached to a cord or rope of about four to six feet in length. Prey cycle is a terrific way of embedding tug-of-war into a wider cycle of exercises that all tie well together, creating a structure around the important game of tug. It includes the following six commands in sequence:

→ **Bark:** The game starts with the dog being taught to bark. Show a driven dog your tug while holding them back from getting it, and soon enough you'll hear vocalizing. You can build that into barking if you don't get the full thing the first time around.

→ **Bite:** The dog barking is our prompt to toss out the tug while holding on to the cord and letting the dog chase and grab it. We think of the tug as a prey animal, a hare for example, desperately trying to get away, running in opposite directions to confuse the predator. We make it hard enough but not impossible.

→ **Pull:** Once the dog has bitten on the tug, we pull on the cord and shake it, again keeping in mind that this is a prey animal desperately fighting for its life. We tug with the dog and soon enough drop the cord, letting the dog win.

→ **Carry:** The victorious dog gets to carry the tug around, showing off their win with lots of praise and encouragement.

→ **Hold:** Next, we stop the dog's movement, asking the dog to sit still with the tug in their mouth. We engage in a fake attempt to take the tug, asking the dog to hold. We see the dog resist the fake attempt by turning away or biting down harder.

→ **Out:** After lots of practice and confidence, begin introducing the out command, which requires the dog to drop the toy. There are many ways of teaching this—for example, using a treat, waving another toy, walking the dog until it drops the toy, or asking for a lie-down command that will distract the dog from the toy. Once out is mastered, we teach the dog to out and then immediately bark again, beginning a new prey cycle.

# Pack Drive

I don't know about you, but I would personally have a hard time playing with someone I didn't know. I couldn't really let my hair down with someone I didn't trust enough to be open and real with. Play is vulnerable because we're going back to a childlike, innocent state. Researchers tell us that among the reasons why we're so close to our dogs is because we're both neotenic—meaning we both retain childlike behaviors and attitudes well into adulthood, including a propensity for play.

Harnessing desires for food and prey through play behaviors is what awakens pack drive. Pack drive is the mature desire to please, connect, bond, and belong with a family. Simply put, it's the dog's love toward us. Our dog has a pure desire to please because we've become worthy in their eyes. As pack drive strengthens, the love deepens. We aim to mature the dog so we can rely less on extrinsic motives and more on knowing that it's our relationship, our love, that makes us do things for each other.

Pack drive is a hallmark of maturity and depth in our bond. But until our dogs have healthy food and prey drives, let's not expect love and bond. An infant can love, but they don't truly understand love like an adult because they require that their needs (drives) be met first. While we have dogs who are not really eating, we're not going to have pack drive. If they're not really being channeled in prey, we're not really going to have pack drive. But when the drives are harnessed, the dog matures, and bonds deepen.

One of the ways we start to see a growing bond between us is in how much our dogs are paying attention to us, how quickly they recall to us, and how loosely they walk on leash. We all want to be able to walk our dogs on a loose leash, and yet many of us struggle to do so. Our dogs pull us, chase after moving objects, and might even exhibit leash aggression.

I hope you realize by now that leash manners are not just a matter of training. Rather, they reflect attitude and bond. When we have a bond, we have dogs looking up at their people and minding them, walking on a loose leash because they want to be near.

## Exercise: *Loose-Leash Walking*

All long-line exercises are about preparing us to walk on a loose leash and to engage in one of the most rewarding activities: being able to walk our dogs anywhere with them close and attentive. Let's summarize how you've been gradually working toward walking your dog on a loose leash:

At Stage 1, you will have introduced your dog to the long line and played a fair bit with your long-line exercises. You will have worked toward some loose-leash walking, emphasizing primordial socialization as well as spatial and distal.

At Stage 2, it becomes easier to practice loose-leash walking, progressing to incorporating elements in proximity—for example, being able to walk on a loose leash on a busy sidewalk. You also incorporate interactional—for example, walking on a loose leash with another person and perhaps their dog. You can start going for walks as now the dog ignores things, understands spaces, can work on a loose line, and can perform right and left turns, all while staying engaged with their handler.

The natural extension of loose-leash walking is walking with no leash. At Stage 2, we start working toward this freedom. Choose a space to work your dog and be sure to have treats or toys in your pocket. Visualize your invisible line on the ground, start by grounding with your dog at the top, and begin line exercises like treat toss, hand lure, and this way (see chapter 7) with a long line.

Hold onto the line at first, then drop it and let it drag for a few rounds. Practice in short spurts and end successfully. The goal is to work up to never holding the line and then taking the line off the dog altogether.

By now, you know how to layer the environments as you attempt a new exercise. So when working on loose-leash and eventually no-leash skills, carefully choose the spaces most likely to help you succeed.

At this stage, your dog should not require the leash to stick around. If you've layered things correctly and taken your time, off-leash work will come naturally. This doesn't mean there won't be times where your dog will be distracted by things, run after things, or take a little time to follow. You can step on the line, get a hold of the line, or simply walk away with the confidence that you've raised a dog that will run right back looking for you.

This means that teaching dogs to be loose will involve an element of risk. It is a worthwhile risk in my view, as it means teaching dogs to be free. Psychologically, we must be prepared for contingencies. When I'm in a touchy situation, the sure way for things to go from bad to worse is for me to get upset. So teaching dogs to go off leash means I need to take measured risks, help my dog succeed, and stay calm no matter what.

# Defensive Drive

With the gradual strengthening of food, prey, and pack drive, we see the emergence of a healthy defensive drive. Healthy defensive drive is not fear or aggression. It is not frantic reactivity. It is a healthy desire to protect that which we care about, and by now, our dogs care about us in deep and meaningful ways.

Defensive drive is a hallmark of a mature and bonded dog, and a healthy defensive drive response means the dog perceives potential threats accurately and modulates their response. When people with a new dog tell me that their dog is being protective of them by barking at everyone, I tell them that is unlikely, as dogs should not overreact to normal situations. The dog is most likely freaked out for not being regulated and is barking out of fear, not defense.

Often, people think it's okay and even good if their dog barks when someone comes to the door, as they want the dog to be a guard dog. Once, when a cleaning lady that my dogs had seen before came into the house, she mentioned being surprised that none of them barked. My dogs didn't see the need to waste their breath as it was her, not some serial home invader, at our doorstep.

The sight of a dog that is appropriately defensive in the later stages of a healthy relationship is very different from a dog that is freaked out. Defensive drive is understated, such as a low growl from the gut. Depending on what is happening, I can ignore the light display of defense—for example, one of the dogs growling because the mail carrier just came by. More often, though, I take note and see what's happening, often thanking the dog for alerting me to things. I praise them if it was something worth mentioning and walk away if not.

Just like other aspects of personality, dogs differ widely in their drives. The myriad combinations of breed, background, temperament, and way of life can produce dogs that are immensely different. One of my dogs, Bruna, has a decent food drive, moderate prey drive, and exceptional pack drive—my affection, approval, and her ability to be with me are everything to her. She is outstanding in helping me with clients, as she's happy to just be around, no matter what. She knows what to do according to what I am doing, without me asking. Being attuned to me and responding accordingly is what makes her the happiest.

# Exercise

At Stage 2, there is less of an emphasis on tiring the dog out, but physical exercise continues to be essential for the dog's physical and mental well-being. We have come to appreciate that when we are exercising our dog, it's never just physical. Any exercise we do with our dog includes physical, social, behavioral, mental, and psychological aspects. Exercise in a new place is not the same as exercise in a familiar place. Exercise around stimuli is not the same as exercise in a quiet space. And so on.

At Stage 1, we stuck to specific places and kept socialization with others primarily at a distance, teaching the dog to ignore things. Now our exercise takes place in new and more places, as we widen the dog's world and progress along the levels of socialization. We exercise while ignoring things in closer proximity and work toward interacting with people and animals. Whether we like to walk, run, jog, swim, or hike, or we're talking about a disk session, ball playing, or tug-of-war, we're taking our exercise to new places and coming in closer contact with other parties.

# Training

At Stage 1, we avoided formal training, relying on setting the dog up to succeed at each outing and capturing any good behavior with praise and rewards. The dog has grown in self-esteem thanks to the structure and success created for them. Because we have thoughtful creatures who are bonded to us in a healthy way, our training need not be relentless. We do not need to kill ourselves with endless repetitions.

Therefore, we continue to emphasize the dog's capacity to think. Any time I do not need to say something, I stay quiet and let the dog think about what needs to be done. Staying quiet means it matters when we do speak, easing our transition into more structured and formal ways of learning. Our dog is also increasingly shifting from working for extrinsic rewards, such as food and play (food and prey drive), to intrinsic rewards, like pleasing their people (pack drive).

We have a dog who has grown in strength and drive, giving us more that we can work with. This is a time to channel our dog's prey drive in games of ball and tug and other activities that are physically, mentally, and psychologically fulfilling. As our dogs grow stronger, our approach is also "stronger" in that we apply discipline and redirect the dog as needed. Exposure is also an appropriate time for the pressure and challenge that both dog and handler are likely to feel in group classes as well as in structured activities and sports. Decompression after new or strenuous activities continues to be important.

We will start to see dogs that are functionally obedient, meaning they listen without having been programmed into responding to cues. So if obedience training is your thing, go for it. But if you've done Way of Life in stages, you will see how little traditional training is needed for sound and stable dogs. When dogs have foundations, when they have experienced exposure to things in measured ways with us as a safe base, they are now thoughtful enough to know what needs to be done on their own.

This includes our dogs' growing capacity to work off leash. If we have done things correctly this far, there's no reason why our dogs can't sustain being trained to be off leash. After all, they are bonded. They're happy to be with us, so why would we worry? In training, as in the socialization and drive exercises, we begin introducing drag-line work. The line isn't just something for me to grab if I must; it also has an anchoring effect on the dog. With time, we work on easing both our and our dog's reliance on the leash.

## Exercise: *From Do Something To Basic Obedience*

At Stage 1, we used the do something exercise (chapter 7) to encourage dogs to volunteer behaviors that we could reward them for. At Stage 2, we begin to attach words to the behaviors they've become good at volunteering and lure them into doing others. Also, any good obedience trainer will tell you to proof your basic obedience cues with these three indicators:

→ **Distance:** You're able to direct your dog further and further away from you.

→ **Distraction:** You're able to direct your dog with distractions around.

→ **Duration:** You're able to ask your dog for greater duration on each of the cues.

We expose the dog to obedience in cue form, teaching common commands, including the following:

→ **Sit:** Sitting is one of the most volunteered behaviors, and likely, our dog will have volunteered it many times over during Stage 1. While playing with do something, attach the word "sit" anytime the dog sits. Eventually, we cue the dog to sit and offer a reward. We can also lure the dog's nose in an upward motion, guiding the dog into a sit position to help this along.

→ **Stand:** It is possible that the dog may have volunteered standing while we played our do something exercises. In that case, we simply attach the word "stand" anytime the dog stands for us. We can also lure the dog into a stand by drawing the treat away from a seated dog's nose and then keeping the fist closed a moment for the dog to realize that standing is what gets rewarded.

→ **Stay:** With your dog sitting or standing, say "stay" while you continually treat the dog. Eventually, space out the treats while still asking for the dog to stay. Progress to stepping away from the dog while asking the dog to stay. Make sure you end the stay command with a release word such as "okay!" or "break!"

→ **Lie down:** Lying down can also be a commonly volunteered behavior while we practiced do something. In that case, we simply attach the word "down" anytime the dog lies down. We can also lure the dog into a down by drawing the treat from a seated dog's nose to the floor and then keeping the fist closed a moment for the dog to realize that lying down is what gets rewarded.

→ **Come:** By now, we matter to the dog. By keeping its world simple at first, we imprinted ourselves as the focus of the dog's world. This means we have a dog who comes gladly, so it will be easy to attach the cue "come" to this behavior.

→ **Get out:** Teaching dogs to leave our space is just as important as asking them to come in. However, it can be a little harder on the dog to be asked to leave than to be asked to come, and that's why it's not something we start with. Revisit the get out exercise from chapter 9, and make a game of throwing treats out of your inner circle, asking the dog to get out and quickly calling them back in.

## Exercise: *Heeling And Turns*

Continue to work your long-line exercises (including recalls, dual recalls, treat tosses, hand lures) as well as simply working on a long line, going back and forth and eventually working toward shortening the line, walking on a loose line, and gradually progressing toward heeling.

Heeling means the dog walks parallel to us, usually on the left, the right side of their head against our left leg and no more than a few inches apart. Just as with any command, when the dog is performing the behavior easily, introduce the cue. As you become more and more comfortable with loose-leash walking and heeling, work on introducing turns, including right and left turns.

→ **Right or Supportive Turns**
With the dog on your left, turn to the right, *away* from your dog. Praise the dog for following. Your dog must do a somewhat-wide turn around you, and because of that, Sam Malatesta used to call this a "supportive turn." Other trainers dub it an "emphatic right turn," as you are suddenly turning in the opposite direction to get the dog to follow.

→ **Left or Confrontational Turns**
With the dog on your left, turn to the left, *into* your dog. In this case, your dog must sidestep to give you room and then find their place next to you, which is why Sam called this a "confrontational turn." Praise the dog for doing so.

## Exercise: *Tie-Out*

The tie-out is a frequently used exercise in many sport and obedience disciplines. The idea is for the dog to sustain the vulnerability that it is likely to feel being tied to something. Think about all the situations in which a dog could be tied out—the groomer's, the vet's, sporting events, obedience class, and just about any situation where whether for a moment or longer, we need the dog secured.

This exercise is for the later stages of Exposure, and as usual, we begin in a restricted area without distractions and work our way to busier places while protecting the dog from intrusions. Living in a city and before pandemic times, I recall often seeing dogs tied to a restaurant or patio fencing with people passing by and sometimes walking over and touching the dogs while the owners were dining. This is not a proper way to tie out a dog. Dogs should feel safe from unwanted invasions.

# Sport

Remember at this stage, we are challenging our bond because that is how it grows and strengthens. It's okay for us to be in situations with our dogs where we're not seeing eye to eye or where we argue. This happens a lot in sport. In herding class, it could be the dog deciding to blow you off and do their own thing with the livestock. In agility, the dog might run around in circles instead of along the obstacles as directed. In scenting class, the dog could scope the premises and mark instead of looking for scent.

Think about it—you're both under the stress that comes with learning something new. We're in a new space with new people and other dogs. The dog must do something, and our job is to walk the dog through it safely and effectively. We're also under performance pressures—our teacher is showing us the ropes (however effectively), and other students are watching, evaluating, and judging us.

At Stage 2, the dog will start to be able to handle these more complex situations. This means we can participate in group classes and sport classes after having introduced the dog to the disciplines at Stage 1. Chapter 7 details different sports available for dogs and handlers of all kinds, and hopefully at this point, you've done some preliminary investigating to see what speaks to you and what's available in your area. Now, you can begin incorporating sport and possibly trialing into your Exposure stage, keeping a close eye on how your dog responds to these new and strenuous situations.

By now we know that when we put the pressure on, we go back to decompressing. If I am asking much of my dog in some avenues, I will ask for less in others. So make sure that after these taxing outings, the dog is getting plenty of time in the crate to be alone, rest, and fully integrate what they have learned.

Drive development at Stage 1 involves optimizing food drive and shifting the emphasis toward prey drive as a maturing drive and one that will pave the way to emerging pack drive, the motivation to bond, please, and belong. We practice our exercises at higher levels of socialization, introduce our dogs to off-leash work, and elevate our participation in sport.

## CASE
# Pixie and Dixie, the Boxer-Shepherd Sisters

Boxer-shepherd mixes Dixie and Pixie were found behind a restaurant and taken to the city shelter. These sisters were estimated to be about 10 months old but weren't considered bonded enough to be adopted out together. Thus, Dixie went to my client, an active woman who loved fitness and being out with her dogs. A few months later, she got wind of the fact that Pixie was still at the shelter and didn't hesitate. She turned up with Dixie in tow only to lose her a few moments later, as Dixie had taken off to the kennel where she and Pixie had been. It was clear to my client that she had to keep the sisters together, and so Pixie came home with them.

Fast-forward to when this client got in touch: the sisters were about seven years old and exhibited a range of issues, making it nearly impossible for my client to go anywhere with them. Pixie and Dixie were restless, constantly running the fences in the yard, reactive to dogs and kids on the streets, and had killed a few squirrels, raccoons, and stray cats:

*I have two shepherd-mix dogs. They are amazing dogs. However, their prey drive is starting to become a huge problem. They have issues with anything that is smaller than they are: cats, other dogs, squirrels, raccoons, skunks, kids. I would love to be more active with them like we used to, but because of this issue it is nearly impossible to take them anywhere, especially with other dog owners leaving their dogs off leash. I really need help.*

# The Issues

As usual, I began with this client by exploring the sisters' way of life, including physical and psychological aspects. The client was clearly in love with her dogs, and the lack of a family hierarchy was part of the problem.

Adopting siblings isn't normally considered a good idea, as sibs raised together can display dysfunctions commonly referred to as "littermate syndrome." These issues are believed to occur because fraternal bonds hinder the formation of healthy connections with humans and deter the development of skills to deal in a human world. The siblings can be inseparable, or they can be in an all-out war, sometimes requiring that one be rehomed. In this case, the two sisters had been together from the beginning with only a brief time apart. They never had the chance to individuate, meaning to become their own dog without being blended with the other sibling.

In addition to that, there were no crates and no schedules, no structure to speak of. I coached my client to rethink the idea that the girls had high prey drive—maybe they did, but the aggression she witnessed was essentially redirected frustration. As you know by now, we manage first and label later.

# A New Way of Life

One of the first things I coached my client on was to not allow herself to entertain the thought that her dogs were "amazing" while the problem behaviors were still happening. She had to begin with an emotional distance from the dogs, that polite indifference rather than showering them with love.

We introduced a new level of structure in the household, which included setting a schedule and crating the girls. It involved separating the sisters, who had lived together 24/7 for the last six years. The beginning stages were very difficult. It was about three weeks of escape attempts, barking, and soiling in the crate. I know many would back off and say this is too much or consider this cruel to the dogs. It isn't cruel—the behavior was a normal response of the dogs challenging my client's right to separate and crate them because in their eyes, she didn't have the foundational relationship to make that decision. My client held on, in spite of vehement protests from her parents, whom she lived with.

To support their individuation, we set separate schedules for the dogs, including dedicated exercise and bonding time, crating, and hangouts in designated parts of the house for each dog. It was weeks before the girls left the property, but when they went out into the world again, they did so with a completely different mindset. Who else had changed? My client, of course.

## The Results

After their initial fierce resistance, the sisters finally let go and allowed calmness and peace to wash over them, relieved that someone finally understood how they needed to be treated. At seven years old, the girls were becoming more mature physically. They still put up a good bit of resistance—after all, it had been years of living constantly together, being treated as one, and not being allowed to individuate and mature on their own. So, that needed some time to come undone. But I could tell from their eyes and graying faces that they were ready for some peace and that they wanted someone to make the decisions for them. While they wanted to be challenged and engaged with, they also needed time to rest and recuperate in private.

Because one could no longer feed off the other, the girls eventually settled down. It was several weeks of them sleeping for hours on end in their crates, decompressing from years of stress. For the first time, my client was able to understand each dog as an individual and to appreciate each one's personality, and she began noting things that she'd never seen before.

Their fence running ceased. They became indifferent to dogs and cats on the street. When alone outside, instead of being on the prowl for critters, they hung out on the deck close to the kitchen door. With time, we brought the girls back together by gradually reintroducing them and reintegrating them. By now, each one had been worked with as an individual. Each one was bonded to her person, was calmer, and had her prey drive channeled in the correct exercises.

By the time my client had to leave the sisters to travel overseas, we had established a way of life that worked for the dogs and the entire family. This allowed my client's parents to keep the sisters during her absence rather than board them at a facility. Maintaining a schedule and hiring a seasoned walker who was given specific instructions helped Pixie and Dixie be able to sustain a long absence from their owner. Their behavior not only didn't regress; it continued to improve, allowing the family to begin exposing the girls to more, particularly to children in the extended family, which they were able to do successfully now that they had a healthy way of life and solid relationship foundations.

# For Reflection

1.  How would you describe your dog's food drive at this stage? How is their weight and physical condition?

2.  How would you describe your dog's prey drive at this stage? How would you describe the quality of your engagement and play with your dog?

3.  In what ways are you seeing pack drive, or even defensive drive, emerging in your dog?

4.  How is your approach to exercising your dog evolving? What are your preferred ways of giving your dog a good workout, and what ways does your dog respond to most positively?

5.  Of the exercises and variations of exercises explored so far, which have proven challenging? Why do you think that is? How can you strengthen your dog's understanding of those exercises?

# SOLIDIFYING AND ENJOYING OUR BOND

# CHAPTER 12

# Relationship, Mission, and Mindset at Stage 3

Love one another, but make not a bond of love:
Let it rather be a moving sea between the shores of your soul.

—**KHALIL GIBRAN,** Lebanese author and poet

*M*any years ago when I still volunteered at my local humane society, I was asked by the K9 staff to coach a new volunteer, David, who apparently had pestered them with requests for additional training. For several months, I coached David on handling the more challenging shelter residents, and with the keenness and capacity he was showing, I encouraged him to grow his learning by fostering. A year or so later, he was ready to foster now that he'd secured a rental home with a small yard. He brought home Snickers, an American foxhound who was found as a stray and taken in by a local shelter before being transferred to ours.

David is one of the people I coached the most intensely, speaking to him once a day on average for the first year that he had Snickers. Snickers had already been returned after two failed adoptions that included multiple bite incidents. He developed severe anxiety, was fitted into a ThunderShirt, and put on antidepressants. Sadly, but not surprisingly, nothing seemed to help.

When David brought Snickers home, he immediately started the decompression process, which meant weaning him off the medication under the supervision of a vet. It also meant several hours in the crate alternating with outings in the yard, mostly alone but always under David's watchful eye. Snickers tried escaping several times, from the crate and from the yard. He also had eye problems and did not particularly welcome David giving him his eye drops.

David understood that Snickers would stop trying to escape once he felt safe in the daily structure, so he stuck to his guns. David didn't talk nor expect much in those early days. He simply worked to establish a predictable routine and met the dog's basic needs. He located a park for vigorous exercise sessions and a quiet alley near the house where they spent many weeks doing their exercises, hanging out, and eventually playing.

As expected, Snickers began calming down, and David noted fewer episodes of barking in the crate or escaping from the yard, signaling that it was time to do more. For a while, every change of environment caused Snickers to regress and revert to the anxious ways of the past. David had to learn patience and not pile unfair expectations on him.

In about six months, he got the dog ready for adoption but, unfortunately, was not allowed to participate in Snickers' adoption process. So David decided to keep Snickers, whom he renamed Doug, as he wasn't about to let months of hard work fall into the wrong hands.

Adopting Doug gave him the opportunity to finish his training and integrate him into his life as a mature, bonded, and fully off-leash capable animal. Thanks to this "failed" foster experience, David was able to learn the entire process of working with a dog from early decompression days to Foundations and Integration, applying the process almost to perfection. He was able to finish Doug's rearing, turning the once-medicated hound into a sound, strong, and spirited dog who lived free until his last breath.

At Stage 1, we established solid foundations by keeping things simple and structured. At Stage 2, we challenged our emerging bond to strengthen and deepen our relationship through exposure to new places, people, animals, and activities. Stage 3, Integration, is the last stage in our rearing and relationship. We polish all the work we have done, transitioning our dogs to maturity, freedom, and inclusion.

It's important to remember that integration is not an either-or situation. From the start, the dog was integrated in our home; the question is one of degree. This entire method is built on gradually increasing that level of integration in accordance with the dog's psychological maturity.

The process is also iterative in that we go back and forth between stages as opposed to solely following a linear progression. For example, when we expose the dog to new things, we go back to decompression and more crate time— those foundational pieces—allowing the dog time to adjust to changes. The same is true as we progress toward Integration.

Integration is the state and relationship we've wanted and worked for all this time. It brings simplicity and ease, knowing we've raised a sound, strong, and spirited dog we can trust and include in our life. We've done our job. Now, we get to enjoy our bond and let it solidify and age like a good wine.

## The Adulthood Stage

Integrated dogs are adult and mature dogs, not merely because of their chronological age. They are dogs who have been extensively schooled at Stage 2. They would have done this and that, come with us to visit friends and family, gone to the garage sale, gone to this class or this sporting practice, and so on. The dog is with us, doing different things and behaving.

At Stage 3, our dogs are "graduating." Now, they can be trusted with increasing levels of freedom and rewarded with greater assimilation into our homes and lives. Adulthood is about being thoughtful, trustworthy, and functionally obedient. This is not the mechanical obedience that would have been conditioned or trained into the dog. It is the natural obedience that comes with regard, respect, and having raised our dogs right.

# Relationship

Going back to the concept of the family hierarchy, let's reflect on how we did our job as parents and leaders and where our dogs are in terms of maturity. How are they doing in terms of soundness, strength, and spirit? How good of a job have we done maturing them? What level are they at? What level are we at? Our aim at Integration is nothing less than us comfortably and elegantly in charge and our dogs matured to a place where they can assist us and team up with us.

Our relationship is different at this stage, having been tried and tested at Stages 1 and 2. The bonds between members of a wolf pack are known to be extremely deep, forged in the challenges that they take on as a family—hunting, risking their lives, fighting off intruders, raising their young, and dealing with the elements. Those events create ties that bind, which is what we are creating throughout the first two stages.

In the safety of deep bonds, our dogs reveal themselves for who they truly are—beyond what we thought or taught. We see them and understand them better, in their preferences, idiosyncrasies, imperfections, and personalities. Anything less than Foundations, Exposure, and Integration will only show you a dog who's pretending. But when the dog is honest and has earned their place in the family, I am glad to accommodate their preferences in a way that I couldn't at the start when they were still neurotic and problematic. A mature dog gets to choose.

# Mission

Our mission at Stage 3 is to mature and graduate our dogs to adulthood, meaning they are sound, strong, and spirited. Our dogs are easy around people and social situations and can be trusted to seek us out if unsure. They're nonconfrontational. They're open to new experiences, knowing they're safe with us and that we've succeeded together. They're bonded to us, staying close without direction, but at the same time independent.

At maturity, all drives fall in balance in a way that's genuine for that specific dog. The dog has a healthy food drive. The dog engages in their preferred versions of prey drive. Based on that, the dog has a healthy capacity to be intimate with their person and, accordingly, defend in a way that's healthy, as opposed to frantic and fearful.

In a similar vein, we have strong socialization at all levels. Our dogs can sustain different environments and stimuli near and far. Should they have to deal with invasive interactions, our dogs take them in stride, knowing we are there to keep them safe. One of the ways we can tell a dog is fully integrated is that they don't regress in new spaces. My girls Bruna and Nejra are excellent examples of this; despite often being in new places and around new people when I am working with clients, they remain at ease.

Our mission here is also to free the dog and work with diligence on the capacity for the dog to be off leash. How do we know that we have a good relationship between human and dog? Here are a few questions to help us find out:

→   What happens when we don't have a leash on the dog?

→   What happens when we don't have incentives such as toys or food?

→   What happens if we're quiet and not modulating our voice to get attention?

→   What happens when it isn't just us and our dog?

Where is the dog? What does the picture look like?

We also work toward greater independence, appreciating that a dog that's clingy is not necessarily bonded, just insecure. Bond requires independence. We have dogs we can board or leave at home for long hours if necessary. The dog can now fully participate at home—on our couch, in our bed, included with us, minimally crated, without a leash on, having a measure of choice and freedom. Anyone who has a dog who stays close, does not bother, and is not bothered, knows the joy I'm talking about.

# Mindset

Sam Malatesta trained hundreds, if not thousands of people, but only a handful were able to genuinely finish their dogs. I am seeing the same thing in my own practice. This is because at each stage, we need to keep a certain mindset toward our dogs, which means not letting our emotions or ambitions get the better of us. Every dog has the capacity to be a fully integrated dog, but this is a hallmark of a dedicated handler, and that's not everyone, although I want to believe that it could be.

Our mindset at Integration is that we continue to be the objective handler, dedicated trainer, and supportive teacher. However, our relationship is different now; it has deepened, and we mean much more to the dog. We've now become the dog's safe place. We've now become their role model, partner, and friend—but as any good leader does, we need to continue earning that approval each day.

With that said, I press on you to not let your emotions get the better of you and not be excessive in your feelings toward your dog. There is a level of extreme emotion that owners often put on puppies and dogs that just isn't appropriate—not at the start, not at finishing, and not ever. It is love to figure out the best way to love our dogs.

# Dealing with Aging, Retirement, and Death

A dog's life follows stages: puppy, teen, young adult, mature adult, senior, and geriatric. In German shepherds, for example, the life expectancy is 11 to 13 years, making the dog a senior at around eight years old. As dogs age—just as with people—they not only start to weaken physically, but they also weaken psychologically and start slowing down. They are not geriatric yet; the dogs could even be quite healthy, happy, and having the time of their life, but they're still aging.

## Changes in Senior and Geriatric Dogs

At this stage, dogs become more vulnerable. If you're sensitive to how your dog's eyes look, you will see more frailty in those eyes. The concerns with safety and security that you grappled with at the start could come back in older years when the dogs know their body and mind are slowing down. We will need to go back to protecting our dogs and supporting them, almost like we did at the start.

One of my girls, Kizzy, recently celebrated her 11th birthday, and for about two years, I have been noticing that although her activity level when out and about has not changed much, her need for sleep and rest has increased significantly. When everyone else is up in the morning, ready to go outside for the first outing of the day, Kizzy is still stretched out on the couch, often sleeping in late and coming down when she's ready to start the day. It's wonderful to have raised her in a way that she can be who she is, especially in her golden years.

Issues we once dealt with could resurface, and past anxieties could manifest again. I have lived with Bob for over a decade, and now that he's at that age, there are issues we once dealt with that are rearing their ugly heads again— including anxiety during car rides and possessiveness over toys.

At the same time, something has been happening to make me reflect on whether this resurgence of issues I thought had been dealt with has to do with perhaps too much laxity, too much freedom, and not enough structure. On several occasions when working out in the yard and garden, not far from my van that was open with access to crates, I lost Bob, only to find him tucked into one of the crates in the van. This is the dog who never really cared for crates and preferred the big kennels outside. Could it be that he missed some of the space and privacy afforded by a crate? Could it be that he missed a measure of structure and containment? It helped me to reflect on that and I fine-tuned things accordingly.

## Getting New Puppies

Feeling that their older dogs are getting up there in age, people will sometimes get new puppies while their senior dogs are still around and in their later years. In and of itself, that's not wrong, but what I don't like is when we ask geriatric dogs to put up with this new puppy—to put up with their replacement, basically. When clients tell me they have their senior dog and new puppy together, it makes me cringe. Here is a recent example:

*We have a new rescue puppy. She is four months old. So far, she has been great. We live on 10 acres, so she is outside a lot. Our issue is she has food aggression toward our senior dog and has attacked her twice over food. She came from a place where she was not well fed, so I'm assuming it derives from that. Is this something you could help with?*

When I tell these potential clients that I recommend junior and senior be predominantly separated, they don't always stick with me. They think the puppy can be taught by the older dog and that the older dog needs the entertainment of this young puppy, when in fact, neither wants the other. The young puppy just wants to be young, doesn't want to be bossed by the old dog, and is now unsure of who's really in charge. The old dog doesn't want to have to manage and educate a young puppy; they just want to be old and relax in their old age, but they know you're outsourcing the work onto them. Both lose trust and respect for the owners in that situation. Those are crucial ideas to keep in mind as our dogs age.

## Retirement from Sport

As someone who's in sport, I often see people keeping their dogs engaged in sport beyond what is healthy. I recall a colleague who brought to class her two dogs—the senior one and the young buck. The senior dog was barking in a frantic way and being corrected for it, but it was clear that he was exhausted; he'd had enough already. A few months later, we heard he'd passed away.

Some people in sport think it's okay to bring a dog that old to those situations, watching their younger siblings going at it with full force and vigor. They think including the dog this way means they are still giving them a rich life even though they're old. That's not how old dogs want to get down in their later years; of that, I am sure. Retiring a dog from sport is painful. I get it. It could even be painful for the dog, but we want to retire from sport early enough to give the dog a little bit of juice in their retirement, to adjust to the change, and to enjoy the next chapter.

That is the most important gift to give our senior dogs—is that they understand that they're free to be seniors. What does that mean? They're free to not engage in things if they don't want. They're free to not have to put up with a young dog and have the obligation to raise them. They're free to not have to perform in competitive sport venues.

Of course we can continue to challenge our dogs in their senior years, but when they start becoming a little harder to handle in these venues, they are trying to tell us something. I vote for retiring on a high note. Isn't that one of the enduring wisdoms of dog training?

Our expectations need to change for older dogs. Raising dogs means riding out with them the seasons of their life, from beginning stages when we did fun stuff together to the time where we settle down and take things easy. It bothers me deeply to see old dogs thrown in with young dogs, taken here and there as if they still want to deal with our human BS.

We think we're doing them a favor by pretending old age does not exist. It really reflects the place we live in—our culture's disregard for the wisdom of the ages and our lack of reverence for seniors and their preference for being rather than doing. So while we don't want to retire a dog too soon, we can be aware of what the dog is telling us so we can choose that time and retire on a good note.

## Understanding at the End

Part of life is death, and that's true for everyone. When you're looking at those final months, weeks, and days with your dog, the best advice I can give you is to go in with the same attitude of maturity as you did when your dog began aging. End of life requires a healthy mindset when interacting with the dog just as well, and here we're saying it's all right for the dog to leave when it's time.

There's nothing harder than the loss of a dog we are close to, but there's also something to be said for understanding that the loss is part of the love. Our time is short-lived, and we knew that going in. We embody the right attitude to the very end, so when it's the dog's time to go, we're not the ones holding them back. We also know to move on at the right time and begin a new way of life, with new dogs who cannot wait to become the sound, strong, and spirited dogs produced by the Way of Life method.

At Stage 3, we have raised an adult we can trust, partner with, and rely on. We have a sound, strong, and spirited dog we can enjoy life with, and because the doors are open for a dog like that, new opportunities for learning and growth are continually available. Contrasted with the fragility of childhood we started with, we are now in a strong and grown-up relationship, and our mission is to enjoy this time of adventure and freedom. When we near the end, we face it with the knowledge that it was a life well lived. We did our duty and raised a sound, strong, and spirited dog.

# For Reflection

1.   How would you describe your role toward your dog since you began this journey? How do you feel this role might change as you contemplate your dog's aging, retirement, and eventual passing?

2.   Summarize and recognize your accomplishments with your dog to date. Identify the challenges and growth opportunities that still lie ahead.

3.   At Stage 3, we are asked to think of our dogs as adults. How does seeing your dog this way change your perception of the dog? How does it change your practical approach to dealing with your dog?

4.   What has been your experience with off-leash dogs, whether your own or others? What is different about this approach to and mindset about off-leash dogs?

5.   Which aspects of Stage 3 feel accessible to you, and which ones are you excited about? Which aspects feel challenging? What are you apprehensive or nervous about?

# CHAPTER 13

# Managing Space and Boundaries at Stage 3

Turn lions into pussycats and pussycats into lions.

—**LEO BELLINO,** German shepherd breeder and conformation show handler

*It's a little early for fireworks yet, but Maya can tell that a noisy night is upon us. It's a holiday weekend, and we had a few introductory cracks and crackles earlier, so she knows what's coming. She seeks my gaze, and our eyes meet. "I'm down for the night," she says, her body aiming toward the basement stairs.*

*"Okie dokie," I say. "See you in the morning?"*

*"Yep," she nods, making her way down to the basement with the big crate she still likes to call home.*

*Maya is a finished dog—mature, wise, and fully integrated, which means I trust her with many decisions. She has freedom of choice, and when it comes to fireworks, her choice is to retreat to her crate for the night.*

*When we'd first started this healing process, she suffered from a fear of thunderstorms and fireworks. But instead of letting her act on these fears, I took charge and crated her before the events began. I conveyed to Maya that hunkering down calmly is how I wanted her to deal with things that scared her. She started to* understand that if she was unable to deal with her insecurities constructively, she could not be included in those moments.

When we started moving toward Exposure, she'd become calmer and much of her reactivity was gone. During thunderstorms or fireworks, I'd have Maya on leash, with her mat and chew toys nearby. She often chose to just sleep at my feet and ride out these episodes. Any time she'd tremble mildly to hear the sounds, I was sure to not react, controlling my thoughts and feelings, staying calm and in the moment. I tell my students all the time that when we acknowledge a reaction, we reinforce it. Maya's slight trembling was decent enough coping behavior. She wasn't losing her mind in fear as she once did.

As we moved to Integration, I let Maya choose how she wanted to deal with the situation. Having become deeply bonded and clearheaded, her phobias were downgraded to mild displeasure, which she chose to deal with by retiring to her crate for the night. But there's another powerful factor that helped Maya make that choice: the independence that had been instilled in our relationship. She could do her thing. I did not need her around, and she knew it.

At Integration, we have worked with the dogs, so they have all the tools they need to succeed. Here's the thing though: we're not asking for perfection. As Maya's fear of loud noises suggests, a finished dog still carries limitations. I mean, who among us doesn't have shortcomings? The important thing is that an integrated dog, like Maya, can recognize their limits and deal with them constructively.

With spaces and boundaries, we started strict and simple, eventually expanding the dog's world and educating the dog in these expanding spaces. Now, the dog has graduated, and with maturity comes a different level of handling. At this stage, the dog is an adult, and we can trust them to act maturely instead of based on dysfunctions and insecurities. The dog is not going to make stupid decisions. They're going to think wisely and, thus, deserve that freedom we've all worked for.

It will always be our responsibility to manage our dogs so that they continue to be the sound, strong, and spirited dogs we've raised them to be. For example, after a busy day in sport and with clients, my dogs are quite tired, maybe even a little irritated. It would be wise for me to not ask for more, instead crating them with their dinner and letting them rest for a few hours. That doesn't mean that every time we come in from anywhere, they need to be crated. At Integration, we can use the crate flexibly as we let our schedules change a little more. The idea is not to continue to live on the same schedule for 15 years, but rather to give the dogs safety at the start so that when schedules do change, they can roll with the punches.

When it comes to the leash, again remember we started with the dog being always on leash (Stage 1), to practicing dragging the line and removing the line (Stage 2), to being predominantly off leash (Stage 3). Our way of life and the connection it created is what keeps us together. Freedom is something to be practiced, so let's not give up too quickly if we have incidents of the dog not handling freedoms responsibly.

At this point, we've taught the dog that open doors and gates do not mean they can cross out. They do not mean that what is happening outside is fair game. One of my girls, Nejra, came to me with a wandering habit that got her into trouble. She'd strayed away from her original home, was caught by local animal control, taken to the nearest shelter, and then identified and subsequently surrendered by her former owners.

When I was ready to start trusting her with open doors, Nejra did wander out a few times, never going far, but leaving the yard all the same. One of these times, I happened to be inside, and it was Bob's mild but insistent vocalizing that cued me to check on what was happening.

Sure enough, I saw Nejra in the front yard smelling and marking. I fetched her without any upset; no need to make a big deal of the transgression. I returned her to the yard without closing the gate. Nobody panicked, and no one got angry. If the dog I worked with diligently through the stages ventures off like this, that doesn't mean it's the end of freedom. As with any other trait we cultivate, handling freedom responsibly takes preparation, practice and, as I said before, a measure of risk.

When we are finishing our dogs, it is important that we keep a place for them to retreat to. That's why we keep the crate around permanently. Then, an older dog has a way out of any situation that is uncomfortable or that they don't wish to deal with—boisterous kids, the younger dogs, a deafening action film, or as with Maya, thunderstorms and fireworks. The dogs will have earned the power to make that decision.

Today, I see this at play with Bob, who retreats upstairs when one of my friends comes with his big dog in tow. Bob just can't be bothered with these kinds of interactions, and while I wouldn't allow them anyway, he's the one managing by going upstairs. Thoughtfulness and independence are what allows our finished dogs to make such wise choices on their own. This is the essence of an integrated dog.

Are integrated dogs still on a schedule? A minimum of routine inspires security for any dog. At the same time, dogs that have been raised following the stages are dogs with tremendous stamina because they are clearheaded and not stressed. So the dogs will have earned their way out of the boot camp existence of their younger years.

# The Three Circles at Stage 3

I hope that by now, you've come to appreciate the power of the three circles and how they apply in all aspects of the Way of Life, including managing space and boundaries, socialization, and drive development. At this point we have a dog that knows its place in any space. While we are less concerned about managing or policing the dog, get into the habit of seeing these three circles in any space where you find yourself with your dog.

## The Inner Circle

I go to training venues where people are generally serious about their dogs. But then I watch them waiting in line for their turn in the field, and their dogs just can't sit still. They whine, whimper, pull to check someone out, and so on, unable to sit next to their person.

I took to heart what Sam Malatesta used to say to his students: "If your dog isn't sitting calmly and proudly next to you, I'm sorry but you have nothing with your dog."[12] Sounds harsh, doesn't it? But it's true. Why would my dog—whom I have fed, trained, and looked after—not sit quietly and pay attention to me?

The key to this is that we are calm and that we have done our work right from the start up until this point. We have protected the inner circle from intrusion. We have taught the dog that it is safe to come in and that it's a space where we can just be together quietly.

## Exercise: *Grounding*

The grounding exercise is one I encourage you to continue using as needed throughout your dog's life. It's an opportunity for you and your dog to hang together, breathe, and take things in until you're both in sync and good to tackle the next thing:

→ You just stepped out of the house and are about to go for a walk.

→ You're about to load the dogs in the van, heading to an all-day hike.

→ You just arrived at the sport venue for a trial.

→ You've walked a fair bit already and could use a break.

→ You just got back home after running a few errands with the dog in tow.

These are all opportunities to bring your dog into your inner circle and reset. I hope you appreciate by now how foundational the grounding exercise is and how important it is to practice it in different places and with different levels of socialization present. You work toward a place where your dog is calm at your side, no matter what, no matter where, no matter whom you're talking to.

---

12  Sam Malatesta and Souha Ezzedeen, "One with Dog: Sam Malatesta's Whelping Box Approach to Rearing and Training Dogs," (unpublished manuscript, Canadian Intellectual Property Office: Copyright Registration #1130736, 2016), 27.

At Stage 3, you continue to ground with your dog in different environments (spatial), inside and outside the house with people, animals, and things at a distance (distal), or with stimuli nearby (proximal). A new focus in the early stages of Integration is grounding with your dog off leash, where the only thing keeping them there is your bond.

If you have multiple dogs, multiple dogs can ground around you—with the understanding that the respect you taught them means some will be in your inner circle and others in your tranquil circle, but all are within correct boundaries and neither one is infringing upon the other. When you teach dogs to respect your space, they learn to appreciate their own space and that of others.

Along with the inner circle being a safe place for dogs to come in, it is also safe to be asked to get out. The expression I use is "okay, go on now." Because access to that space is not taken for granted, our dogs respect that space, ask to come in, and can tell when it's a good time and when to steer clear.

## Exercise: *Come Here, Get Out*

For those of us with multiple dogs, respect for the inner circle can make all the difference in terms of keeping the peace between the dogs. No one dog can stake a claim on being in that space. My Malinois Nejra loves being close, right there in my inner circle. That might appear fine enough until we realize that in a multidog situation, this could be construed by the other dogs that they cannot come in because the space is occupied, unless of course I call them in. That's why I love playing this game with multiple dogs.

Begin with two dogs around you in the tranquil circle. Send dog A a little further out with a treat toss, call dog B into your inner circle, and spend a moment with that dog there. When dog A returns after finding the tossed treat, see to it that they give you space. Ask them to stay out, or ignore their attempts at butting in, all while making sure that dog B stays there in your inner circle. Then send dog B out with a treat toss, calling dog A to come into your space. Send dog A back out as you call dog B back in, and so on.

# The Tranquil Circle

When our dog is out with us, being within the tranquil circle is the default location. Our dog is now accustomed to finding their spot within a short distance from us, minding their space, ours, and that of others. This is where the dog wishes to be. It is where the dog is serene and in good company.

The dog automatically finds their spot and stays out of trouble when they can see that we are occupied elsewhere. For example, any time I am out gardening, I move to different spots around the yard, the front, the back, this bed, that bed. As I move, the dogs move with me and lie down a few feet away, some closer and some a little further, all of them in my orbit. I don't need to ask; this has become habit.

We're also less dogmatic about things at this point. This means that as the dogs mature and grow in independence, they get to choose to be further away from me. They get to go near the boundaries a little more, particularly windows and entry/exit points. They can now be trusted in these spaces.

In addition, we can begin giving dogs a way out. As my dogs mature and some of them have begun aging, they all know that it is okay to leave a space if they need to. Maya knew she could leave my space and find her crate on stormy nights. Kizzy knows it's all right for her to sleep in and not start the day with everyone else. Note that the dog needs to sense that you bless that independence. You're allowing the dog that measure of choice and are not needy of their presence.

## Exercise: *Mat Time*

At Stage 3, you strengthen your dog's capacity to park themselves around you in any given situation, with the added challenge of doing this off leash and with more than one of your dogs, if that's your situation.

→   With spatial socialization, your off-leash dogs find their place in your orbit without encroaching upon each other in different places and environments and without much introduction needed to that new environment.

→ With distal socialization, the dogs can do so with stimuli at a distance, which they've become pros at ignoring.

→ With proximal socialization, they can do so with stimuli considerably closer, which the dogs also ignore. But at times, they will move away from the stimuli, especially if the exposure is experienced as confrontational.

→ With interactional and potentially oppositional socialization, they learn to still hang in the tranquil circle, even as you engage with others or are potentially fending off an intrusive person or dog.

## The Territorial Circle

While at this point our dog is allowed near the territorial line, here's the thing: they don't really want to be there. The dog is mature enough to know that their place is in the tranquil circle, and the dog does not step beyond the territorial circle without checking in with you. When out in the yard, the dog stays within the center of the yard near the house and not by the fences. If the dog does happen to be at a boundary, we don't have abuses of power resulting in inappropriately defensive behavior.

It is important that the dog can make decisions within a space but that the dog does not decide to leave a space. For example, if I am taking the garbage bins out from the driveway crossing the sidewalk onto the boulevard to the street, Bruna follows me down the driveway and then stops of her own volition. I do not need to tell her; she stops, knowing the sidewalk is the territorial line.

When someone is at the door, she and the other dogs stand away from the door—again from their understanding that the territorial boundary is not their concern. When we're on hikes and we come across people (often with dogs), my dogs find their way back to me. It's all right if we're occasionally taken by surprise. We're less concerned with avoiding people and animals at this stage, but the dogs know to stick with me and walk on by quickly.

By now, minding us around doors, gates, and around any other territorial boundaries is second nature to the dogs. The mind me and territorial line approach (TLA) exercises are now about reinforcing our dogs' understanding that they do not necessarily accompany us to that territorial line, much less walk through with us. When crossing into new spaces, all dogs need at this point is a pause and permission to follow us. We can keep doors and gates open, and we don't have dogs flying through, ensuring both safety and liberty. Imagine what happens when you open a front door, gate, or car door—you don't have dogs leaping out into dangerous situations.

## Exercise: *Territorial Line Approach*

The idea of TLA is emphasizing to the dog that it should hang back as we approach a territorial line. Another person approaching us signals a territorial line. Other dogs approaching us signals a territorial line. Doors, gates, thresholds, and other physical or natural boundaries are all territorial lines.

At Stage 3, continue to build on this exercise and the variations in chapter 9. However, you eventually get to a place where you don't need to stage this as an exercise as much. You can walk more naturally toward those territorial lines with your dog that gets it and circles behind you and lets you lead the way, in both safety for themselves and deference toward you, whether on or off leash.

We started off with heavy regimentation at the start precisely to end up in a place of true freedom, choice, and agency for our dogs. While we continue to manage to ensure everyone's safety and success, our dogs are increasingly capable of managing themselves, and we can trust them to do so wisely. Stage 3 is simply about solidifying experiences and practicing what was learned at Stage 2 in different situations, at different levels of socialization, and with dogs increasingly off leash.

## CASE
# Nimbus the German Shepherd

Several years ago, I was introduced to Nimbus's owner, an ambitious young man who was going to school and working full-time while still dedicating himself to raising his young pup, a German shepherd. We worked together for a while but then lost touch. I was glad to hear back from him but was dismayed that Nimbus wasn't doing well.

Turns out Nimbus's owner had met someone special. They were in love, had moved in together, and now did not see eye to eye on how Nimbus should be dealt with. Finally my client's partner contacted me, hoping we could pick up where we'd left off all these years ago:

*My partner trained with you a few years ago when he first got Nimbus. In the past two years, I have moved in with him. We are not on the same page with regards to handling the dog. This has led to the dog's increased anxiety as well as reactivity to both humans and dogs. We would like to seek your help in training for both of us to better handle Nimbus and to see him be a more stable dog.*

## The Issues

Indeed, Nimbus had become anxious, stressed, and quick to react to people and animals. He was also potentially dangerous around people; one could not walk by too close without him wanting to grab someone's arm. At home, he paced restlessly, whined, and barked at neighbors. He was hard to handle, impossible to settle, and howled and hollered as if he were being tortured anytime anything would be asked of him.

Even with my experience with Maya and other anxious dogs, I had never encountered anxiety of this scale. More than once, it was suggested that Nimbus ought to be medicated. Given how bad he was, there were times even I couldn't help but wonder if that was the only way. Eventually, with time and incredible dedication by my clients, Nimbus proved us right. Medication wasn't needed; his issues were cured by a change in how he lived—and a change in how his owners lived too.

The differing psychological stances of the owners stressed the dog out, and he suffered from the inconsistencies in how he was handled. The man wanted to do things as I'd originally coached him, while his new partner thought that crates were cruel. Their arguments over Nimbus went on for a couple of years, and Nimbus steadily deteriorated, given the lack of consistency and the constant tensions, which he knew were about him.

## A New Way of Life

By the time my clients had contacted me, they were prepared to make changes, as the quality of life of all members of the household was at an all-time low. We first worked on bringing their mindsets into alignment so that they were both thinking and acting in the same way.

Unless we regulate inside, we cannot expect a dog to be responsive to being regulated outside. Therefore, we crated Nimbus, established a schedule for him, and began seriously challenging him in his outings. Even in their small apartment, when he was out of the crate, he was still blocked off from certain spaces.

We revved up a weak food drive and strengthened his prey drive, tugging and playing ball with him. We discovered that Nimbus was one of those dogs who would want to take his ball with him to heaven. It soothed him to have a ball, and we let him carry it around inside as well as on his walks, which helped tremendously with his reactivity.

## Results

Nimbus's case is a reminder that even a dog set up well with foundations can regress if there's not a consistent approach being applied. As a coach, it was a real thrill for me to see not only Nimbus change but his people change as well. While becoming more and more consistent in handling, they each developed their unique style and cultivated their own bond with the dog. Nimbus doesn't have just one person he looks up to but two.

One of the first signs of improvement was how deeply Nimbus slept, inside or outside the crate, as his anxiety receded. I kept getting videos of Nimbus snoring, sleeping soundly, on his back, sometimes his tongue sticking out in relaxation. He got better all the time at being calm inside and outside the house, ignoring the neighbors, ignoring strangers, dealing better with other dogs. He started to become silly and spirited and, at the same time, more mature and respectful of boundaries.

Over time, his capacity to adjust to new situations grew, and he has boarded with me several times, gaining in confidence each time. It's been a thrill getting videos of him walking loosely in a busy neighborhood and being described by his owners as "pleasant" and "chill."

It took two years, but Nimbus was successfully decompressed, and he and his owners now have solid relationship foundations. Because Nimbus is sounder and stronger than ever before, he responds well when asked to do things, such as leaving something alone that would previously have made him reactive.

Among other successes, my clients have been able to take Nimbus camping, and he successfully met one of their neighbors, a woman who'd followed Nimbus's progress and had made herself available to help socialize him properly—something they had been cautious about due to his anxiety and potential aggression. We must trust that all that good work will pan out, and indeed it did with this German shepherd dog and his family.

# For Reflection

1.  What does your schedule with your dog look like? How has your schedule changed since Stage 2? What are the ways your dog could be better integrated into your work and/or life?

2.  When it comes to space and boundaries, what are the things that you are still working on consistently? What are the things that are easy or innate for your dog now?

3.  What is the role of crating and decompression like for your dog now?

4. What differences do you see in yourself and in your dog as you incorporate the exercises into your way of life (rather than focusing on them specifically for training)?

5. How are you seeing your dog become more independent and thoughtful? What does their decision-making tell you about their personality?

# CHAPTER 14

# Socialization at Stage 3

When a man's best friend is his dog, that dog has a problem.

—**EDWARD ABBEY,** author and environmental advocate

66 *We have a dog that would be good for you," said my humane society supervisor, knowing I was always down for a challenge.*

*"Already?" I thought to myself. I'd just placed my last foster in what hopefully was a good forever home and wondered if I could use a break before the next project.*

*"We're a bit concerned that he doesn't have a good chance if he stays here," he added, sensing my hesitation.*

*"Who is it?" I asked.*

*"It's Bobo, the dog from Taiwan."*

*Bobo was a Formosan mountain dog who'd begun life as a free-roaming dog and then was plucked off the streets of Taiwan and brought to Canada. After about a year of trials and travails with Bobo, he was eventually surrendered to the shelter where I volunteered. I agreed to foster him, renamed him "Bob," and we began our Foundations work.*

*He presented with many issues, including extreme reactivity and combative behavior to dogs and people, refusal to be confined, and possession over food and toys. He was ferocious and tenacious, and especially aggressive to being touched. Crating was one of the hardest parts for him, as he was able to get out of many of the crates*

I tried him in. If your dog is quite big or strong, learn from my mistake and always go for the ironclad option.

Once we figured out what worked for him—which was in my outdoor kennels or crated in the van—he began to rapidly adjust, and we moved into Exposure. My own dogs at the time, Rama and Maya, and a former foster I was boarding named Goliath, were instrumental in helping Bob get back into being around dogs. Since then, he's become a kind of ambassador dog and has helped me with many fosters and boarders.

We have both come a long way since those early days, but there remains caution to be taken around Bob, particularly if being touched by strangers. Yet, one of my proudest moments with Bob was at a local store that allowed dogs. While I was busy bagging my things with Bob hanging behind me politely in territorial line fashion, I turned around to see one of the cashiers hugging Bob, her face next to his.

Despite a powerful combination of particular genetics and a difficult youth, Bob acted as a mature and integrated dog would do in the face of such oppositional and confrontational behavior on the part of a stranger. He gave me a moment to assess and deal. He didn't so much as growl and, if anything, was even more polite than usual, knowing he was in a place with a higher level of expectation.

As soon as I saw what was going on, I asked the woman to leave him alone and to ask next time whether touching the dog was okay. The interaction ended without a problem, but it confirmed that Bob had been raised right and could be trusted to let me deal, even in difficult situations.

It's important to understand that this entire time we've been raising our dogs right, it's not to ask them to put up with what they're not designed to accept. When we raise our dogs while understanding the limits of their tolerance, we nurture their very capacity to be tolerant. Contrary to what some might think, I am good with having dogs who don't wish to be social and who happen to be selective in who gets to touch them. But what they need to be is safe in an event such as the one I share here.

At Stage 3, our dogs are capable of being alone, ignoring things as needed, and interacting with others as appropriate. All the work we did to make our dogs stable means they can be honest with us, making choices and expressing preferences about socialization. If there are ways of interacting or people and animals that do not interest them, it is our place and privilege to respect those wishes, lest we undermine the bond we worked so hard to nurture. They continue to work for food and toys as a form of enrichment and stimulation, but they're also happy to listen with minimal incentive. By now, their pack drive, or love for us, is deep.

Therefore, we continue to give dogs opportunities for alone time, time in the crate (even if minimal), and time alone outside, even if just a little here and a little there, which I promise you, they appreciate even more as they mature. Our primordial socialization is so solid by now that the dog can sustain any of the higher rungs of socialization. They can handle new places. They can ignore all kinds of stimuli near and far and even those that invade our space.

The dog is capable of being handled by other people in various capacities, another form of oppositional socialization. As we have a dog who is bonded and independent, we can put the dog through potentially challenging experiences—being on a tie-out, handed off to someone else for boarding, or dropped off for medical treatment or grooming—without issues. The dog trusts the situation because they trust their human.

# Primordial

Primordial socialization continues throughout the lifetime of the dog. We continue to be the ones handling our dogs, managing them, taking them places, training and sporting with them, having them vetted, grooming them—so on and so forth. The daily activities of care continue, and the quality of these interactions send signals about our attitude and relationship. Continue to foster that strong bond.

# Spatial, Distal, and Proximal

With a dog we are finishing, we work on expanding exploration even more—different environments, different people, different animals and so on—based on what's available and what we want to do. With a fully integrated dog, we can come into a new place, and our dog looks up to us for guidance and adjusts instantaneously, simply because they have us there. When we start going to new places, and the dog is happy rather than apprehensive and hesitant to check out something new, this is a strong sign that the dog is maturing. My emphasis on ignoring things, whether near or far, means that at finishing, my dog's first response to people, animals, and things is to ignore them. At Stage 3, this has become a way of life.

With that said, I encourage you to always familiarize yourself with a space before introducing your dog. When I arrive at a park or trail, even a familiar one, I step out on my own first, look at the premises, see what's going on, and gauge the environment. Are there people over there, or kids over here? I see a bunch of unruly dogs over there—maybe I am better off waiting until they're gone. I get a feel for the environment and then take my dogs out because that allows me to handle them with that much more poise and confidence, translating into them feeling the same. The idea of having finished dogs doesn't mean we don't constantly strive to make things successful for them.

# Interactional

When I introduce people to my dogs, they're often surprised, sometimes even a little hurt when the dogs ignore them. However, when introductions do happen, the people are even more pleasantly surprised at how calm and well-mannered the dogs remain.

As our dogs have more experience interacting with others, this becomes a time when we know their preferences and act accordingly. Stage 3 is about authenticity and us understanding our dogs better. Some are more social than others, some enjoy rambunctious playmates, and others like to simply hang out. Take note of these preferences and manage accordingly. Just because the dogs are integrated doesn't mean we should impose our preferences. If anything, this is a time for even greater respect.

## Exercise: *Having People Over At Stage 3*

One of the pleasures of living with dogs who have been raised to be sound, strong, and spirited is having them participate in our social life with family, friends, and community.

In the early stages of Integration, continue to strengthen the dog's capacity to ignore things that are close and to gauge how the dog is dealing. If you've taken your time with gradual socialization, your dogs should find *you* more interesting and relevant than just about anything. I see this in my own dogs: people will talk to them, try to make eye contact with them, or engage, but my dogs will carry on ignoring them, diverting their eyes, and pulling closer to me.

At Stage 3, intensify opportunities for your dog to interact more freely with your guests. You can start by sending the dog over to say hi and then calling them back to you, reinforcing the idea that you're the one regulating the interactions.

With time, let the dog interact more freely, knowing they're orbiting around you and primarily paying attention to you. Begin allowing the dog out of the crate for longer periods while visitors are around, interacting or simply hanging out. Start with the dog on leash, eventually working your way to having the dog loose around your guests.

Ask your visitors to continue checking in with you on how to deal with your dogs and to take their cues from you. However, if you've come this far, it means you can relax the rules with your guests a little more and let things happen, including oppositional forms of socialization such as someone reaching toward the dog, following the dog, or wanting to touch the dog.

Of course, you're watching and paying attention. A dog you've raised right and exposed gradually might put up just fine with these experiences, or they might find them unpleasant and seek you out. Read the dog and their desire to continue participating. Always try to stay one step ahead of the dog's needs, evaluating their comfort and enjoyment. Decide for the dog when the time is up instead of waiting for the dog to come tell you that they've had enough. Otherwise, party on and enjoy, as both you and your dog have earned it!

# Oppositional

One of the first things people often allow with a new puppy or dog is for other people and animals to come into the dog's space and interact with the dog. Such "confrontations" are considered oppositional socialization, and we underestimate how much they deplete and damage dogs if permitted.

Mature, finished dogs can handle the invasion of their space, though we don't want to make a habit out of it. If someone gets in their faces, they can handle it. If someone wants to pet them, they can handle it. That doesn't mean we overdo it; if we keep it to a minimum, we know the dog can take it, should it happen. We continue to remember that their preference is for us, they're not public property, their space ought to be protected, and their socialization regulated.

Our goal as handlers is essentially to protect the space of our dogs and minimize the likelihood of intrusions. What should we do if we come across loose dogs? Unless I know the people, and we are working toward introducing the dogs so they can have an enduring friendship, I ignore them, and we walk on. When we are going about our day normally, we don't stop and greet and make a big fuss over every stranger we pass. It should be the same for our dogs. When loose dogs approach, I keep walking because I am signaling to my dogs that I did not allow or bless this meeting and that they can follow or get left behind.

## Exercise: *Let It Happen*

As you progress with Stage 3, continue to protect your dog's space but begin to be a little less adamant about it. Start to let things happen and see what you've got. At this point, you've instilled in your dog the idea that your space is sacred and safe, and the dog knows that is the status quo. Invasions of that space are only momentary interruptions, which is what allows the dog to deal with these constructively.

When beginning to practice this, keep it restricted to interactions with people. (We'll talk about engaging with dogs in the next exercise.) I'll give you an example with Nejra and Kizzy—Nejra being a very social dog, and Kizzy the opposite. While their personalities are different, both girls handled the oppositional socialization well.

I happened to be hanging out not far from a community center with Kizzy and Nejra. Out came one kid, followed by another one and then another. All were running toward us. I quickly calculated that this might be a nice opportunity for some socialization with children. I calmly asked my girls to lie down and stay, and I also regulated the behavior of the kids, asking them to touch the girls a certain way, handing them treats to give the girls. There was much loud chatter and laughter, and my girls took it all in stride because everything we'd done had prepared us for something like this. I was also clearly vibing that "spirit of adventure" I mentioned earlier. I kept the interaction controlled and short, and the girls yet again experienced a jump in confidence for having taken on the challenge of oppositional socialization successfully.

## Exercise: *Engaging With Dogs At Stage 3*

As you work in the later stages of Exposure, allowing your dog to begin interacting and playing with other dogs, you will see friendships develop between your dog and their dog friends. Just like us, dogs don't just immediately like other dogs and want to play with them. Some dogs are extremely social and playful with other dogs, but gradual introductions pave the way for lasting relationships.

As a side note, therefore, I don't recommend day cares and dog parks: They completely violate the principle of gradual introductions. It is no wonder so many dogs are considered bad with other dogs—they're simply not given the benefit of phased acquaintance. Friendships do matter to dogs but playing with strangers is not something they want. Sound dogs that have healthy bonds are generally not interested in striking up immediate friendships with strangers.

Just as we start to allow occasional oppositional socialization with people, we do the same with dogs. This begins with us being a little less adamant about protecting our dogs' space. Remember they're primarily focused on you. They've become sound, strong, and spirited. Not only are their food and prey drives strong, but so are their pack drives. As well, defense drive kicks in at maturity, which means that your dogs should have enough spunk and presence to fend off intruding dogs and be strong enough to just go past them because you've taught them that level of respect.

Therefore, imagine you're on a trail, and you come across loose dogs. Your dogs are loose too, but they're around you and have pulled even closer because they see the incoming dogs. Keep on walking, giving your dogs a little time to circle around the incoming dogs, check them out quickly, and then follow you. If you don't stop to meet these unfamiliar dogs, you convey to your dogs that you don't quite approve of this visit. It's okay for them to have a sniff, but we aren't going to linger or engage.

In closing, socialization at Stage 3 is about solidifying all levels of socialization: primordial, spatial, distal, proximal, interactional, and oppositional. At the same time, we continue to govern our spaces and our dogs' behavior in these spaces, setting them up for success, respecting their personal space, and continuing to guide and protect them.

## CASE
# Taco the Orphaned Street Pup

I am lucky that former clients who resonate with my work often refer me to their friends. That is how I met this client, a fiery young lawyer now residing in the U.S., whom I connected with before her pup was even in the picture. Soon after her new puppy Taco arrived, she'd sent me this message:

*We were in Mexico traveling the Baja coast over the weekend. It's incredibly poor in some of these areas, and there are stray dogs everywhere you go. A man living across the street from a taco truck had four orphaned puppies roaming his property, and when he saw us with our dog, he told us to take one of the puppies because their mom had died. So, that's how we ended up with the new addition to our family, Taco.*

I was thrilled for her, knowing she would be the kind of person who would do right by her dog. However, concern creeped in as I read along:

*I didn't know what to expect when taking home a stray puppy, but he's a total gem. Taco follows me everywhere like I'm his mom. He is super easygoing and likes to interact with the 14-year-old German shepherd we have. He's very attached to me and gets vocal when he's not around me or is being held by someone else.*

## The Issues

This message turned on all kinds of warning bells in my head. New dogs shouldn't be following us around, nor do I have them meeting or interacting with the other dogs in the house, especially if these other dogs happen to be geriatric and deserving of their space. One could already see the signs of overattachment, which didn't bode well for Taco's capacity to grow into a sound and strong dog.

While my recommendations for foundations made sense to the client, they didn't go down well with her partner. Despite his mounting frustrations with Taco's house-training difficulties, he still wasn't comfortable crating the pup and saw no issue with having him interact with the older dog. Of course, I could only advise, and it was up to them to decide. She tried applying what she could from all she'd read—working on traditional obedience training (as in conditioning) while continuing with their prevailing way of life.

A few weeks later, she reached out to me again, this time in a very different set of circumstances. She and her partner had split up, and she was moving out with Taco in hand. Of course, now other concerns weighed in the balance, including emotional upheaval, her job stability, and finding a suitable place to live. She was heartbroken and lost, but I also knew that deep down, she was relieved she could do right by Taco now.

Even though the less-than-ideal conditions lasted only a few weeks, they still took their toll on the very young and impressionable pup. The client had to repair her foundations before doing much more. Taco was restless and unable to settle himself or enjoy the deep sleep so endearing of puppies. Getting him engaged in anything was a challenge. He had little interest in playing with toys, tugging, or chasing a ball.

Taco had always been interested in food, but he was so scattered and stressed that he couldn't quite work for food. Any time my client would try to engage him with treats, he would rapidly lose interest or get frustrated, not having the wherewithal to concentrate. On their walks, he was oblivious to his owner and obsessed with whatever the ground offered. Keeping him from devouring food and garbage they passed on the street caused battles. Whenever she did manage to get him engaged in play or to go on a walk, it rapidly escalated to Taco relentlessly nipping her body and tearing her clothes.

## A New Way of Life

We began working together remotely, addressing all aspects in the way of life including the pup's schedule, socialization, and daily manner of handling. As I expected, she dedicated herself to creating a new way of life for Taco—not taking anything for granted, asking questions, and double-checking her decisions. She started by bringing things back to a place of safety and simplicity. In these early days, she crated Taco heavily, giving him the chance to settle himself, let his guard down, and fall asleep, catching up on weeks of insufficient rest.

She also knew she had to dial down exposure and return to a place where it was just mom and pup. In the process, she realized that what she called "the abundance of positive socialization experiences with dogs, people, and kids" was the very reason he'd become skittish and apprehensive about being touched by anyone other than her.

Now, she built a bubble around him, teaching him to see things at a distance and ignore them and to come close to things and ignore them. She kept their outings simple and managed his food intake and physical exercise to begin revving up his food motivation, which made it easier to manage him around the littered streets of the neighborhood.

As Taco began to ease up and mature, she knew she could start expanding his social circle. She identified people in her neighborhood who seemed to have nice dogs, dogs they seemed to have good relationships with, and built rapport with them, creating a network for herself and her dog. Taco was able to enjoy socializing with other dogs and people, as his confidence grew, knowing that anything his owner showed him was safe and good.

# Results

After several months of investing in solid foundations, keeping things simple, structured, and successful, little Taco was developing beautifully despite unfavorable beginnings as an orphan—which many say doom a dog to a lifetime of difficulties and insecurities. Our work together has only strengthened my enduring belief in the power of Way of Life.

He was maturing into a sound and open young dog, ready for the major challenge of relocating with his owner. He flew across the country crated in cargo as if it were nothing. He took the new experiences of the airport, flight, and arrival at the new destination in stride.

At the same time, my client experienced a few setbacks during this relocation, which only elevated her learning. One example was Taco's reaction to her parents when she arrived at their home in Toronto. On the one hand, they could barely contain their excitement at meeting Taco. On the other hand, she knew it was her job to manage and set the right expectations. It was a little too much and too soon for Taco, and he wanted nothing to do with his "grandparents." He expressed this by barking quite aggressively whenever someone other than his owner was near the room he was being crated in.

Changes of environment can cause dogs to regress and withdraw. Socializing with new parties is taxing on dogs in ways we don't always appreciate. That's why when we're in a new place, we dial things down and let the dogs adjust before moving up the rungs of exposure. Once Taco recovered from the change of environment, the confidence of weathering things took his self-esteem and their bond to another level. He has since come around to his grandparents, who visit regularly and bring along his favorite chews.

This client learned that the better she manages Taco, the better he becomes. And she knows that she will need to manage him less as time goes on because he will have been raised correctly and fully integrated. As she's transitioned into the adolescent stage with him, she is now able to expand his world and engage full-on in sport. She has noted an elevation in the drive and power he brings to working for food, tugging, and engaging with her in ways he hadn't before. To keep harnessing his growing energy, she located a facility to pursue scent work and agility, and they also share a life of outdoor adventures. Now, she proudly calls him a "go-anywhere, do-anything" dog.

# For Reflection

1.  Now that you have a strong relationship foundation, how has your dog been handling the different levels of socialization? Where have you seen the most progress? Are there any specific locations or situations where the dog regresses?

2.  In which new ways can you build the levels of socialization into your day-to-day life and outings with your dog? Consider visiting different parks and hiking trails, trying new sports venues, taking the dog to work, meeting friends and family (and their dogs), taking road trips, staying in hotels, and so on.

3.  What have you found out about your dog's preferences when it comes to socialization? What are the situations the dog loves to participate in? What are the ones they prefer to avoid?

4.  What has your experience been like as friends interact with or strangers encounter your functionally obedient dog?

5.  What is one surprising and wonderful thing you've learned about your dog as you are finishing your dog with Stage 3?

# CHAPTER 15

# Drive Development at Stage 3

And the day came when the risk to remain tight in a bud was more painful than the risk it took to blossom.

—**ANAIS NIN,** French-born American diarist, essayist, and novelist

66 *So how much do you know about herding?" asked Kathy, my new herding teacher.*

*"Not much at all," I said, "other than I've been wanting to do this for the longest time, and I think my dog would be good at it."*

*"You know," she said, looking relieved, "it can be a good thing to not know much about something. You go in with a more open mind!"*

*What I thought would be an activity that Maya and I would enjoy while I was on sabbatical from the university ended up being a passion that has lasted to this day. Here I am more than a decade and four dogs later, still trying to wrap my head around this sport.*

*In my view, herding is a sport of kings, just like chess is above all board games. When I hear friends go on about how much they love their sport, sure, I am thrilled for them. But I and others in herding know that there is no other dog sport quite as challenging for the dog, human, and their relationship. As Kathy says, the "tools"* used in this game, the livestock animals, are alive and have hearts and minds of their own. It is our job to treat them "like fine china."

At first, Maya sure gave me a run for my money in the herding arena. Her instincts to round up the animals and tell them what to do roared in her, and though I thought I had good relationship material with her, we were tested yet again as we brought livestock into the picture. We slowly learned the basic herding commands— driving the sheep from a point to another, holding them still, putting them in pens, and sorting them into groups. We worked on different stock, mustering the courage to herd cattle, and humbled by the precision and persistence required for ducks and geese. Some of the most memorable moments in my career as a dog handler and in my existence as a human being took place on Kathy and her husband Dave's farm, with my dogs and our classmates.

About 18 months into our newfound passion, Maya's aging body forced her retirement. It was a bit difficult at first, but all the work we'd done and obstacles we'd overcome allowed Maya, for the first time, to enjoy the peace of a low-stress life. We stayed active in different ways appropriate to her retired status.

Luckily, herding opportunities presented themselves even past her retirement, like the time when I was headed to my favorite drive-through with Maya riding shotgun. We arrived at the intersection but found it backed up with traffic because a large flock of Canada geese had decided to set up camp. I saw the situation, and clearly so did Maya; she could tell something needed to be done. I stopped the car, flashed my signals, stepped out, and waved to the impatient drivers to stay put.

Out came Maya, flawlessly rounding up the flock, zooming around cars to make sure she'd not missed any strays, and gently moving the geese to the park by the road. The Canada geese, otherwise known to be temperamental, moved nicely with neither protest nor irritation—exactly the response proper herding achieves. When Maya was done, she checked back in with me instead of continuing to "play" with the geese: "All done?" she asked with her big eyes.

"Yep, all done!" I said ecstatically. "Smart girl you are." Back into the van she hopped as the drivers clapped and cheered. It was a real YouTube moment for us that she felt equally proud of.

At Stage 3, we have a balanced manifestation of drives, one that reflects a dog's authentic disposition and personality. Each dog is unique, and the logic of layering and progression, couched in a relationship that changes accordingly, is what helps reveal each dog with as much clarity and honesty as possible.

Integration is about putting all the pieces together—we channeled food and prey drive, and paved the way for pack and defensive drive. Now at maturation, we have all drives in balance.

All along, our exercises were not meant just for the sake of doing them. Rather, they were practiced lightly and consistently as a way of creating long-lasting habits that come in handy in our day-to-day existence with our dogs—for example, being calm at our side, minding us at doors, hanging behind us at boundary lines, walking nicely on leash, and obeying with little incentive.

Our exercises take a different shape at this point in that they become practiced here and there, as a way of staying fresh and as a fun, playful thing to do. At this point we work toward the dog's capacity to exercise and perform various exercises off leash and at any level of socialization. We explore new spaces, work near and far things, and prepare our dogs for the possibility of oppositional socialization.

# Food Drive

A finished dog continues to have food drive; this is a zest and enthusiasm for life that does not go away. The dog is down for food any time food is presented, even if they just ate or if the food is not the most appealing. The dog is willing to try any food and is not picky or choosy. Anyone who trains with me knows that my dogs get animated around food no matter what's happening and that they'll do anything for treats. Even if they're older, even if they're finished dogs, they still have that food drive, which continues to come in handy in our training, socialization, and sport.

# Prey Drive

Strengthening and channeling prey drive is also something we continue to do at Stage 3. A grown dog doesn't cease wanting to play. I find the opposite to be true; there's something about being sound, strong, and spirited that makes dogs even more playful, able to let their hair down and have a good time.

Working on prey games continues to be something we do over a lifetime, including treat tosses and hand lures, ball playing, tugging, and prey cycle games—all according to the level of interest shown by the dog. Even as the dog ages, there continues to be opportunity for us to get silly and play. In the end, this is how you should be thinking about prey drive: that it's very simply the desire to play in whatever ways suit a particular dog.

# Pack Drive

Only when food drive is satisfied and prey drive is harnessed can a dog truly be able to love in the way that we humans understand it. At Stage 3, the dog is happy to perform to please you for the joy of your approval and satisfaction, and in fact, that approval is better than any food or toy incentive you could provide. This is a relationship that you can settle into with intimacy, trust, and love, while continuing to engage in activities that strengthen your bond.

Here's a recent example with Kizzy that underlines the power of pack drive. Rather suddenly, Kizzy appeared extremely bothered by slippery and shiny floors: at the vet's office, at our scent training location, and at our pet store. I experimented with shoes and kept her nails short and paws shaved. My scent trainer assisted us with floor mats, and at a trial once, we asked the judge if we could turn the lights off.

My attitude to Kizzy was that I loved her, supported her, and at the same time, was not going to give this fear much weight. I took note of it but did not dwell on it. I didn't make a big deal of these fears but also communicated to her that she could do better and that she could be better, if she chose. She felt it, and with the desire to overcome that is core to pack drive, Kizzy worked through her fears on her own. Our scenting trainer often remarks how Kizzy has been working nicely, ignoring the shiny floors. Recently, Kizzy was taken to the back of our vet clinic for a routine visit without concern, the vet remarked. When we love, we work on getting better for those we love.

# Defensive Drive

All dogs, regardless of breed, can act in a defensive manner. It is healthy and natural, but if they're acting in a defensive manner when I first get the dog, that's problematic. That is coming from a place of fear and anxiety, not defensive drive. A dog's natural desire to protect is nurtured, comes with time, and follows a correct progression in the development of drives.

Defensiveness is not frantic. Defensiveness is not panicked. Defensiveness is "I think I hear something outside that you might want to pay attention to." It's a confident display of maturity, and it tends to go hand in hand with pack drive because, as dogs start to become deeply bonded with us, their desire to protect us naturally emerges.

# Exercise

Integration, once achieved, is the way of life we've been working toward. Finishing Stage 3 doesn't mean the work stops, though; just like any relationship, it takes consistent work. Now, though, we focus that work on maintaining and enjoying our bond as we live together. As the dog ages, we also adjust our way of life as needed.

Physical exercise continues to be an important, healthy part of the everyday routine, and at this point, we know how to manage all aspects of our outing, including physical, social, mental, and psychological.

Think of your outings as a sandwich:

→ The start of the outing (top piece of bread) and the end of the outing (bottom piece of bread) are the same in that they are the more challenging, yet crucial, pieces.

→  At the start, our dogs are understandably excited, and we need to manage that with low expectations, patience, and light control.

→  At the end, our dogs are tired and wired, and we need to manage that with lower expectations and greater control.

→  The best part is the middle of the outing, the tasty filling, where the dog is in optimal performance. This is where we work best and where we can relax a little. But without the bread on either side, the sandwich falls apart, right? So how we get to the outing and what we do afterward matter.

At this point, we have worked with our dog on whatever prey activities get them going and engaging. Whether it's disk, ball, tug-of-war, or something else, we are consistently engaging our dog in physical exercise that is also mentally stimulating, psychologically challenging, and relationally bonding.

We are also free to enjoy our preferred activities, knowing we have prepared and educated our partner to participate with us. Whether walks, runs, or hikes, we can engage in these activities in various places, with various amounts of socialization and with minimal leashing. Our dogs heed the principles of the three circles—respecting our space, staying close, and keeping off the outer boundaries—whether they have a line on or not.

# Training

A well-trained dog is not necessarily a well-behaved one. I've spoken with many clients who call me to ask about all types of anxiety and aggression, but somewhere in the conversation they emphasize that their dog knows sit and other commands. Clearly, this training—which we now know is only conditioning— has left some gaps if the dog is having behavior issues. By the same token, a well-behaved dog with foundations and exposure has not necessarily been "trained" in a traditional, formal kind of way. And yet, the dog will have a handle on key commands such as sit, stay, recall, down, and heel, as well as come here and get out, in both on- and off-leash capacity.

At Stage 3, our training focuses on solidifying our off-leash work, where it's important that our attitude backs up the training. So, when we're cutting our dog loose, are we scared? Are we worried about what could happen? I don't cut a dog loose until they've been tested on the leash and drag line extensively; it's not something that suddenly we're going to do. It's done gradually, offering the dog little impressions of what's to come and helping me gain confidence about the outcome.

At the same time, we need to understand that while the dog values its freedom, the line we have on the dog also acts as a source of safety. So when it is time to let the line drag or take it off, we're gradually asking the dog to step up their independence, individuate, and take responsibility for their own behavior.

As well, our dogs can handle vulnerability-inducing exercises such as being put on a tie-out, handed to another handler, or being boarded, which would have been introduced at Stage 2. Can we tie our dogs and have them handle the experience well? How about with various kinds and levels of distraction available? How about in different places, with different things happening near and far, and with people interacting with us or even with them? How do they take to being handed off to someone? How do they deal with being boarded?

Raising our dogs right means we develop in them such soundness that they naturally become well behaved and begin to display functional obedience. This functional obedience shows up early in the process but becomes really apparent at Stage 3. Just like functional medicine is not about separate body parts but rather how the whole is working together, dogs become organically and naturally obedient with minimal training in this process. This is only achieved by going back to the root cause of things rather than playing whack-a-mole with every individual issue that surfaces.

As the dog grows in functional obedience, we then associate their natural behaviors with specific cues so that we can direct the dog when needed. This gives us a language that we both understand, one that the dog developed with us instead of one that was imposed on them. In essence, that is my philosophy about training.

At Stage 3, we continue to participate fully in group and sport classes, now being a little less concerned with activities being taxing on the dogs. The dog has practice now, and if we continue to balance times of pressure with rest, the dog can handle the psychological vulnerability of being physically tired.

## **Exercise:** *Off-Leash Simulated Long-Line Work And Turns*

All the long-line exercises you've been practicing from the beginning have prepared you and your dog not only to walk on a loose leash but eventually on a drag line and then without any leash, no matter where you are or what is going on.

Continue playing your games and practicing your long-line exercises with and without a line. Keep in mind that your dog's desire to stay with you and focus on you is not just a matter of practice but also a question of how well you've addressed all the elements in the Way of Life method.

→ **Spatial:** Practice in different environments.

→ **Distal:** Practice with action at a distance and strengthen your dog's off-leash capacity.

→ **Proximal:** Work your way to where you can walk with your dog dragging the line, then without a line near people, and then near people and dogs.

→ **Interactional:** Challenge your loose dog by engaging with others as you walk.

→ **Oppositional:** Challenge your dog to continue walking loosely next to you, dragging a line first and then without a line, in situations such as people passing by and touching your dog without asking, loose dogs coming into your space, children running toward you, and so on.

Just as in Stage 2 (see chapter 11), start any exercises holding the line and then dropping it, holding and dropping. Then take it off, continue the exercises a few times, and hook it back on again. This kind of practice helps the dog understand that they are expected to act the same whether the leash is there or not. This way, you can work toward your dog being off leash in a controlled way, always making sure the dog is set up to succeed.

Continue to use your dog's food, prey, and pack drives in the direction of success. Off-leash work is challenging, and you're almost going back to basics, using food, toys, and of course your praise, as you work on your long-line exercises with a line dragging and eventually no line at all.

The idea is to get to a place where your dog walks next to you, around you, behind you, and with you—in either the inner or tranquil circle—in a way that is organic and natural, like two friends walking together. You get to a place where it's not about doing the exercises anymore but simply enjoying a way of life where the dog is safely and responsibly free almost constantly.

# Sport

Remember what I said earlier: Sport will sweeten your bond, but it won't solve your problems. Sometimes, people struggle with their dogs in part because the dog doesn't have a healthy outlet for their natural tendencies. And sometimes, people active in sport struggle because they've not given sport its correct place in the way of life and did not engage in sport in a manner consistent with developmental stages.

At Stage 3, with all drives in balance, we are active in sport, and the dog can perform at the top of their skill since we've instilled in the dog a strong sense of self as well as confidence in us as the dog's handler. Sport can be a very rewarding part of a dog's life—and their humans' too! Be sure to remain open to new and different sport opportunities to widen your dog's experiences and to give the dog a chance to find what they love. In addition, as part of bringing all aspects of the way of life in balance, it's important to allow dogs to participate in activities that are noncompetitive and nonperformative, where they can just be dogs.

Drive development at Stage 3 is about bringing all drives in balance in accordance with maturity and authenticity. Because the dog has been raised to be sound, strong, and spirited, they show us who they really are and what they care about. We have a dog we can exercise in various ways and participate full-on in sports and activities of our choice.

## CASE
# Toby the Pembroke Welsh Corgi

These clients, a married couple, did everything right. Or they thought they did. They chose a Pembroke Welsh corgi, a breed they identified with culturally but had also researched thoroughly, finding these dogs described as happy, intelligent, and fun.

Due to little experience with dogs, they were turned down by a few breeders, but one did agree to sell them a male pup they named Toby. They brought Toby home and a few months later, contacted me:

*My husband and I have a five-month-old male corgi. While he's overall well behaved—when you have him at home and he's in a good mood, great little guy— we're experiencing aggression. It's a common trait in corgis, and sometimes it's definitely territorial, and others it's out of the blue. We don't think he's a bad-natured dog since the aggression comes and goes, but he does nip, bite, and lunge at us.*

## The Issues

At only a few months old, Toby had already aggressed on his humans several times. He displayed barrier aggression at the fences in their yard and was extremely unpredictable—nice enough one moment and vicious the next. He resource guarded everything—food, toys, anything he could use to get into an argument. When in the yard, he would hide under the cedars and dig his heels when called out, goading his owners into an argument while using the cedars as a shield. Though little, he was a powerhouse on leash and pulled my clients on their walks. They were at a loss and blamed the restrictions on training and socialization created by the pandemic. At the same time, they could tell something was off in their relationship. "I don't think he trusts us," she said to me on our first call.

On closer assessment, we quickly identified psychological as well as physical aspects that were contributing to the issues. My clients agreed that neither one had the right attitude about the dog. They appreciated the fact that not being on the same page made matters worse. The woman had wanted a corgi for the longest time, specifically a Welsh corgi because she is Welsh. She adored Toby and coddled and pampered him. In contrast, the man wanted to teach Toby manners, train him, and be the disciplinarian.

My clients also thought their dog's behavior was normal, on grounds that aggression, they thought, "is a common trait in corgis." I explained to my clients that the "aggression" that these kinds of dogs are known for is natural when directed at livestock—but not at humans! Problems reflect a combination of breed plus way of life. As a student of sheep herding for many years, I've come to appreciate the tenacity and meanness that is present in a proper herding dog, at the proper time. Herders cannot let themselves get intimidated by the livestock. Sometimes, herders even have to defend themselves against the livestock. Their lives depend on this capacity, and so, too, does the farmer's life. Therefore, it's that level of power inside, combined with a dysfunctional way of life, that can bring out the worst in these dogs.

At a physical level, we had the common lack of structure in the day-to-day life, premature training, and failure to challenge the dog and meet his needs as a smart and driven working dog. For example, my clients left a tiny crate open in the middle of a larger enclosure, and Toby would shuffle around, at a loss as to what exactly was expected of him in this big space. He lacked a schedule and structure that would meet his need for order and predictability. He also needed an outlet as he was not stimulated and challenged in the way an intelligent and driven breed like a corgi should be.

## A New Way of Life

We went to work introducing the physical and psychological changes needed to help Toby. I was happy that both husband and wife were open and committed to all the changes proposed, which began with adjusting their attitudes and bringing them into alignment. She had to get off the coddling, and he had to get off the idea that the only way to relate to a dog was through training. Other changes included scheduling and crating Toby properly to bring the aggressive incidents to a halt, controlling his learning environment and giving everyone a breather from months of conflict.

We replaced the arrangement with the x-pen and small crate with a large crate. We set a schedule that included outings with specific training exercises as well as hikes, aiming to get Toby tired out physically and challenged mentally. It was interesting that both my clients were athletes but didn't realize how athletic their dog was. They started to hike with him, at times taking him on challenging trails. I coached them on using the natural environment to challenge Toby, having him climb on rocks, cross logs, and walk through streams and muddy spots. The schedule also included stretches of time alone in the yard, which sometimes he spent under the cedars, though eventually he would come out.

My clients also learned to handle the dog in a way that helped improve his attitude while keeping them safe, which mostly consisted of leaving him alone. Thus, all attempts to get into fights were ignored. If Toby wished to spend the evening by the cedars, he was welcome to do so. If he wished to continue chewing his antler bone, that would be fine. They also had a long line on him, allowing a safety buffer when they did need to handle him.

They were able to manage all aspects of Toby's aggression except around food, having trouble feeding him in his crate without unleashing a possessive reaction. At this point, Toby boarded with me, which gave him a positive handler transference experience and the opportunity to socialize with dogs for the first time. Each one of my dogs enjoyed Toby and his company, sensing that at the core, he was a smart and charismatic character.

The boarding also gave me the chance to figure out a handling mechanic for feeding—a standard operating procedure—that would not trigger his reaction. If we can stop a dog from acting out a behavior, that behavior eventually falls off the dog's repertoire. Before bringing Toby to his crate for mealtimes, I would prepare the crate so that the food was already inside at the very end of the crate, with the door propped open. Upon bringing Toby over, I would get close enough for him to know the food was there. His focus now solely on the food, I could unclip his leash, knowing he'd go straight for the food and start eating. At that point, I'd approach quietly and close the crate behind him. When my clients were able to implement this mechanic, aggression around food eventually dissipated.

## Results

During this time, Toby sure gave us all a run for our money, but my clients showed remarkable courage and commitment, resulting in solid relationship improvements. One of the very first signs of improvement was the safety, calmness, and ease created by having Toby crated properly. Once he knew he did not have to decide whether to be inside or outside the crate, shuffling around the x-pen, he began to sleep well, at times on his back with his legs in the air. Gradually, the atmosphere at home began to change as everyone adjusted to a new normal, and they were able to go longer and longer without incidents.

Eventually, my clients were able to introduce sports, which they knew would help Toby tremendously now that they had foundations with him. They appreciated that sport alone was not the solution, but that it would be a great way to channel his drives.

Toby was a lot more than what these clients, who only had average experience with dogs, had bargained for, but they learned a lot in this process and knew that they'd both changed as people. When we last spoke, the couple mentioned that they were hoping to take on a rescue dog in the future, knowing that, after working on Toby's way of life, they'd have the skills to help the dog have a successful and fulfilling life.

## For Reflection

1.  How have you been witnessing growth and development in your dog's drives, especially pack and defensive drives?

2.  How is your approach to exercising your dog evolving? What are your

preferred ways of giving your dog a good workout, and what ways does your dog respond to most positively?

3.  How is your approach to training your dog evolving? Now that your dog is functionally obedient, how do you plan on continuing training, both to keep that relationship strong and to challenge your dog mentally?

4.  When it comes to off-leash exercises and transitioning to off-leash walking, hiking, or otherwise living (where it's allowed), how are you feeling? Are you a little nervous or confident? Remembering that your psychological state affects your dog, how can you prepare yourself for successful off-leash outings?

5.  What are your dreams for the future with your dog? For example, if you've successfully been engaging in one sport, what is another that you might be interested in trying out?

# Epilogue

Treat me as I am,

and that I shall remain.

Treat me as I wish to be,

and that I shall become.

—**KARL SCHMIDT,** author, photographer, and animal welfare advocate

*B*efore Maya came into my life, there was Rama. If it wasn't for him and the confidence he gave me, I wouldn't have taken on a challenge like the one Maya presented. I don't think I would have adopted her and dedicated myself to working through our issues together. I would have never become the person I am.

Rama was a German shepherd mix whom we were blessed to share our lives with for over a decade. I happened to be on the lookout for a male shepherd, and even though Rama was a mix, his description on the shelter website was such that I immediately applied to visit with him. Turns out he'd been found as a stray by a Good Samaritan who fell in love with him, kept him as long as he could, and then realizing he couldn't keep up with such a large and energetic dog, brought him to one of the local shelters. The detail provided on the animal surrender form showed just how fond the person was of Rama and the many reasons why.

Rama was a big, sturdy, and rambunctious boy. He was smart and at the same time didn't seem to have a care in the world. My first memory of him when I walked toward his kennel was him stretching in downward-dog position, looking straight into my eyes. I adopted him promptly, and he was my mate for a year before Maya joined us.

Rama is that rare dog who makes ignorant dog owners, like the one I was, look good and feel good about themselves—I really thought I understood this whole dog thing. He was of such easygoing and noble character that he rarely did anything to get in trouble.

At the dog park, instead of getting into fights with the hordes of unstable dogs around, he would insist on playing ball with me. "Can't you tell I'm occupied?" he seemed to be telling the other dogs.

Any time I'd be frustrated with something he did, I'd ask him to go lie down, and he'd always oblige. I didn't know enough to see the little signs of stress, the subtle indicators that our way of life could be better. Instead, I relied on obedience I hadn't really earned.

When Maya joined us, she wasn't prepared to go along like Rama. "I don't think so, lady," was her attitude from the beginning. Rama was the better dog by many contemporary standards. Maya was, by far, the better teacher. In between her issues—which were nothing but cries for a way of life she could get behind—and other troubles that followed, we entered a stressful phase as we moved from the U.S. to Canada. Rama was the buffer of our tensions, taking things in stride for all of us. Maya and I adored him, as did many of our friends, both human and canine, who knew him.

Rama never asked for much, all the way to the end. One Monday in a frigid February, he lost his balance and fell. When this happened again the next morning, I knew something was up. Deep down, I could feel he was leaving us. Still, we ran tests, ruled out possibilities, and established that Rama was in fact dying, bleeding internally of what must have been a ruptured splenic tumor. I didn't have to weigh a difficult decision nor consider invasive and costly treatments. The end was here. That Thursday, Rama was deeply asleep and almost gone when our vet came to help him along.

I end with this story of Rama because his temperament made him an exceptionally tolerant and kind dog while at the same time being fun, strong, and adventurous—the ideal dog, really. We all know that dog who made our job a breeze, causing us *to wonder why the others didn't. And yet, dogs like Rama are the exception, not the standard, so why do we expect them all to act this way?*

*At the same time, I saw how even Rama became much sounder and stronger when Maya compelled me to rethink our way of life. Even the already excellent dog that he was became better and all around happier. Regardless of who they are, how challenging or easy, let us raise our dogs right.*

I opened this book with memories of deep fulfillment and joy with dogs as well as memories of guilt and shame. Like millions of others, I lived with a dog that exhibited behavioral issues, some of them severe. Behavioral issues, such as those suffered by my girl Maya, have grown exponentially in the last decades, affecting people and dogs of all walks of life, here in North America and all around the world. Both people and dogs ache when dogs aren't psychologically healthy, when they're not sound, strong, and spirited. Everyone ends up living restricted and stressful lives instead of the life of joy and freedom that came promised with that dog.

Despite unprecedented interest in dogs and tremendous progress in their scientific study, the fact remains that we're nowhere near a real solution to the issues we're witnessing. This is because the focus is on coercing certain behaviors through conditioning, medicating, and using tools that hurt without considering the dog's way of life. Way of life is anything but insignificant. In my world, way of life is everything.

As you near the end of this book, I know that I have left you with much to think about. Few things in life make me as happy as helping dogs with issues heal, and I hope that this process has been healing for both you and your dog. But I feel I am here for a wider purpose and that is to change the conversation on raising dogs and living with them. And so I want to leave you with the following key takeaways.

## 1.   Dogs Always Reflect Their Way of Life

First, do yourself, your dogs, and your world a favor by always considering that dogs reflect their relationships and ways of life. Behaviors are mirrors into their ways of life. Of course, dogs are greater or lesser representations of their breeds and a product of their backgrounds and early rearing experiences. But they are also the way of life we gave them. They are who they have become with us. This is the piece that we don't talk about, and yet it's the only one we can change.

So anytime you're dealing with behavioral issues—anxiety, reactivity, fear, noise phobias, or whatever could be manifesting—make it less about the dog and more about the situation. Too often we think that issues are isolated from the broader context, but issues are fundamentally a product of that context. Sometimes people are offended when I say we need to go back to Foundations. "Our relationship is fine, thank you!" they say. "Now if we could only fix this problem…"

I love that, today, there are so many varied ways of engaging with our dogs, whether it's agility courses or learning to scent. But we need to do more, and that's being careful about what we're doing when we're not training and what we're doing when we're not sporting. We need a deeper awareness of the connection between how dogs live and how they behave, between the quality of their relationships and the health of their mind and spirit. I hope we get to a place where we stop judging dogs, writing them off, and euthanizing them based solely on the image they present while overlooking their way of life.

## 2.   Training Dogs Isn't the Same as Raising Them

The dogs we have today, whether mutts or purebreds, all come from a long line of breeds that were created for specific functions. And of course, there are dogs out there still performing vital working roles all over the world. But most dogs today are bought or adopted with the intention that they just be part of the family. And if they're going to be our friends and family, living with us in our homes instead of as workers who live outside and work for us, then they can't just be trained. They need to be raised. Being a great family member *is* the new job, and this requires raising.

I surmise that we've overlooked raising because it is akin to parenting, and traditionally we have not thought of spending time with a dog as "parenting" them. With parenting—as the name suggests—it is more about the parents than the kids. I promise you: our dogs are looking to us to "parent" them and not just train them. They're looking for familial safety in this chaotic and confusing world, a world that they know has not always been kind to them.

## 3.  In Raising Dogs, We Look to Their Ancestors

I also believe we struggle with raising dogs because we don't have models of how to raise them—or we think we don't. Humans love to impose our way of thinking on everything, I'd say we're even obsessed with this kind of control. But this arrogance is shortsighted. How much thought have we put into how dogs and their ancestors do things? As far as I'm concerned, canid mothers, and mammals in general, are the teachers, the real experts we should be consulting.

Of course we cannot possibly raise our dogs exactly the way wolves raise their cubs. But there is an undeniable structure and progression that every wolf pack follows when raising their young. The stakes for them are life or death if that relationship isn't rock solid. If we want a bonded relationship with our dogs built on comparable loyalty, love, trust, and joy, then perhaps we can look to the wisdom of wolves as a blueprint for how to achieve that in a way that our dogs can understand and contribute to.

Admittedly, we can apply these ways at best imperfectly. Still, I sincerely believe that trying to do things their way, at least in spirit, is better than thinking we know better. So in the new ethic of rearing dogs—of dogmanship—I propose a focus on them and their ways. I know there is a way of living with dogs that brings out the best in them. I've experienced it with my own dogs and dozens of foster and client dogs. There is an ethos in living with dogs that not only helps them be all that they can be but helps us as well.

# 4.   We Are in Control of Way of Life

In this book, I define "way of life" as the daily leadership and management of the dog, one that's inspired by the ways of dogs and their ancestors. Once we get on board with this concept, we realize that way of life is something that we can control; it is the only thing we truly can do something about.

Way of life includes our mindset and the relationship we have created, consciously and unconsciously. Way of life includes how we manage space and boundaries, how we socialize, and our development of drives through exercise, training, and sport. We have control over all these aspects. All parts work together, and when you begin aligning your way of life, you will see changes you did not expect and surprising improvements that you didn't train into the dog. Dogs are just waiting for a way of life they can get behind so that they can show us all they have.

When we're in charge of the way of life, it helps dogs relax. All dogs need that sense of safety, which transcends all breeds and backgrounds. In addition, the present is more powerful than any past, so leave behind any notions of a dog that is "ruined" by a rough past or misguided training. You don't have to take my word for it—this is not about belief but about direct experience. See for yourself what happens to the dog when you change your mind. Belief is nothing; experience is everything.

# 5.   There Is No Magic Bullet

Not long ago, I was on a call with clients who hadn't gone on a date in four years, held hostage at home by a Samoyed with severe separation anxiety. We had a long conversation about their current way of life including their attitude, the present state of their relationship with their dog, and their approach to managing space and boundaries, socialization, and drives. There were long pauses as the clients took all this in.

Finally, the woman said, "So there's no magic bullet."

Her statement was more affirmation than question, and it seemed like a lot for her to absorb. She and her spouse had been hoping and praying for that one magic trick that would make the dog get over something as pernicious as codependence.

So the next takeaway is that there are no magic bullets in the business of healing dogs and their issues. I realize this might be difficult—perhaps too much to ask. It sucks to imagine setting aside everything we've done, all that hard work, and starting from scratch. You might have come here wanting a few tips and tricks rather than a whole makeover. You wanted a few renovations here and there; I offer a teardown and rebuild.

But I promise, it's worth it.

## 6.   Change Begins with Us

This leads me to my final takeaway. If you've read all this way, I know you realize that before anything, *you* need to change to make this happen.

I talk to people all the time who want their dogs to change but who do not wish to think, feel, or live any differently themselves. But for our dogs to change, we need to be the ones changing first. There is empowerment in the idea that if we could screw things up so bad, we can also remake them into something amazing.

Is that too much to ask? Is the love of our dogs—a love so grand it's found across pop culture, poetry, and history—not enough motivation for us to change? Your dog's happiness is worth the change. It is a love so deep, so fulfilling, so universal. Your dog deserves that you look deeply and with humility for ways to give back a fraction of what dogs give us.

And if you need any more persuading, just think of this: The level of freedom your dog experiences is equivalent to yours—as there is nothing more restricting than having a dog with problems, a dog you can't leave behind, a dog you can't trust, or a dog you can't do things or go places with. That's no life for either one of you.

This approach is not difficult, but it is different. What's difficult is living with a dog with problems. What's difficult is living with a dog that is sad, neglected, confined, and unhappy. If you're experiencing behavioral issues like the ones in the client stories I share throughout, your dog is asking you to change—or maybe insisting that you do!

I can guarantee—from my own experience and that of my clients—the joy, pride, confidence, and fulfillment that you will feel at the conclusion of this journey are truly life-changing. Without a doubt, going through this process transforms not only your dog but you as well. The deep bonds created when we take the time to raise our dogs, instead of just trying to fix their problems, opens possibilities we never imagined possible. Love moves mountains. Deep bonds create miracles.

I wish you well on this journey of knowing yourself, healing your dog, and discovering who you both truly are.

# References

Addams, Jessica and Andrew Miller. *Between Dog and Wolf: Understanding the Connection and the Confusion.* Wenatchee: Dogwise Publishing, 2012.

Aloff, Brenda. *Aggression in Dogs: Practical Management, Prevention, & Behaviour Modification.* Self-published, Brenda Aloff, 2002.

American Animal Hospital Association. "Busy Dogs Are Good Dogs." Pet Behavior Brochure Series, 2016.

American Animal Hospital Association. "Crate Training: Create the Perfect Canine Cave." Pet Behavior Brochure Series, 2016.

American Animal Hospital Association. "Home Alone: Solving Separation Anxiety Problems." Pet Behavior Brochure Series, 2016.

American Animal Hospital Association. "Fido Was First: Training Your Dog for Baby's Arrival." Pet Behavior Brochure Series, 2016.

American Animal Hospital Association. "The Social Scene: Introducing Your Puppy to the World." Pet Behavior Brochure Series, 2016.

American College of Veterinary Behaviorists. *Decoding Your Dog: The Ultimate Experts Explain Common Dog Behaviors and Reveal How to Prevent or Change Unwanted Ones.* Edited by Debra Horwitz, John Ciribassi, and Steve Dale. New York: Houghton Mifflin Harcourt, 2014.

American Kennel Club. "Canine Good Citizen (CGC)." American Kennel Club, accessed April 17, 2023. https://www.akc.org/products-services/training-programs/canine-good-citizen/.

Amiot, Catherine E. and Brock Bastian. Toward a Psychology of Human-Animal Relations. *Psychological Bulletin*, 141, no. 1 (2015): 6–47. https://doi.org/10.1037/a0038147.

Arluke, Arnold. "A Sociology of Sociological Animal Studies." *Society & Animals*, 10, NO. 4 (2002): 369–374. https://doi.org/10.1163/156853002320936827.

Arnold, Jennifer. *Love Is All You Need: The Revolutionary Bond-Based Approach to Educating Your Dog*. New York: Random House, 2016.

Bandura, Albert. "Social Learning Theory of Identification Processes." In *Handbook of Socialization Theory and Research, 1st ed.*, 213-262. Edited by D. A. Goslin. New York: Rand McNally, 1969.

Beck, Alan and Aaron Katcher. *Between Pets and People: The Importance of Animal Companionship*. West Lafayette: Purdue University Press, 1996.

Becker, Karen Shaw. "The Mistakes Dog Owners Make About Separation Anxiety." Mercola Healthy Pets, October 25, 2019. https://healthypets.mercola.com/sites/healthypets/archive/2019/10/25/how-to-help-a-dog-with-separation-anxiety.aspx.

Becker, Karen Shaw. "11 Ways To Help Soothe Your Noise Phobic Dog." Mercola Healthy Pets, February 26, 2020. https://healthypets.mercola.com/sites/healthypets/archive/2020/02/26/dog-noise-phobia.aspx.

Bekoff, Marc. *Canine Confidential: Why Dogs Do What They Do*. Chicago: University of Chicago Press, 2018.

Bender, Allie and Emily Strong. *Canine Enrichment for The Real World: Making It A Part Of Your Dog's Daily Life*. Wenatchee: Dogwise Publishing, 2019.

Blakeslee, Nate. *American Wolf: A True Story of Survival and Obsession in the West*. New York: Broadway Books, 2017.

Bowlby, John. *The Making and Breaking of Affectional Bonds*. New York: Routledge, 1976.

Bowlby, John. *A Secure Base: Clinical Applications of Attachment Theory*. New York: Routledge, 1988.

Bradshaw, John. *Dog Sense: How the Science of Dog Behavior Can Make You a Better Friend to Your Pet.* New York: Basic Books, 2011.

Bradshaw, John. *In Defence of Dogs: Why Dogs Need Our Understanding.* New York: Allen Lane, 2012.

Bradshaw, John. *The Animals Along Us: How Pets Make Us Human.* New York: Basic Books, 2017

Braitman, Laurel. *Animal Madness: How Anxious Dogs, Compulsive Parrots, And Elephants in Recovery Help Us Understand Ourselves.* New York: Simon & Schuster, 2014.

Bretherton, Inge. The Origins of Attachment Theory: John Bowlby and Mary Ainsworth. *Developmental Psychology* 28, no. 5 (1992): 759–775. https://cmapspublic2.ihmc.us/rid=1LQX400NM-RBVKH9-1KL6/the%20origins%20of%20attachment%20theory%20john%20bowlby%20and_mary_ainsworth.pdf.

Brassey, Charlotte. "Tackling the Canine Obesity Crisis." BBC News, September 10, 2017. https://www.bbc.com/news/science-environment-41161424.

Breitner, Jill. "Why I Don't Use A Crate When Training Dogs." Dogster, August 11, 2016. https://www.dogster.com/lifestyle/why-i-dont-believe-in-crate-training.

Brophey, Kim. "Ethological Contributions to Aggression in Dogs." Virtual conference session. Aggression in Dogs Conference, 2020.

Brophey, Kim. "The Problem with Treating a Dog like a Pet," TEDx UNC Asheville. April 4, 2018. Video, 19:15. https://www.ted.com/talks/kim_brophey_the_problem_with_treating_a_dog_like_a_pet.

Brophey, Kim. *Meet Your Dog: The Game Changing Guide to Understanding Your Dog's Behavior.* San Francisco: Chronicle Books, 2018.

Canadian Kennel Club. "Canine Good Neighbour (CGN)." Canadian Kennel Club, accessed April 17, 2023. https://www.ckc.ca/en/Raising-My-Dog/Responsible-Ownership/Canine-Good-Neighbour-Program.

Chen, Angus. "Dog People Live Longer. But Why?" WBUR National Public Radio, October 26, 2019. https://www.npr.org/sections/health-shots/2019/10/26/773531999/dog-people-live-longer-but-why.

Clothier, Suzanne. *If a Dog's Prayers Were Answered … Bones Would Rain from the Sky: Deepening Our Relationships with Dogs.* New York: Hachette Book Group, 2002.

Clothier, Suzanne. "He Just Wants to Say 'Hi.'" Suzanne Clothier Relationship Centered Training, July 2012. https://harmonydogpark.ca/wp-content/uploads/2012/07/He-just-wants-to-say-hi-rude-dogs.pdf.

Clothier, Suzanne. "Aggression Basics." Suzanne Clothier Relationship Centered Training, accessed April 17, 2023. https://suzanneclothier.com/article/aggression-basics/.

Clothier, Suzanne. "Aggression & some reasons behind it." Suzanne Clothier Relationship Centered Training, accessed April 17, 2023. https://suzanneclothier.com/article/aggression-reasons-behind/.

Clothier, Suzanne. "That Darned Dominance Debate." Suzanne Clothier Relationship Centered Training, accessed April 17, 2023. https://suzanneclothier.com/article/darned-dominance-debate/

Clothier, Suzanne. "If Only That Hadn't Happened, This Dog Would Be Fine." Suzanne Clothier Relationship Centered Training, accessed April 17, 2023. https://suzanneclothier.com/article/hadnt-happened-dog-fine/.

Coppinger, Raymond and Lorna Coppinger. *Dogs: A New Understanding of Canine Origin, Behavior, And Evolution.* Chicago: University of Chicago Press. 2001.

Coppinger, Raymond and Mark Feinstein. *How Dogs Work.* Chicago: University of Chicago Press, 2015.

Cook, Amy. (2019). "We Need To Stop Calling It 'Socialization.'" Play Way Dogs, February 2, 2019. http://playwaydogs.com/we-need-to-stop-calling-it-socialization/.

Cooke, Lucy. *Bitch: On the Female of the Species.* New York: Basic Books, 2022.

Coren, Stanley. *The Intelligence of Dogs: A Guide to the Thoughts, Emotions, And Inner Lives of Our Canine Companions*. New York: Free Press, 2006.

Coren, Stanley. "The Politics of Pet Dogs and Kennel Crates." Psychology Today, March 26, 2012. https://www.psychologytoday.com/ca/blog/canine-corner/201203/the-politics-pet-dogs-and-kennel-crates.

Coulter, Kendra. *Animals, Work, And the Promise of Interspecies Solidarity.* New York: Palgrave Macmillan, 2016.

Crosby, Jim. "Tools for Evaluating Aggression: What Works in the Real World?" Virtual conference session, Aggression in Dogs Conference, 2020.

Cudworth, Erika. "Labors of Love: Work, Labor, and Care in Dog-Human Relations." *Gender, Work and Organization* 29, no. 3 (2021): 830–844. https://doi.org/10.1111/gwao.12814.

Rachel Dale, Sylvian Palma-Jacinto, Sarah Marshall-Pescini, and Friederike Range.(2019). "Wolves, But Not Dogs, Are Prosocial in a Touch Screen Task." *PLOS One* 14, no. 55, e0215444. https://doi.org/10.1371/journal.pone.0215444.

de Waal, Frans. *Are We Smart Enough to Know How Smart Animals Are?* New York: W. W. Norton & Company, 2016.

Derr, Mark. *How The Dog Became the Dog: From Wolves to Our Best Friends.* London: Duckworth Overlook, 2012.

Dunbar, Ian. *Before and After Getting Your Puppy: The Positive Approach to Raising a Happy, Healthy & Well-Behaved Dog.* Novato: New World Library, 2004.

Dutcher, Jim and Jamie Dutcher. *Running With Wolves: Our Story of Life with the Sawtooth Pack.* Washington, D.C.: National Geographic, 2019.

Dodman, Nicholas. *The Dog Who Loved Too Much: Tales, Treatments, And the Psychology of Dogs.* New York: Bantam Books, 1996.

Eaton, Barry. *Dominance in Dogs: Fact or Fiction?* Wenatchee: Dogwise Publishing, 2008.

Ellis, Michael. [Leerburg]. "The Fundamentals of Tug Play." YouTube. April 10, 2019. Video, 8:46. https://www.youtube.com/watch?v=JucgnzD-_Yw.

Ellis, Michael. [Leerburg]. "The Power of Playing Tug with Your Dog." YouTube. September 25, 2009. Video, 10:05. https://www.youtube.com/watch?v=SsWnL4VWZNg.

Ellis, Michael. [Leerburg]. "Michael Ellis Plays Tug." YouTube. January 17, 2013. Video, 3:43. https://www.youtube.com/watch?v=GyKGbJQ-ldc.

Ellis, Michael. [Leerburg]. "Playing Tug with Puppies."YouTube. February 11, 2011. Video, 2:44. https://www.youtube.com/watch?v=nCZLudNFHbo.

Fancher, Robert. *Cultures Of Healing: Correcting the Image of American Mental Health Care*. New York: W. H. Freeman and Co, 1995.

Fenzi, Denise. "Puppy or Piranha? Interactive Strategies for Raising, Training, and Enjoying High-Drive Dogs." Virtual conference session. Aggression in Dogs Conference, 2020.

Fenzi, Denise. "Understanding High-Drive Dogs: When The Abnormal is Absolutely Normal." Virtual conference session. Aggression in Dogs Conference, 2020.

Fenzi, Denise. "Socialization in the World of COVID." Denise Fenzi Blog, September 21, 2020. https://denisefenzi.com/2020/09/socialization-in-the-world-of-covid/.

Fenzi, Denise. "A Five-Minute Read to Raising a Puppy Positively." Denise Fenzi Blog, November 23, 2011. https://denisefenzi.com/2019/11/a-five-minute-read-to-raising-a-puppy-positively/.

Fenzi, Denise. "It's a Puppy, Not a Problem." Fenzi Dog Sport Academy Blog, August 26, 2019. https://www.fenzidogsportsacademy.com/blog/it-s-a-puppy-not-a-problem

Fenzi, Denise. "More on Socialization." Denise Fenzi Blog, March 27, 2019. https://denisefenzi.com/2019/03/more-on-socialization/.

Fenzi, Denise. "Do We Teach Resilience?" Denise Fenzi Blog, February 1, 2016. https://denisefenzi.com/2016/02/do-we-teach-resilience/.

Fenzi, Denise. "Socialization." Denise Fenzi Blog, July 31, 2013. https://denisefenzi.com/2013/07/socialization/.

Fenzi, Denise. "Lyra's Socialization—The Role of Environmental Cues." Denise Fenzi Blog, November 4, 2011. https://denisefenzi.com/2011/11/lyras-socialization-the-role-of-environmental-cues/.

Geber, Tony, dir. *Kingdom of the White Wolf with Ronan Donovan.* 2019; Brooklyn, NY: Market Road Films. Disney+.

Harvey, Jacky Colliss. *The Animal's Companion: People & Their Pets, A 26,000-Year Love Story.* Philadelphia: Running Press, 2019.

Hannah, David and Kirsten Robertson.(2017). Human-Animal Work: A Massive, Understudied Domain of Human Activity. *Journal of Management Inquiry* 26, no. 1, (2017): 116–118. https://journals.sagepub.com/doi/10.1177/1056492616655076.

Horowitz, Alexandra. *Inside of a Dog: What Dogs See, Smell and Know.* New York: Simon & Schuster, 2009.

Horowitz, Alexandra. *Our Dogs, Ourselves: The Story of a Singular Bond.* New York: Scribner. 2019.

Howard, Lauren. "If Your Dog Is Fat, You're Not Getting Enough Exercise." Piece of My Heart Rescue Blog, June 20, 2017. https://pieceofmyheartrescue.wordpress.com/2017/06/20/first-blog-post/.

Howard, Lauren. "Dog Parks—aka "Pawshank Redemption?" Piece of My Heart Rescue Blog, January 6, 2018. https://pieceofmyheartrescue.wordpress.com/2018/01/06/dog-parks-aka-pawshank-redemption/.

Howell, Tiffani J., Tammie King, and Pauleen C. Bennett. "Puppy Parties and Beyond: The Role of Early Socialization Practices on Adult Dog Behavior." *Veterinary Medicine: Research and Reports (Auckland, N.Z.)* 6, (2015): 143–153. https://doi.org/10.2147/VMRR.S62081.

Johns, Gary. "The Essential Impact of Context on Organizational Behavior." *Academy of Management Review* 31, no. 2, (2006): 386–408. https://doi.org/10.5465/amr.2006.20208687.

Jones, Katenna. "Fighting Like Cats & Dogs: Dealing with Inter-Species Aggression." Virtual conference session. Aggression in Dogs Conference, 2020.

Kelemen, Thomas, Samuel H. Matthews, Min (Maggie) Wan, and Yejun Zhang. "The Secret Life of Pets: The Intersection of Animals and Organizational Life." *Journal of Organizational Behavior* 41, no. 7 (2019): 694–697. https://doi.org/10.1002/job.2465.

Kerns, Nancy. "The Benefits of Crate Training Your Dog from an Early Age: A Terrific Management Tool as Well as a Home Away from Home." Whole Dog Journal, December 17, 2010. https://www.whole-dog-journal.com/training/crates/the-benefits-of-crate-training-your-dog-from-an-early-age/.

London, Karen & Patricia McConnell. *Play Together, Stay Together: Happy and Healthy Play Between People and Dogs.* Black Earth: McConnell Publishing, 2008.

Lopez, Barry *Of Wolves and Men.* New York: Scribner, 1978.

Lowrey, Sassafras. "The Dog Park Is Bad, Actually." *New York Times*, February 6, 2020. https://www.nytimes.com/2020/02/06/smarter-living/the-dog-park-is-bad-actually.html.

Malatesta, Sam. "Who's the Dog: Camp Outline." Who's the Dog Blog, accessed April 17, 2023. https://www.whosthedog.net/training-services/camp-outline.

Malatesta, Sam. "Illness and Behavior." Who's the Dog Blog, March 14, 2009. https://www.whosthedog.net/blog/illness-and-behavior.

Malatesta, Sam. "Aggression—The Cure—The Handler." Who's the Dog Blog, March 8, 2009. https://www.whosthedog.net/blog/aggression-the-cure-handler.

Malatesta, Sam. "My Viewpoint on Aggression." Who's the Dog Blog, February 19, 2009. https://www.whosthedog.net/blog/my-viewpoint-on-aggression.

Malatesta, Sam. "Aggression Towards Old Dog." Who's the Dog Blog, December 31, 2008. https://www.whosthedog.net/blog/aggression-towards-old-dog.

Malatesta, Sam. "Food Snarfing." Who's the Dog Blog, October 8, 2008. https://www.whosthedog.net/blog/food-snarfing.

Malatesta, Sam. "A Min Pin of Mettle." Who's the Dog Blog, September 11, 2008. https://www.whosthedog.net/blog/a-min-pin-of-mettle.

Malatesta, Sam. "Alpha Role vs. Alpha Roll." Who's the Dog Blog, July 28, 2008. https://www.whosthedog.net/blog/alpha-role-vs-alpha-roll.

Malatesta, Sam. "Dog Kills New Puppy." Who's the Dog Blog, July 27, 2008. https://www.whosthedog.net/blog/dog-kills-new-puppy.

Malatesta, Sam. "The 'Dirty Water' Analogy for Handler-Dog Training Issues." Who's the Dog Blog, July 25, 2008. https://www.whosthedog.net/blog/dirty-water.

Malatesta, Sam. "To Click or Not to Click." Who's the Dog Blog, July 9, 2008. https://www.whosthedog.net/blog/to-click-or-not-to-click.

Malatesta, Sam. "Prong Collars." Who's the Dog Blog, June 23, 2008. https://www.whosthedog.net/blog/prong-collar.

Malatesta, Sam. "Dutch Government Lifting Pit Bull Ban." Who's the Dog Blog, June 11, 2008. https://www.whosthedog.net/blog/dutch-government-lifting-pit-bull-ban.

Malatesta, Sam. "Fat Dog." Who's the Dog Blog, May 24, 2008. https://www.whosthedog.net/blog/fat-dog.

Malatesta, Sam. "Puppy Mill Breeding Dog Rehabilitation." Who's the Dog Blog, April 30, 2008. https://www.whosthedog.net/blog/puppy-mill-breeding-dog-rehabilitation.

Malatesta, Sam. "6-Year-Old Girl Attacked by Dog." Who's the Dog Blog, April 25, 2008. https://www.whosthedog.net/blog/6-year-old-girl-attacked-by-dog.

Malatesta, Sam. "House Pet Expectation Syndrome." Who's the Dog Blog, April 23, 2008. https://www.whosthedog.net/blog/house-pet-expectation-syndrome.

Malatesta, Sam. "Dog Fostering Tips." Who's the Dog Blog, April 1, 2008. https://www.whosthedog.net/blog/dog-fostering-tips.

Malatesta, Sam. "Managing Dogs Around a New Baby." Who's the Dog Blog, March 24, 2008. https://www.whosthedog.net/blog/manage-dogs-around-a-new-baby.

Malatesta, Sam. "Aggressive Puppy." Who's the Dog Blog, March 20, 2008. https://www.whosthedog.net/blog/aggressive-puppy,

Malatesta, Sam. "Genetics vs. Nurture." Who's the Dog Blog. https://www.whosthedog.net/blog/genetics-vs-nurture-in-dogs

Malatesta, Sam. "Fearfulness in Dogs." Who's the Dog Blog, February 17, 2008. https://www.whosthedog.net/blog/fearfulness-in-dogs.

Malatesta, Sam. "Food Aggression and Resource Guarding." Who's the Dog Blog, February 1, 2008. https://www.whosthedog.net/blog/food-aggression-resource-guarding-in-dogs.

Malatesta, Sam. "Submissive Urination." Who's the Dog Blog, January 20, 2008. https://www.whosthedog.net/blog/submissive-urination.

Malatesta, Sam. "Gentle Leader & Other Training Devices." Who's the Dog Blog, January 15, 2008. https://www.whosthedog.net/blog/gentle-leader-other-dog-training-devices.

Malatesta, Sam. "Poop Eating." Who's the Dog Blog, December 23, 2007. https://www.whosthedog.net/blog/poop-eating.

Malatesta, Sam. "Biting Puppy." Who's the Dog Blog, December 14, 2007. https://www.whosthedog.net/blog/biting-puppy.

Malatesta, Sam. "Teach Your Dog Good Etiquette." Who's the Dog Blog, August 1, 2007. https://www.whosthedog.net/blog/teach-your-dog-good-etiquette.

Malatesta, Sam and Souha Ezzedeen. *One with Dog: Sam Malatesta's Whelping Box Approach to Rearing and Training Dogs.* Canadian Intellectual Property Office: Copyright Registration #1130736 2016.

Masson, Jeffrey Moussaieff *Lost Companions: Reflections on the Death of Pets.* New York: St. Martin's Press, 2020.

McAuliffe, Claudeen. *Mindful Dog Teaching: Reflections on the Relationships We Share With Our Dogs.* Wenatchee: Dogwise Publishing, 2006.

McConnell, Patricia B. *For The Love of a Dog: Understanding Emotion in You and Your Best Friend.* New York: Ballantine Books, 2007.

McConnell, Patricia B. *Tales of Two Species: Essays on Loving and Living with Dogs.* Wenatchee: Dogwise Publishing, 2008.

McConnell, Patricia B. *The Cautious Canine: How to Help Dogs Conquer Their Fears* (2nd edition). Black Earth: McConnell Publishing Ltd., 2005.

McConnell, Patricia B. *The Other End of the Leash: Why We Do What We Do Around Dogs.* New York: Random House Inc., 2002.

McConnell, Patricia B. *I'll Be Home Soon! How to Prevent and Treat Separation Anxiety.* Black Earth: McConnell Publishing Ltd., 2000.

McConnell, Patricia B., and Karen B. London. *Feisty Fido: Help for the Leash-Reactive Dog* (2nd ed.). Black Earth: McConnell Publishing Ltd., 2009.

McIntyre, Rick. *The Alpha Female Wolf: The Fierce Legacy of Yellowstone's 06.* Vancouver: Greystone Books Ltd., 2022.

McIntyre, Rick. *The Redemption of Wolf 302: From Renegade to Yellowstone Alpha Male.* Vancouver, Greystone Books Ltd., 2021.

McIntyre, Rick. *The Reign of Wolf 21: The Saga of Yellowstone's Legendary Druid Pack.* Vancouver: Greystone Books Ltd., 2020.

McIntyre, Rick. *The Rise of Wolf 8: Witnessing the Triumph of Yellowstone's Underdog.* Vancouver: Greystone Books Ltd., 2019.

McIntyre, Rick. *A Society of Wolves.* New York: Voyageur Press, 1996.

McMillan, Brandon. *Lucky Dog Lessons: Train Your Dog in Seven Days*. New York: HarperCollins, 2018.

McMillan, Trish. *Secrets of the Shelter Ninjas: Handling Difficult Dogs Safely.* Virtual conference session. Aggression in Dogs Conference, 2020.

Meisterfeld, C. W. *Jelly Bean versus Dr. Jekyll & Mr. Hyde: Written for the Safety of Our Children and the Welfare of Our Dogs*. Palm Coast: MRK Publishing, 1989.

Millan, Cesar. *Cesar Millan's Short Guide to a Happy Dog*. Washington, D.C.: The National Geographic Society, 2013.

Millan, Cesar, & Melissa Jo Peltier. *Be The Pack Leader: Use Cesar's Way to Transform Your Dog and Your Life*. New York: Three Rivers Press, 2010.

Millan, Cesar, & Melissa Jo Peltier. *Cesar's Rules: Your Way to a Well-Behaved Dog*. New York: Crown Publishing Group, 2010.

Millan, Cesar, & Melissa Jo Peltier. *Cesar's Way: The Natural, Everyday Guide to Understanding & Correcting Common Dog Problems*. New York: Three Rivers Press, 2006.

Miller, Jill Kessler. "I Am Not a Dog Park Advocate." Jill Kessler Miller: Expert Witness in Dogs, Dog Bites and Behavior, October 8, 2015. https://www.jillkessler.com/post/2015/10/09/i-am-not-a-dog-park-advocate.

Monks of New Skete. *Let Dogs Be Dogs: Understanding Canine Nature and Mastering the Art of Living with Your Dog*. New York: Little, Brown and Company, 2017.

Monks of New Skete. *How to Be Your Dog's Best Friend: A Training Manual for Dog Owners*. New York: Little, Brown and Co, 1978.

Morris, Desmond. *Dogwatching: The Essential Guide to Dog Behavior*. New York: Jonathan Cape Ltd., 1986.

Mowat, Farley. *Never Cry Wolf: The Amazing True Story of Life Among Arctic Wolves*. New York: Penguin Modern Canadian Classics, 1963.

Murphy, Kathy. "The Neuroscience of Aggression." Virtual conference session. Aggression in Dogs Conference, 2020.

Orlean, Susan. *On Animals*. New York: Avid Reader Press, 2021.

Pierce, Jessica. *Run, Spot, Run: The Ethics of Keeping Pets*. Chicago: University of Chicago Press, 2016.

Pierce, Jessica and Marc Bekoff. *A Dog's World: Imagining the Lives of Dogs in a World without Humans*. Princeton: Princeton University Press, 2021.

Pike, Amy L. "Medical Causes of and Medication Interventions for Aggression in Dogs." Aggression in Dogs Conference, 2020.

Pina e Cunha, Miguel, Arménio Rego, and Ian Munro. "Dogs in Organizations." *Human Relations* 72, no. 4, (2019): 778–800. https://doi. org/10.1177/0018726718780.

Pryor, Karen. *Don't Shoot the Dog: The New Art of Teaching and Training*. New York: Bantam Books, 1999.

Raycroft, Mark and Pili Palm-Leis. "Wolf Ways—Marauder, Protector, Companion." Canadian Geographic 139 (2019): 28–36.

Ritland, Mike and Gary Brozek. *Trident K9 Warriors: My Tale from The Training Ground to the Battlefield with Elite Navy SEAL Canines*. New York: St. Martin's Press, 2013.

Rugaas, Turid. *On Talking Terms with Dogs: Calming Signals*. Wenatchee: Dogwise Publishing, 2006.

Safina, Carl. *Beyond Words: What Animals Think and Feel*. New York: Henry Holt & Company, 2015

Salter Ainsworth, Mary, Mary Blehar, Everett Waters, and Sally Wall. *Patterns of Attachment: A Psychological Study of the Strange Situation*. New York: Psychology Press, 2015.

Serpell, James. *In The Company of Animals: A Study of Human-Animal Relationships*. Cambridge: Cambridge University Press, 1996.

Shapiro, Kenneth. "Human-Animal Studies: Remembering the Past, Celebrating the Present, Troubling the Future." *Society & Animals* 28, no. 7 (2020): 797–833. https://brill.com/view/journals/soan/28/7/article-p797_6. xml?language=en.

Shikashio, Michael. "The Many Lenses of Aggression—Is This Party Just Getting Started?" Virtual conference session. Aggression in Dogs Conference, 2020.

Shikashio, Michael. "Troubleshooting Difficult Scenarios in Aggression Cases." Virtual conference session. Aggression in Dogs Conference, 2020.

Shipman, Pat. *Our Oldest Companions: The Story of the First Dogs.* Cambridge: Harvard University Press, 2021.

Stilwell, Victoria. *Train Your Dog Positively: Understand Your Dog and Solve Common Behavior Problems Including Separation Anxiety, Excessive Barking, Aggression, Housetraining, Leash Pulling, And More!* Berkeley: Ten Speed Press, 2013.

Simon, Armando. "The Uniqueness of Mammals." Areo Magazine, November 19, 2020. *https://areomagazine.com/2020/11/19/the-uniqueness-of-mammals/.*

Sykes, Bryan. *Once a Wolf: The Science Behind Our Dogs' Astonishing Genetic Evolution.* New York: Liveright Publishing, 2019.

Tuan, Yi-Fu. *Dominance and Affection: The Making of Pets.* New Haven: Yale University Press, 2003.

Tucker, Nancy. "How Long Is Too Long to Leave a Dog Home Alone?" Whole Dog Journal, April 18, 2018. https://www.whole-dog-journal.com/care/how-long-is-too-long-to-leave-a-dog-alone/.

Todd, Zazie. "Why You Need to Socialize Your Puppy." Companion Animal Psychology, February 25, 2015. https://www.companionanimalpsychology.com/2015/02/why-you-need-to-socialize-your-puppy.html.

Todd, Zazie. *Wag: The Science of Making Your Dog Happy.* Vancouver: Greystone Books Ltd., 2020.

Volhard, Jack and Wendy Volhard. *Dog Training for Dummies.* New York: Wiley Publishing, 2001.

Wallin, David. *Attachment in Psychotherapy.* New York: Guilford Publications, 2007.

Wallin, David and Stephen Goldbart. *Mapping the Terrain of the Heart: Passion, Tenderness, and the Capacity to Love.* Lanham: Jason Aronson, 1998.

Wood, Deborah. *Help for Your Shy Dog: Turning Your Terrified Dog Into a Terrific Pet.* New York: Wiley Publishing, 1999.

Wu, Katherine J. "Wolves Boop Their Snoots to Touch Screens to Feed Their Friends. Dogs? Not So Much." Public Broadcasting Station, May 1, 2019.https://www.pbs.org/wgbh/nova/article/wolves-dogs-touch-screens/.

Wynne, Clive L. D. *Dog Is Love: Why and How Your Dog Loves You.* New York: Houghton Mifflin Harcourt, 2019.

# Glossary

**Agility:** A sport where dogs run across obstacles such as bar jumps, A-frames, and teeter-totters, with the dogs' handlers guiding them along courses of varying degrees of complexity.

**Attachment theory:** A theory developed by John Bowlby highlighting the importance of primary attachments in development and well-being.

**Barn hunt:** A sport where dogs work to sniff out and alert to rats placed in containers within straw structures the dogs have to climb on, as would be found in farms.

**Classical conditioning:** A learning process pioneered by Ivan Pavlov where associating two disparate events is learned through repetition—for example, the sound of a bell and dogs salivating.

**Counterconditioning:** A technique used in animal training that pairs an event with a positive outcome in an effort to change the behavior in response to that event.

**Critical socialization period:** A period of intense learning approximately occurring between three and 16 weeks of age in the development of a puppy.

**Defensive drive:** One of the four drives; a dog's natural desire to protect and defend valued resources including territory, food, objects, and human and animal family members. See also **drives**.

**Denning site:** A safe and hidden space where mother canids such as wolves and coyotes give birth to their cubs and look after them closely for roughly the first eight weeks of life.

**Denning stage:** The roughly eight-week period where wolf cubs develop following birth, in close and exclusive contact with their mothers.

**Desensitization:** A conditioning technique aimed at reducing the intensity of a dog's response to an event.

**Distal socialization:** The third level of socialization, which involves exposure to stimuli, including people, animals, and things, at a distance and without interaction. See also **socialization**.

**Drives:** A dog's natural, instinctual, and inherited motivations. See also **defensive drive**, **food drive**, **pack drive**, and **prey drive**.

**Dock diving:** A sport where dogs jump from a raised platform or dock to retrieve a toy thrown into a pool below (also known as dock jumping).

**Exposure stage:** The second rearing stage in the Way of Life method focused on exposing, socializing, and educating the dog.

**Family hierarchy:** A concept that clarifies relationship dynamics between humans and dogs by examining where each fall in the categories of infant cubs, adolescents and yearlings, adults, betas, and alphas.

**Food drive:** One of the four drives; a dog's natural and instinctual desire for food as a means of survival. See also **drives**.

**Foundations stage:** The first rearing stage in the Way of Life method focused on decompression, establishing safety and success, and laying a foundation of trust.

**Functional obedience:** Natural and nonconditioned obedience and compliance occurring as a result of healthy rearing.

**Handler transference:** The practice of handing over dogs to other people for handling and boarding, as a means of strengthening dogs.

**Inadvertent training:** The unintended training and learning that occurs as a result of poor management and leadership of the dog.

**Interactional socialization:** The fifth level of socialization, which involves verbal and physical interaction with people and animals. See also **socialization**.

**Inner circle:** The smallest of the three circles, consisting of the intimate space around the handler. See also **three circles**.

**Integration stage:** The third rearing stage in the Way of Life method focused on solidifying Foundations and Exposure, assimilating the dog, and working in off-leash capacity.

**Littermate syndrome:** A situation whereby puppies raised together grow to develop tensions and conflicts in their relationships at adulthood.

**Lure coursing:** A sport that involves dogs chasing after a mechanized lure across courses, simulating chasing live prey.

**Negative punishment:** A method of reinforcement for training purposes involving the removal or taking away of an unwanted outcome.

**Negative reinforcement:** A method of reinforcement for training purposes involving the removal or taking away of a desired outcome.

**Obedience:** A sport where dogs learn commands of various degrees of complexity, including common cues such as sit or lie down, adding distance and duration.

**Operant conditioning:** Learning as a result of associating behavior with its consequences.

**Oppositional socialization:** The sixth level of socialization, which involves exposure to invasive and intrusive behavior from people and animals. See also **socialization**.

**Organizational behavior:** A scholarly field of study focusing on the behavior of people in groups and organizations.

**Pack drive:** One of the four drives; a dog's natural and instinctual desire to care for and belong with a family unit. See also **drives**.

**Positive punishment:** A method of reinforcement for training purposes involving the application of an unwanted outcome.

**Positive reinforcement:** A method of reinforcement for training purposes involving the application of a wanted outcome.

**Prey drive:** One of the four drives; a dog's natural and instinctual desire to chase and grab, inherited as part of a dog's hunt for food. See also **drives**.

**Primordial socialization:** The first level of socialization, which involves intimate exposure between human and dog including all start-to-finish care and handling. See also **socialization**.

**Proximal socialization:** The fourth level of socialization, which involves exposure to stimuli, including people, animals, and things that are nearby without interaction. See also **socialization**.

**Rally obedience:** A sport that presents a fun way of practicing obedience where handlers and dogs heel along a course of obstacles presenting cues to perform (also known as Rally-O).

**Recall games:** Training practices such as restrained recall and two-way recall that solidify a dog returning to the handler while being called in a fun and engaging manner.

**Rendezvous site:** Nondenning spots where wolf cubs are taken for their safety, education, and socialization before integration into the pack.

**Shaping:** A reinforcement technique that trains a behavior by rewarding successive, closer and closer approximations of the behavior.

**Social or observational learning:** A set of theories that propose that people learn by observing others, adapting their behavior to their social context.

**Socialization:** A dog's gradual exposure to stimuli and experiences along six rungs. See also **primordial**, **spatial**, **distal**, **proximal**, **interactional**, and **oppositional socialization**.

**Spatial socialization:** The second level of socialization, which involves exposure to different environments without necessarily engaging in these environments. See also **socialization**.

**Sprinter trials:** A sport that involves dogs running a 100-meter sprint, scored based on their height and finish time to determine their speed in terms of kilometers per hour.

**Territorial circle:** The largest of the three circles, consisting of the territorial boundary between a space and another. See also **three circles**.

**Three circles:** A concept developed by Sam Malatesta where space is understood and managed along three concentric circles. See also **inner circle**, **territorial circle**, and **tranquil circle**.

**Three rearing and relationship stages:** The Way of Life method to rearing dogs mirroring stages of canine and human development. See also **foundations stage**, **exposure stage**, and **integration stage**.

**Tracking:** A scent-oriented discipline where handlers lay foot tracks for the dogs to follow as they locate and alert to articles along the track.

**Tranquil circle:** The middle of the three circles, consisting of a 10-foot radius circle around the handler. See also **three circles**.

**Weaning:** A critical event in the life of a puppy where it is stopped from drinking its mother's milk and transitioned to soft and eventually solid food.

**Whelping:** The process of a mother dog or wolf giving birth to pups or cubs, usually occurring in a den for wolves and a whelping box for dogs.

**Whelping box theory:** An approach to dog training developed by Sam Malatesta based on the behavior of the mother dog toward her puppies from whelping to weaning.

# *Acknowledgments*

Love is the way I walk in gratitude.

**— A COURSE IN MIRACLES**

I am honored and humbled to take a moment to acknowledge those who helped me write this book and become the dog trainer, handler, coach, guardian, and steward that I am today. It truly takes a village to write and publish a book and I could not be more grateful for the many people and organizations that made this possible.

Beginning with the team at Book Launchers, including founder Julie Broad, members of the support team Roy Rocha, Elissa Graeser, and Renee Harrison, marketing gurus Sarah Bean and Nicole Larson, audiobook adviser and voice coach Greg Douras, audiobook producer Alex Paris from ADS Studio, and members of the design and production teams – I cannot thank you enough for your expertise, generosity of time and spirit, and your support throughout the publishing process.

I am also deeply indebted to my editorial team at KN Literary Arts namely Emily Krempholtz and my developmental and copy editor Audra Figgins, and Dan Good and Holly Akins at Book Launchers. My beta readers for your wonderful feedback—Annalise Beube, Cathy Collins, Tina Sharifi, Wendy Strickland, and Paul Swiercz—thank you!

My Way of Life™ Dog Training partners including Nour Ezzedeen, Agatha Bayones, Carla Aboumatar, Sunny Trochaniak, and Chris Castillo: You have supported me, my business, and everything it took to get this book out in the world. Thank you so much!

My clients, whom I won't name for privacy: Your belief in me, your openness to the Way of Life method, and your success with it were the reminders I often needed to keep going. Your trials and travails, feats and triumphs, provided wonderful stories for this book and I can't thank you enough for your support and validation.

All my dog training teachers and instructors, my mentors past and present, including Kathy Warner, Christopher Rollox, Karin Apfel, and especially my decade-long and life-changing mentor and teacher Sam Malatesta.

Of course, my family, which has believed in me and supported me from the beginning, including my late grandmother Zabad Saab and my late father Riad Ezzedeen—I know just how much you've been cheering me on from beyond.

Deepest gratitude to my mother, Juhayna Raslan, and my creative and talented entrepreneurial sisters, Layla and Nour. I hope to be always worthy of the immense love and support that you have given me.

I couldn't have done this work, while juggling a full-time academic career and a growing business, without the support of my dearest friends Paddy Aker, Shaz and Stephanie Arad, Robeena "Beany" Benfield, Cathy Collins, Shaunna Drew, Dr. Jumana Kawar, Dr. Kristin Lamoureux, the late Dr. Janet L. Nixdorff, Rev. Laurie Jane Nevin, Sam Novid, Wendy Strickland, Dr. Paul M. Swiercz, Cesar Villanueva, and Dr. David Zarnett.

And of course the dogs who are the ultimate reason for this book—my own dogs, foster dogs, client dogs, and all the dogs I dealt with as a volunteer. You dwell in my heart and mind. Deepest love and gratitude to Flora, Foxy, Rex, Clio, Jada, Jasmin, Rama, Maya, Murphy, Erdo, and Beau: It matters not how much time we had; your impact on me was for a lifetime. Till we meet again.

And the current crew, Bob and "the girls" Kizzy, Bruna, and Nejra, this book came at your expense in many ways. You displayed such patience as the days went by without us being able to spend the time together that I would like and that you deserve. I hope this book makes a real difference for your kind, for you have all waited too long to be truly understood.

With deep and everlasting gratitude.

Souha Ezzedeen PhD
Toronto, Canada
September 7, 2023

# *About the Author*

S ouha Ezzedeen, PhD, is a human-dog relationship coach, dog trainer, academic, business owner, creator of the Way of Life Method, and forever student of the art and science of raising sound, strong, and spirited dogs. She holds a doctorate in management and organizational behavior; is a tenured associate professor, educator, and researcher; and is the founder of Way of Life™ Dog Training, a Toronto-based coaching business focused primarily on canine behavioral issues.

Inspired by challenges with several dogs, particularly her German shepherd Maya, Souha draws on nearly 20 years of diverse experiences with dogs, coaching dog owners in designing ways of life that heal behavioral issues and unleash deep bonds with their dogs.

Souha lives in Toronto, Canada, with her four dogs—German shepherds Kizzy and Bruna, Belgian Malinois Nejra, and Taiwanese mountain dog Bob. Together, they enjoy hiking and swimming, and have been active in herding and scenting for several years.

# Index

## A

adolescence 5, 163, 164, 213
adolescent stage 172, 265
adult 37, 43, 48, 57, 59, 64, 67, 75, 136, 140, 164, 166, 169, 170, 216, 233, 236, 240, 242
Adulthood Stage 233
Afghan hound 14
aggression 2, 9, 13, 15, 17, 20, 27, 30, 33, 41, 57, 131, 133, 174, 217, 218, 226, 237, 252,
        272, 276, 277, 278, 279, 292, 296, 297, 298,
   food aggression 27, 237
   wildlife aggression 15, 16, 189, 225
agility 14, 151, 154, 156, 157, 175, 224, 266, 284
Ainsworth, Mary Salter 28, 29, 291, 301
Airedale 14
Akita 14
Alaskan malamute 14
alpha female 52, 58, 59, 63, 68
alpha male 52, 58, 59, 60, 63, 66,
American bulldog 13
anxiety 2, 3, 5, 9, 13, 17, 18, 22, 23, 25, 26, 28, 29, 31, 77, 94, 95, 111, 132, 140, 187, 207,
        231, 237, 250, 252, 271, 272, 284, 286, 290
attachment figure 29
attachment styles 29
   insecure attachment 29
   secure attachment 29
attachment theory 28
Australian shepherd 153
authenticity 258, 276

## B

baby gate 91, 96, 105, 107, 116, 174, 175
balanced training 19
ball play 140
barn hunt 151

basenji  14
basset hound  14
beagle  14
behavioral fostering  7, 10, 83, 87, 113, 114, 231, 232, 255, 256
behavior modification  18, 20, 28, 208
Belgian malinois  14, 162, 313
Bernese mountain dog  14
beta female  35, 37, 57
beta male  35, 37, 57
Bichon frise  15
biddability  31
bloodhound  14
boarding  93, 148, 171, 187, 191, 192, 205, 206, 256, 257, 278, 306
body harness  100
border collie  14
Bowlby, John  28, 290, 291, 305
boxer  13
breed  11, 12, 13, 15, 17, 21, 24, 27, 40, 44, 45, 55, 73, 97, 109, 133, 138, 151, 154, 163, 173, 208, 212, 213, 219, 271, 276, 277
breeder  8, 11, 45, 46, 47, 87, 109, 117, 241
Brophey, Kim  13, 291
bull terrier  13

## C

cairn terrier  14
cane corso  14
canine drives  42, 43, 136
Canine Good Citizen  2, 289
Canine Good Neighbor,  *See Also Canine Good Citizen*
Cardigan Welsh corgi  14
Cavalier King Charles Spaniel  15
chew bones  89, 98, 265
chihuahua  15
choice  37, 38, 61, 96, 100, 144, 173, 174, 235, 241, 242, 247, 249, 276
chow chow  14
classical conditioning  19
cockapoo  13, 84, 207, 211
cocker spaniel  14
codependence  287
collar  25, 89, 100, 297
  Martingale collar  89
  prong collar  23, 78, 132
come here exercise  120,
conditioning  18, 19, 20, 23, 24, 28, 30, 33, 148, 263, 272, 283, 305, 306, 307
coonhound  14
corgi  12, 14, 276, 277
corrections  2, 169, 170,
counter conditioning  19, 208, 305

crate  19, 26, 82, 83, 87, 89, 90, 91, 92, 93, 94, 95, 96, 97, 98, 101, 103, 104, 105, 107, 110, 111, 117, 122, 123, 126, 127, 128, 129, 130, 135, 136, 144, 146, 148, 156, 171, 173, 174, 175, 176, 177, 188, 192, 199, 206, 208, 209, 212, 224, 226, 232, 233, 237, 241, 242, 243, 244, 247, 251, 252, 257, 259, 277, 278, 279, 291, 296
   travel crate  96
crate time  110, 135, 233
crating  78, 82, 92, 93, 94, 95, 96, 97, 98, 108, 109, 110, 112, 132, 137, 155, 157, 190, 208, 212, 226, 227, 243, 252, 263, 278
critical socialization period  11

**D**

decompression  61, 75, 81, 84, 87, 91, 94, 95, 112, 114, 127, 131, 140, 145, 191, 206, 232, 233, 252, 306
defensive drive  77, 218, 228, 269, 271, 306
defensiveness  77, 174
denning site  60
denning stage  60, 61
desensitization  19
discipline  21, 44, 47, 148, 149, 150, 151, 153, 166, 168, 169, 170, 171, 172, 191, 220, 309
disk  219, 272
distal socialization  101, 103, 108, 126, 127, 133, 150, 167, 185, 201, 207, 210, 248
distance  14, 24, 42, 45, 61, 81, 84, 101, 103, 104, 106, 108, 111, 121, 123, 124, 125, 126, 127, 128, 129, 130, 133, 141, 147, 150, 152, 178, 179, 181, 185, 186, 189, 193, 194, 195, 197, 198, 201, 203, 208, 214, 219, 226, 246, 247, 248, 264, 274, 306, 307, 318
distraction  121, 141, 147, 152, 204, 273
dock diving  153, 306
dog daycares  9, 21, 41, 261
dog parks  21, 40, 199, 261
dominance  35, 36, 47, 56, 168, 292
Do Something Exercise 149, 221
drives  6, 7, 21, 42, 43, 44, 45, 65, 81, 111, 136, 137, 140, 142, 147, 149, 166, 167, 171, 172, 195, 212, 213, 216, 219, 234, 261, 269, 271, 275, 276, 279, 286, 305, 306, 307, 308, 316
   defensive drive  77, 218, 228, 269, 271, 306
   food drive  19, 43, 44, 83, 132, 136, 137, 138, 139, 140, 141, 153, 157, 166, 188, 213, 219, 225, 228, 234, 251, 269, 270, 306
   pack drive  43, 77, 167, 168, 195, 196, 204, 213, 216, 218, 219, 220, 225, 228, 257, 270, 271, 306
   prey drive  43, 47, 84, 136, 140, 141, 144, 153, 158, 166, 189, 196, 212, 213, 214, 219, 220, 225, 226, 227, 228, 235, 251, 269, 270, 306
duration  58, 60, 90, 99, 152, 221, 307

**E**

English foxhound  14
English pointer  14
ethology  28
exercise  6, 26, 33, 37, 38, 42, 44, 47, 48, 78, 90, 91, 96, 100, 102, 103, 104, 105, 106, 107,

116, 117, 120, 121, 123, 124, 126, 128, 130, 135, 136, 137, 142, 143, 144, 145, 146, 147, 149, 150, 153, 158, 179, 181, 182, 183, 184, 185, 187, 195, 196, 198, 203, 206, 210, 212, 213, 214, 215, 218, 219, 220, 221, 222, 223, 227, 232, 245, 249, 260, 264, 269, 271, 272, 276, 286
exercise pen  96, 116, 318. *See also* x-pen
exposure stage  309

# F

family hierarchy  34, 36, 57, 63, 76, 80, 136, 165, 170, 226, 234, 318
fear  3, 18, 22, 27, 29, 33, 40, 41, 60, 80, 144, 157, 165, 168, 174, 193, 218, 241, 242, 270, 271, 284
fireworks  29, 31, 174, 241, 242, 244
flirt pole  144
food drive  19, 43, 44, 83, 132, 136, 137, 138, 139, 140, 141, 153, 157, 166, 188, 213, 219, 225, 228, 234, 251, 269, 270, 306
food possession  139, 255
force-free  19
foundations stage  309
free feeding  139
French bulldog  13
functional obedience  273

# G

geriatric dogs  237
German shepherd  1, 13, 14, 84, 108, 241, 250, 252, 263, 281, 313
get out exercise  222
golden retriever  14
Great Pyrenees  14
greyhound  12, 14, 82
grooming  90, 119, 180, 200, 201, 257
grooming table  119
grounding exercise  102, 107, 130, 196, 214, 245
guarding  3, 13, 14, 15, 60, 139, 187, 298

# H

handler-dog box  39
handler transference  192, 205, 278
hand lure exercise  142, 143, 214, 217, 222, 270
head halter  2
heeling  222, 223
herding  10, 13, 56, 135, 151, 152, 155, 194, 224, 267, 268, 277, 313
hiking  103, 106, 114, 144, 145, 146, 179, 180, 183, 193, 205, 210, 212, 266, 280, 313, 319
hunting  13, 14, 43, 53, 55, 59, 60, 62, 63, 64, 65, 67, 138, 150, 234

# I

inadvertent training  38
inner circle  39, 100, 102, 104, 107, 108, 125, 134, 146, 178, 179, 180, 181, 196, 199, 222, 245, 246, 309
insecurity  155, 174
integration stage  309
interactional socialization  167, 179, 195, 198

## J

Jack Russell  14
jogging  144, 146
Johns, Gary  27, 295
juvenile  43, 56, 76, 79, 84, 140, 166

## K

Kopinak, Sharon  8, 161

## L

Law of Effect  19
learning theory  19
leash reactivity  3, 27
Let It Happen Exercise  260
lie down  102, 105, 150, 152, 247, 261, 282, 307
littermate syndrome  226
London, Karen B.  20, 293, 296, 299
lone wolf  65
long line  99, 104, 106, 116, 120, 141, 214, 217, 222, 278, 284
loose-leash walking  143, 217, 223
Lorenz, Konrad  29
lure coursing  153, 307

## M

Malatesta, Sam  8, 10, 38, 40, 45, 124, 223, 235, 245, 296, 297, 298, 299, 309, 311
Maltese  15
mammalian factor  54
mat time exercise  181
maturation  5, 65, 70, 163, 164, 178, 179, 180, 212, 269
McConnell, Patricia  20, 296, 299
McInyre, Rick  54
medication  4, 22, 24, 28, 232
milling crowds  197
mind me exercise  106, 146, 182
mindset  4, 6, 33, 34, 48, 81, 82, 83, 112, 120, 146, 157, 163, 170, 227, 236, 239, 240, 286
mission  6, 8, 33, 34, 36, 48, 64, 65, 77, 85, 88, 165, 172, 174, 185, 234, 235, 240, 320
Mowat, Farley  54, 55, 300
multiple dogs  104, 246

# N

negative punishment 19
negative reinforcement 19
Newfoundland 14, 191
no-pull harness 23, 89, 100

# O

obedience 2, 9, 31, 57, 80, 125, 135, 147, 151, 152, 153, 154, 156, 166, 171, 214, 220, 221, 223, 233, 263, 273, 282, 306, 308
  functional obedience 273
observational learning theory 290. *See also* social learning theory
operant conditioning 19, 28
oppositional socialization 42, 125, 171, 180, 182, 200, 205, 210, 214, 248, 257, 260, 261, 269, 308
organizational behavior 7, 19, 27, 313
outdoor kennel 96, 97, 116, 188

# P

pack drive 43, 77, 167, 168, 195, 196, 204, 213, 216, 218, 219, 220, 225, 228, 257, 270, 271, 306
Pavlov, Ivan 19, 305
personality 2, 6, 11, 16, 24, 27, 33, 45, 46, 58, 82, 83, 138, 151, 162, 213, 214, 219, 227, 253, 269
phobia 290
  crate phobia 94
  noise phobia 284
play 9, 40, 44, 47, 55, 63, 90, 129, 136, 137, 140, 143, 144, 149, 153, 156, 167, 201, 202, 203, 204, 205, 212, 213, 214, 215, 216, 220, 228, 244, 261, 264, 268, 270, 316
politeness 31
Portuguese water dog 14
positive punishment 19
positive reinforcement 19, 168
possession 27, 139, 255, 318
predator 55, 70, 215
prey cycle exercise 214, 215
prey drive 43, 47, 84, 136, 140, 141, 144, 153, 158, 166, 189, 196, 212, 213, 214, 219, 220, 225, 226, 227, 228, 235, 251, 269, 270, 306
primordial socialization 42, 100, 101, 117, 118, 120, 122, 130, 133, 184, 186, 200, 207, 209, 210, 217, 257
protection 13, 56, 60, 68, 151, 153
proximal socialization 167, 182, 185, 197, 198, 201, 202, 248
psychoanalysis 28
psychotropic medication 22
public transportation 195, 196, 197
punishment 2, 19, 168, 169, 307
  negative punishment 19
  positive punishment 19

puppy mill 12, 96, 101, 186, 187, 191
puppy playgroups 40
puzzle toys 89

# R

rally-obedience 152, 308
reactive dog(s) 3, 20, 27, 29, 30, 40, 80, 109, 111, 144, 154, 155, 165, 187, 192, 207, 211, 218, 242, 250, 251, 255, 284
reactivity 3, 20, 27, 29, 30, 40, 80, 109, 111, 144, 154, 155, 165, 187, 192, 207, 211, 218, 242, 250, 251, 255, 284
rearing stages 5, 6, 137
recall games 101, 120, 121, 180
  dual recall 120
  simple recall 120
reflection questions 6, 7
reinforcement 19, 20, 28, 168, 307, 308
  negative reinforcement 19, 320
  positive reinforcement 19, 168
relationship 4, 5, 6, 11, 21, 26, 27, 30, 32, 33, 34, 37, 43, 45, 48, 49, 59, 61, 74, 75, 76, 77, 81, 82, 84, 90, 102, 118, 137, 138, 148, 155, 156, 157, 163, 164, 165, 167, 170, 172, 173, 200, 202, 203, 208, 213, 216, 219, 227, 228, 233, 234, 235, 236, 240, 242, 252, 257, 266, 267, 268, 269, 270, 271, 277, 279, 280, 284, 285, 286, 306, 309, 313
rendezvous site 63
resource guarding 3, 15, 139, 187
retrieving 13, 214
rewards 19, 45, 138, 220
right/left turns 222, 223
running 1, 10, 17, 44, 53, 63, 117, 120, 121, 142, 144, 153, 187, 213, 215, 225, 227, 245, 261, 274, 308

# S

safe refuge 115
saluki 14
scent detection 151
scent hounds 14
secure base 29, 161, 198
senior dogs 209, 237, 238
separation anxiety 3, 13, 25, 28, 29, 31, 187, 286
shaping 19, 42
Siberian husky 14
sit 30, 103, 106, 140, 147, 149, 150, 152, 182, 184, 211, 215, 221, 245, 272, 307
Skinner, B.F. 19
sociability 31
socialization 6, 11, 40, 41, 42, 44, 48, 61, 62, 63, 69, 81, 83, 90, 93, 100, 101, 103, 104, 107, 108, 111, 114, 115, 117, 118, 120, 122, 123, 124, 125, 126, 127, 129, 130, 131, 132, 133, 141, 145, 147, 150, 153, 166, 167, 171, 172, 179, 180, 181, 182, 184, 185, 186, 193, 194, 195, 196, 197, 198, 199, 200, 201, 202, 203, 205, 206, 207, 208, 209, 210,

214, 217, 219, 221, 225, 235, 244, 245, 247, 248, 249, 257, 259, 260, 261, 262, 264, 266, 269, 272, 277, 286, 292, 294, 295, 305, 306, 307, 308

distal socialization  101, 103, 108, 126, 127, 133, 150, 167, 185, 201, 207, 210, 248

forced socialization  40

hyper socialization  40

indirect socialization  124

interactional socialization  167, 179, 195, 198

oppositional socialization  42, 125, 171, 180, 182, 200, 205, 210, 214, 248, 257, 260, 261, 269, 308

passive socialization  124

primordial socialization  42, 100, 101, 117, 118, 120, 122, 130, 133, 184, 186, 200, 207, 209, 210, 217, 257

proximal socialization  167, 182, 185, 197, 198, 201, 202, 248

spatial socialization  101, 103, 107, 111, 122, 123, 185, 193, 201, 247

social learning theory  290. *See also* observational learning theory

solo time  26, 96, 101, 102, 110, 116, 117, 122, 124, 176, 177, 191, 206, 208

soundness  30, 31, 33, 48, 111, 138, 157, 174, 234, 273

sound sensitivity  27, 208

spiritedness  30, 31, 33, 48, 111

sport  2, 6, 8, 16, 21, 24, 30, 33, 42, 44, 45, 48, 136, 140, 150, 151, 152, 153, 154, 155, 156, 157, 158, 166, 171, 172, 210, 212, 213, 223, 224, 225, 238, 243, 245, 265, 267, 269, 273, 275, 279, 280, 286, 305, 306, 307, 308

sprinter trials  153, 308

stand  52, 118, 119, 152, 162, 182, 221, 248

stay  25, 32, 36, 62, 64, 98, 99, 104, 105, 132, 140, 147, 149, 152, 170, 178, 179, 181, 188, 206, 210, 211, 218, 220, 222, 246, 259, 261, 268, 272, 274

strange situation test  29

strength  30, 31, 33, 35, 37, 48, 53, 59, 67, 68, 78, 80, 83, 88, 89, 94, 111, 144, 145, 157, 166, 174, 200, 205, 220, 234

swimming  144, 313

## T

territorial circle  38, 106, 108, 182, 248, 309

territoriality  13, 15

territorial line approach exercise  183, 184, 248, 249

this way exercise  143, 146

Thorndike, Edward  19

three circles  38, 39, 100, 108, 112, 116, 120, 178, 190, 209, 244, 272, 307, 308, 309

ThunderCaps  23

ThunderShirt  23, 231

thunderstorms  29, 31, 174, 241, 242, 244

tie-out  167, 223, 257, 273

tracking  56, 150, 151, 153, 213

training  2, 4, 5, 6, 7, 11, 18, 19, 20, 26, 28, 29, 30, 32, 33, 35, 36, 37, 38, 42, 44, 48, 49, 57, 64, 87, 92, 93, 99, 105, 109, 111, 116, 125, 135, 136, 139, 144, 147, 148, 149, 151, 157, 166, 171, 172, 184, 195, 209, 211, 212, 213, 214, 217, 220, 221, 231, 232, 239, 244, 250, 253, 257, 263, 269, 270, 272, 273, 276, 277, 278, 280, 284, 286, 289, 291, 296, 298, 305, 306, 307, 309, 311

tranquil circle  39, 99, 104, 105, 106, 108, 179, 180, 181, 182, 192, 246, 247, 248, 275, 309
treat pouch  195
treat toss exercise  214
tug-of-war  62, 153, 215, 220, 272
tug toys  111, 144

## U

unintended learning  38

## V

veterinarians  8, 22, 41
vet visits  200, 201

## W

Warner, Kathy  8, 311
weaning  11, 46, 47, 59, 63, 169, 232, 309
West Highland terrier  14
whelping  11, 46, 59, 69, 87, 115, 309
whelping box theory  46, 87
withdrawal symptoms  95
Wolf 06  68
Wolf 8M  66
Wolf 21M  67
Wolf 826F  68. *See also* Wolf 06
wolf cubs  35, 63, 65, 138, 163, 306, 308
wolf den  60
wolf packs  5, 35, 36, 53, 54, 56, 57, 58, 69, 169

## X

x-pen  91, 96, 110, 175, 278, 279

Printed in the USA
CPSIA information can be obtained
at www.ICGtesting.com
LVHW090214221023
761758LV00040B/547